FEMALE-
FRIENDLY
SCIENCE

Pergamon Titles of Related Interest

Bleier FEMINIST APPROACHES TO SCIENCE

Bleier SCIENCE AND GENDER: A Critique of Biology and its Theories on Women

Rosser FEMINISM WITHIN THE SCIENCE & HEALTH CARE PROFESSIONS: Overcoming Resistance

Rosser TEACHING SCIENCE AND HEALTH FROM A FEMINIST PERSPECTIVE: A Practical Guide

Rothschild MACHINA EX DEA: Feminist Perspectives on Technology

Rothschild TEACHING TECHNOLOGY FROM A FEMINIST PERSPECTIVE: A Practical Guide

Related Journals
(Free sample copies available upon request.)

ISSUES IN REPRODUCTIVE AND GENETIC
  ENGINEERING: Journal of International Feminist Analysis
WOMEN'S STUDIES INTERNATIONAL FORUM

The ATHENE Series

General Editors
Gloria Bowles
Renate Klein
Janice Raymond

Consulting Editor
Dale Spender

The Athene Series assumes that all those who are concerned with formulating explanations of the way the world works need to know and appreciate the significance of basic feminist principles.

The growth of feminist research has challenged almost all aspects of social organization in our culture. The Athene Series focuses on the construction of knowledge and the exclusion of women from the process—both as theorists and subjects of study—and offers innovative studies that challenge established theories and research.

On Athene—When Metis, goddess of wisdom who presided over all knowledge was pregnant with Athene, she was swallowed up by Zeus who then gave birth to Athene from his head. The original Athene is thus the parthenogenetic daughter of a strong mother and as the feminist myth goes, at the "third birth" of Athene she stops being Zeus' obedient mouthpiece and returns to her real source: the science and wisdom of womankind.

FEMALE-FRIENDLY SCIENCE

Applying Women's Studies Methods and Theories to Attract Students

SUE V. ROSSER

PERGAMON PRESS
Member of Maxwell Macmillan Pergamon Publishing Corporation
New York ■ Oxford ■ Beijing ■ Frankfurt
São Paulo ■ Sydney ■ Tokyo ■ Toronto

Pergamon Press Offices:

U.S.A.	Pergamon Press, Inc., Maxwell House, Fairview Park, Elmsford, New York 10523, U.S.A.
U.K.	Pergamon Press plc, Headington Hill Hall, Oxford OX3 0BW, England
PEOPLE'S REPUBLIC OF CHINA	Pergamon Press, 0909 China World Tower, No. 1 Jian Guo Men Wai Avenue, Beijing 100004, People's Republic of China
FEDERAL REPUBLIC OF GERMANY	Pergamon Press GmbH, Hammerweg 6, D-6242 Kronberg, Federal Republic of Germany
BRAZIL	Pergamon Editora Ltda, Rua Eça de Queiros, 346, CEP 04011, Paraiso, São Paulo, Brazil
AUSTRALIA	Pergamon Press Australia Pty Ltd., P.O. Box 544, Potts Point, NSW 2011, Australia
JAPAN	Pergamon Press, 8th Floor, Matsuoka Central Building, 1-7-1 Nishishinjuku, Shinjuku-ku, Tokyo 160, Japan
CANADA	Pergamon Press Canada Ltd., Suite 271, 253 College Street, Toronto, Ontario M5T 1R5, Canada

Copyright © 1990 Pergamon Press, Inc.

Library of Congress Cataloging in Publication Data

Rosser, Sue Vilhauer.
   Female-friendly science : applying women's studies methods and theories to attract students / by Sue V. Rosser. -- 1st ed.
     p.   cm. -- (Athene series)
   "Bibliography / by Faye Chadwell": p.
   ISBN 0-08-037469-7 (alk. paper) : -- ISBN 0-08-037470-0 (pbk. : alk. paper) :
    1. Science--Study and teaching (Higher) 2. Women in science.
I. Title. II. Series.
Q181.R683 1990
507.1'1--dc20   89-28903
                                           CIP

Printing: 1 2 3 4 5 6 7 8 9   Year: 0 1 2 3 4 5 6 7 8 9

Printed in the United States of America

The paper used in this publication meets the minimum requirements of American National Standard for Information Sciences—Permanence of Paper for Printed Library Materials, ANSI Z39.48-1984

To
Joan Altekruse
a mentor who strives to
make medicine female-friendly

Contents

Acknowledgments   ix

Introduction   xi

1. **Crisis in Higher Education:** The Disconnection of the
    Higher Education Reports From the Student Majority   1

2. **Feminist Theories and Methods:** How to Make Course
    Content and Pedagogy Less Alienating for Women   10

3. **The M. Butterfly Dilemma:** Similarities and Differences
    Between the African-American, Marxist, Non-Western, and
    Feminist Critiques of Science   22

4. **Women's Ways of Knowing:** Research by Women Scientists
    Reflecting Women's Studies Scholarship   34

5. **Toward Inclusionary Methods:** Connecting to Students by
    Changing Approaches in Teaching Science   55

6. **Sexism in Textbooks:** New Subtleties Replace Overt
    Stereotypes by Sue V. Rosser and Ellen Potter   73

7. **Warming up the Classroom Climate for Women**   92

8. **Conclusion:** What I Learned From the Bag Lady Scientist
    and the Nobel Laureate James Watson   106

References   113

Supplemental Bibliography: by Faye Chadwell
                                 Feminism and Science   123
                                 Feminist Pedagogy   134
                                 Feminist Theory   141
                                 Women and Science   143

Indexes   149

About the Author   161

Series List   163

Acknowledgments

It is almost impossible to acknowledge the numerous individuals who contributed either directly or indirectly to making *Female-Friendly Science* a reality. Ideas suggested in a different context by colleagues, remarks by strangers overheard in an airport or mall, and daily kindnesses of friends and family provided the supportive, stimulating background that under-girded my work and influenced me in subtle indirect ways. Because of the very nature of their contributions, I cannot begin to list the individuals responsible for these indirect effects, although I would never doubt the importance of their influence.

Several people have contributed to *Female-Friendly Science* in very direct ways. Faye Chadwell was primarily responsible for the extensive bibliography, Cathy Eckman and Nancy Washington aided her. I appreciate the immense effort and countless hours she spent in carefully tracking down each reference. I am grateful to Ellen Potter, coprincipal investigator of the grant for the research that led to Chapter 6. Although the entire textbook research project was collaborative, the part of Chapter 6 that centered on science activities was largely her work. Also, I would like to acknowledge that much of the material in Chapter 5 was originally published in the special issue, Feminism and Science in Memory of Ruth Bleier, of the *Women's Studies International Forum*, which I edited (Sue V. Rosser, 1989a). Similarly, material in Chapter 7 was first published in the *Feminist Teacher* (Sue V. Rosser, 1989b).

I am particularly indebted to those people who contributed to and supported my work on a daily basis both professionally and personally. Jean

Ayers typed the manuscript, covered numerous details, and put things back together when everything fell apart in the office. Charlotte Hogsett supported me at every step of the project. She helped me to hone the ideas, gave suggestions for improvements in each chapter, and encouraged me when I faltered. My parents, John and Elizabeth Vilhauer, helped me realize my potential. My daughters, Meagan and Caitie, inspired me with the desire to fight for a future in which both the world and its science and technology will be more female-friendly.

Finally, I would like to express my gratitude to Pergamon Press for its demonstration of confidence in me by its continued publication of my work. The editors of the Athene Series, Gloria Bowles, Janice Raymond, Renate Klein, and Dale Spender, continue to give their valuable time to ensure that feminist scholarly manuscripts are reviewed and published. Renate was particularly instrumental in helping with this book, as she has been with all books on feminism and science which Pergamon has published. Lisa Tantillo, the Athene Acquisitions Editor, handled all the details conscientiously and with good humor. Phyllis Hall began the Athene Series, steered it through its early formative years, and ensures that it remains female-friendly. All these people are responsible for this book, and I am grateful to each of them.

Introduction

A combination of demographic and economic forces has produced a unique opportunity for the scientific and feminist communities to initiate a dialogue. A severe shortage of American-trained scientists is predicted for the mid-1990s. Women and minorities represent the most qualified and eligible groups from which that shortage is likely to be filled, according to the Office of Technology Assessment. The scientific community is open to evaluating its current teaching methods and course content to explore alternative methods to attract these individuals.

During the past two decades, the feminist community has sharpened its critique within the academy, extending women's studies to the scientific disciplines. Development of feminist pedagogical techniques and of feminist theory to include the consideration of race and class with gender have provided increasingly sophisticated approaches to include women and people of color. The pedagogy and theories developed for women's studies have reached the point at which they may be successfully applied to problems outside that field.

The purpose of this book is to explore the potential of feminist pedagogical methods and theories of women's studies to attract women and people of color to science. The exploration begins with an evaluation of the current reports surrounding the crisis in American higher education. The crisis and its correlated dearth of scientists and engineers is accurately depicted in the reports. However, the back to basics solutions suggested by their authors are unlikely to attract the women and minorities needed to fill the shortage. An examination of feminist scholarship and pedagogy developed for teaching women's studies courses reveals information and techniques that contrast with the back to basics approaches advocated in the reports. Comparing the feminist critiques of science with African-American, Marxist, and non-Western critiques reveals the similarities among them as well as the unique features that each perspective provides.

The recent attention to women's ways of knowing raises the question of whether or not successful women scientists have developed approaches and theories different from those used by traditional male scientists. Extension of these theories and adaptation of pedagogical techniques could lead to specific changes in curricular content and teaching methods used in science courses that will attract more women and people of color to the study of science. Specific guidelines for textbook selection and exercises for faculty to raise their sensitivity to gendered and racist language, sexist behaviors, and sexual harassment help to create a classroom climate that is conducive to learning. The ultimate effect of these inclusionary theories and methods may reach beyond their original aims. Not only are more women and people of color likely to become scientists, but more men may also choose careers in science, because these methods have been shown to be attractive to white males. What is more important, however, is that the new theories may help to make science more accessible, varied, and humane. As more people from differing races, classes, ethnic backgrounds, and genders become scientists, the science they evolve will be reflective of their rich diversity of perspective.

Chapter 1

Crisis in Higher Education

The Disconnection of the Higher Education
Reports From the Student Majority

The 1980s marked the decade of reports and critiques of problems in higher education for undergraduates in America. A scathing report, "To Reclaim a Legacy: A Report on the Humanities in Higher Education," was issued by the secretary of Education, William Bennett, in 1984. In addition, the Carnegie Foundation for the Advancement of Teaching (Ernest L. Boyer, 1987), the Association of American Colleges (1985), and the National Institute for Education (1984) produced well publicized reports written under the auspices of government agencies or foundations. Well-known professors at premier universities contributed their critiques of the students, faculty, and curricula to provide an insider's view for the public debate. The two most controversial and widely read of these books are Allan Bloom's *The Closing of the American Mind: How Higher Education Has Failed Democracy and Impoverished the Souls of Today's Students* (1987) and *Cultural Literacy: What Every American Needs to Know* (1987) by E. D. Hirsch, Jr.

Although they differ in tone and severity of criticism, all these reports and books identify similar problems. Students are disengaged from their studies, self-centered, and ignorant of national and cultural traditions. Faculty have become too specialized; their research orientation has led them to abdicate responsibility for coherence in the undergraduate curriculum. Because students and faculty have fallen prey to the "me first" individualism of the 1980s, a lack of intellectual community on campus and a dearth of commitment to societal concerns is evident.

Disconnection and disengagements among students, among faculty, between students and faculty, and among students, faculty, and the curricula

1

are the common themes in the reports and books. Fragmentation and alienation are manifested most directly in failed attempts to provide an integrated
learning experience such as a freshman core or general education requirements for undergraduate students. Although most of the reports deplore
these failures and suggest specific requirements, they do not explore the
disconnections within our society in general, and within higher education
in particular, which have led to this situation. And although they point out
the increased fragmentation of knowledge into specialized areas, the reports
do not consider the larger implications. Correlated with the increasing specialization of knowledge are a depersonalization of knowledge and a separation of the academy from the polity. Because the educated individual
tends to know more and more about a narrower and narrower field, it is
difficult for him or her to apply such detailed, specialized knowledge to
areas that may be important in personal and community life.

The current debate also fails to link changing trends in student demo-
graphics to the need for curricular reforms pointed out by women's studies
and ethnic studies. Some of the books and reports simply ignore women
and minorities entirely; others show outright hostility to women, women's
studies, and ethnic studies. As Nancy Hoffman (1987) notes, most often
the references to women are limited to statistics, showing that women now
account for the majority of undergraduate students and choose majors and
careers different from those of previous generations of women students. The
reports ignore the obvious implication that modifications in curricula and
methods may be needed to serve a diverse population effectively.

Bloom does not ignore women, minorities, feminism, women's studies,
or ethnic studies; in The Closing of the American Mind, he is overtly hostile
to them. He does not advocate education for the masses—a unique corner-
stone of American education made possible by universal compulsory education laws mandated in the early twentieth century—or even for the majority. Instead, his target audience "consists of thousands of students of
comparatively high intelligence, materially and spiritually free to do pretty
much what they want with the few years of college they are privileged to
have—in short, the kind of young persons who populate the twenty or thirty
best universities" (p. 22). Bloom, who frequently admits that he is an elitist,
deplores the 1960s as a period when colleges "were asked to change their
content and their standards, to eliminate elitism, racism and sexism as 'perceived' by the students" (p. 347). For Bloom, the American university
reached its highest point in the 1950s, just before the disintegration of standards and elitism in the 1960s:

> One of the myths is that the fifties were a period of intellectual conformism
> and superficiality, whereas there was real excitement and questioning in the
> sixties. McCarthyism—invoked when Stalinism is mentioned in order to even
> the balance of injustice between the two superpowers—symbolizes those

gray, grim years, while the blazing sixties were the days of "the movement" and, to hear its survivors tell it, their single-handed liberation of the blacks, the women and the South Vietnamese. Without entering into the strictly political issues, the intellectual picture projected is precisely the opposite of the truth. (p. 322)

As Bloom traces the current crisis of higher education to the decomposition of the university which began in the sixties with the demands of students to eliminate elitism, racism, and sexism, he praises the natural sciences as the area within the university that has maintained standards because it is mainly the preserve of white males. For example, he states,

The humanities and social sciences were debauched and grade inflation took off, while natural sciences remain largely the preserve of white males. Thus the true elitists of the university have been able to stay on the good side of the forces of history without having to suffer any of the consequences. (p. 351)

Bloom's racist, elitist, sexist attitude shows a clear disconnection with the demographic trends for the increasing majority of students who are female and/or a minority member. The natural sciences may become extinct if they continue to remain the "true elitist" white male preserve.

SHORTAGE OF SCIENTISTS

At the same time that the reports are deploring the condition of American higher education, the Office of Technology Assessment (OTA) and the National Science Foundation (NSF) predict a severe shortage of American-trained scientists for the mid-1990s. Demographic trends predict a significant drop in the number of white males of college age (Sheila E. Widnall, 1988) who have been the majority of the students in science and engineering.

Based on current participation rates, the future pool of science and engineering baccalaureates is projected to show a significant drop (NSF, 1987). The peak of U.S. graduate students available from traditional pools has passed; a 26% decrease in the pool is predicted by the late 1990s. Hidden in these statistics is the fact that the percentage of minority students in this age cohort will increase substantially. Because this group is currently underrepresented in science and engineering graduate programs, a projection based on the current participation of various groups would show an even more severe drop in the production of scientifically trained personnel at the Ph.D. level.

The percentage of B.S. degree holders in science and engineering who attain the Ph.D. degree has also fallen, from about 12% to 6% over the past 20 years (NSF, 1987). In engineering, the number of Ph.D.s obtained by U.S. citizens per year fell by more than 50% between 1970 and 1984 (NRC, 1986); currently more than 50% of Ph.D.s in engineering awarded each year go to foreign nationals (NSF, 1987). In science, the actual number of Ph.D. degrees awarded to male U.S. citizens has continued a downward trend since 1970. In engineering, increased competition is already evident, constituting a major reason for the significant decrease in U.S. students attaining the Ph.D. in engineering.

An OTA report (1985) described the pipeline for students in the natural sciences and engineering in which the attrition of women is dramatic relative to that of men:

> The report described an initial cohort of 2000 male and 2000 female students at the ninth grade level. Of that original cohort, only 1000 of each group will have sufficient mathematics at the ninth grade level to remain in the pipeline. When the two groups are followed to the end of high school, 280 men and 220 women will have completed sufficient mathematics to pursue a technical career. A major drop in women students occurs with career choice upon entering college, with 140 men and 44 women choosing scientific careers. After a career choice is made, a larger percentage of women than men actually complete their intended degree in science and engineering: at the B.S. level, 46 men and 20 women receive degrees. Data show that women enter graduate school in the same proportion relative to their percentage of B.S. degrees as do men in the various technical specialties. (The number actually entering graduate school from each cohort is estimated from their current presence in graduate schools since entry data are not available). However, some combination of attrition and stopping at the M.S. level rather than going on for the Ph.D. creates another major drop for the women students in the pipeline. Of the original 2000 students in each group, five men and one woman will receive the Ph.D. degree in some field of the natural sciences or engineering. (Widnall, 1988, pp. 1740–41)

Although Bloom sees the strength and maintenance of quality standards within the natural sciences as a consequence of their remaining a white male preserve, the NSF and the OTA recognize that this situation must change for the United States to have enough scientists and engineers. These agencies recognize that women and minorities must be recruited into the pool of potential scientists in much larger numbers if there is to be any hope of alleviating the dearth of scientists.

Maximization has often led to discrimination while minimization may lead to differential needs not being met. These agencies must also recognize that women and minorities, who are now the majority of students, are not attracted to science and that the United States faces a severe shortage of scientists which will not be filled by retaining science as the preserve of the white male. Perhaps this atmosphere will create appropriate conditions for exploring differences and differential approaches which will not exclude women and people of color.

Unfortunately, the solutions suggested by the authors of higher education reports shed little light on methods which would attract women and minorities to science. In some senses this lack of attention to the current female majority can seem appropriate. Significant legal and personal battles were fought to obtain equality of treatment for women both inside and outside of academia. Much early women's studies and feminist research focused on similarities or lack of differences between men and women. Despite the defeat of the Equal Rights Amendment (or perhaps because of it) and the critique by feminists such as Catherine A. MacKinnon (1987) that "equal treatment" merely perpetuates the male standards and values from which difference is measured, many feminists still take the positivist or liberal feminist (Alison Jaggar, 1983) stance of equality, or no differences, for political discussions.

Following this stance of minimalization, it seems logical not to call for modifications in curricular content or approaches based on differences in sex and race. However, history reveals that exclusion of women and people of color from institutions of higher education and high paying professions was often based on anatomical differences, supposed IQ differences, or differential performance on standardized tests (Stephen Jay Gould, 1981; Janet Sayers 1982). Lack of tolerance for diversity has frequently led to the translation of difference, from the white and/or male norm, as inferior. When the difference could be demonstrated to have a biological basis, as it has many times in history, then biological determinism was used to justify the political status quo and deny access to education for women and people of color. It is not surprising, therefore, to find that considerable debate in feminist circles still centers around whether sex and racial differences should be maximized or minimized (Katherine T. Bartlett, 1988; MacKinnon, 1987).

In adopting a maximalist approach, I do not mean to imply that I assume there are biological differences in the brain or mental functioning between men and women or people of different races. In our society there are certainly differences in the social treatment and teaching of girls and boys and men and women (and of people of different races, classes, and sexual preferences). This differential treatment is likely to be the main factor in the differential attraction of these groups to science, although lack of controlled experimental data makes it impossible to rule out psychological or biological differences as possible contributing factors.

An underlying assumption in this book is that exploration between the differences in traditional approaches to science and those of women and people of color is useful so as to discern whether these female-friendly approaches might make the study of science more attractive. Similarly, pedagogical methods and curricular content from women's studies and ethnic studies will be contrasted with the traditional curriculum, which assumes the white male as a norm, in an attempt to retrieve and develop useful tools to attract individuals to science. I do not assume that any differences suggested necessarily have a biological basis, are linked with a specific genital sex, or imply inferiority or superiority. The differences are explored in an attempt to alleviate the prospective shortage of scientists by filling positions with women and and minorities, who now constitute the majority of students.

CRITIQUE OF BLOOM

Because Bloom's ideas for educational reform demonstrate a clear break between his elitist, 1950s ideal vision and the realities of the new majority of students in the decades of the 1980s and 1990s, it is not surprising that his solutions are inappropriate. Bloom openly states a hostile attitude toward women, feminism, and women's studies that subtly pervades many other reports. Still other reports simply ignore the implications of a female majority and remain silent on the effects on the curriculum of feminism and the new scholarship on women. Although Bloom is on the extreme edge compared to the other reports and books, it is instructive to explore his attitudes toward women and women's studies.[1]

Like most of the other reports, Bloom makes little attempt to use gender neutral language or language that is inclusive of females in his book. His assumption that male language is universal is complemented by his unquestioned androcentric perspective. He assumes students are male (thus flying in the face of the female statistical majority) and will have had experiences or opportunities reserved primarily for men in our culture. For example, in discussing the horrors of rock music, he states:

> It artificially induces the exaltation naturally attached to the completion of the greatest endeavors—victory in a just war, consummated love, artistic creation, religious devotion and discovery of truth. . . . These students will assiduously study economics or the professions and the Michael Jackson costume will slip off to reveal a Brooks Brothers suit beneath. (1987, p. 81)

Use of gendered language and an implicit, unquestioned androcentric perspective are the indirect ways in which Bloom conveys his attitudes toward women. He also directly presents his view of the differences between men and women.[2]

Bloom roots his ideas about women in nature, taking an "anatomy is destiny" approach to women:

> Man in the state of nature, either in the first one or the one we have now, can walk away from a sexual encounter and never give it another thought. But a woman may have a child, and in fact, as becomes ever clearer, may want to

---

[1]Because my expertise is in the area of women's studies, I will critique Bloom's work from the perspective of gender. Undoubtedly, many similar comments could be made from a more thorough analysis of his work with regard to race and class.

[2]In the following section, I quote Bloom extensively so that the reader will have the opportunity to see Bloom's own account of the differences.

have a child. Sex can be an indifferent thing for men, but it really cannot quite be so for women. This is what might be called the female drama. (p. 114)

He deplores the rise of the women's movement, which has tampered with nature, and considers earlier patterns of courtship and marriage as more desirable:

That man is not made to be alone is all very well, but who is made to live with him? This is why men and women hesitated before marriage, and court-ship was thought necessary to find out whether the couple was compatible, and perhaps to give them basic training in compatibility. A man was to make a living and protect his wife and children, and a woman was to provide for the domestic economy, particularly in caring for husband and children. (p. 126)

Louis Menand (1987) points out in his review of Bloom's book that this view makes nonsense of the notion of the natural, since courtship is a historically and culturally specific institution, by no means the universal norm: "This little piece of the argument is emblematic of Bloom's whole critique: the academic in the ivory tower manages, by the exercise of unadulterated rea-son, to produce a philosophical justification for the status quo ante" (p. 40).

After building the case that the biological destiny of women makes them different from men, Bloom proceeds to present his rather traditional views on male/female relationships:

And here is where the whole business turns nasty. The souls of men—their ambitious, warlike, protective, possessive character—must be dismantled in order to liberate women from their domination. Machismo—the polemical description of maleness or spiritedness, which was the central *natural* passion in men's souls in the psychology of the ancients, the passion of attachment and loyalty—was the villain, the source of the difference between the sexes. (p. 129)

He implies that sex is a major factor motivating men toward marriage:

Meanwhile, one of the strongest, oldest motives for marriage is no longer oper-ative. Men can now easily enjoy the sex that previously could only be had in marriage. (p. 132)

With such views about the nature of males and females, it is not surpris-ing that Bloom directly attacks feminism for interfering with nature:

The women's movement is not founded on nature. Although feminism sees the position of women as a result of nurture and not nature, its crucial conten-tion is that biology should not be destiny, and biology is surely natural. It is certain that feminism has brought with it an unrelenting process of conscious-ness-raising and changing that begins in what is probably a permanent human inclination and is surely a modern one—the longing for the unlimited, the unconstrained. It ends, as do many modern movements that seek abstract jus-tice, in forgetting nature and using force to refashion human beings to secure that justice. (p. 100)

Bloom finds that feminism has also been a disruptive force within the academy, that it embodies the "latest enemy of the vitality of the classic texts." He suggests that sexism attracted previous generations to literature:

> But all literature up to today is sexist. The Muses never sang to the poets about liberated women . . . and [this] was also what drew students to reading them. (p. 65)

> The latest translation of Biblical text—sponsored by the National Council of the Churches of Christ—suppresses gender references to God, so that future generations will not have to grapple with the fact that God was once a sexist. (pp. 65–66)

He registers his disapproval of the feminist critiques of the classics:

> Another tactic is to expunge the most offensive authors—for example, Rousseau—from the education of the young or to include feminist responses in college courses, pointing out the distorting prejudices, and using the books only as evidence of the misunderstanding of woman's nature and the history of injustice to it. (p. 66)

He further expresses disapproval of the "images of women" approaches to teaching literature:

> Moreover, the great female characters can be used as examples of the various ways women have coped with their enslavements to the sexual role. (p. 66)

Bloom also blames feminism for the downfall of the family:

> Ninety percent or more of children of divorced parents stay with their mothers, whose preeminent stake in children has been enhanced by feminist demands and by a consequent easy rationalization of male irresponsibility. So we have reproduction without family—if family includes the presence of a male who has any kind of a definite function. (p. 105)

What is most telling and regrettable about Bloom's attack on feminism is that he has undertaken it without doing his homework on either the classics or women's studies. In her excellent, probing review in *The New York Times*, Martha Nussbaum (1987) demonstrates that Bloom was silent about well known classical references (Epicureus, Musonius) that support the importance of the education of women. She documents his use of a not widely accepted interpretation of Plato's *Republic* to support lack of access to equal education for women. Nussbaum (1987) points out that Bloom's vague use of the term "ancients" implies "the major Hellenistic philosophers, Epicurean, Skeptic, and Stoic" (p. 23) agreed that machismo was the central natural passion in men's souls when, in fact, they differed widely on this point.

Bloom and, to a lesser extent, the authors of the other reports in higher education leave us in a paradoxical situation. They seem to advocate curricular content and methods that have been shown to secure academia as the preserve of the white middle to upper class Western male. Aside from the racism and sexism (and perhaps illegal discrimination) implied by these approaches, they also do little to alleviate the problem of the predicted dearth of scientists and engineers. One cannot hope to attract women and minorities using curricular content and methods demonstrated to exclude and repel those very groups. There are other curricula and methodological approaches within higher education, but ignored by the reports, that might begin to solve the problem.

Chapter 2

Feminist Theories and Methods

How to Make Course Content and Pedagogy
Less Alienating for Women

The racism and sexism expressed overtly by Bloom (1987) make it likely that his solution to the crisis in higher education will continue to exclude rather than attract women and minorities to higher education in general and to science and engineering in particular. Although the authors of the other reports are not as clearly sexist and racist in their solutions, they do fail to make a connection between the changing demographic profile of the potential student pool and methods to attract the students to higher education. While several reports note the statistical increase in the percentage of women and minority students projected for the 1990s, they stop short of exploring the research and approaches that higher education has already developed for these groups.

During the past two decades, the feminist community has sharpened its critique within the academy, extending women's studies to the scientific disciplines. Development of feminist pedagogical techniques and of feminist theory to include the consideration of race and class with gender have provided increasingly sophisticated approaches to include women and people of color. The pedagogy and theories developed for women's studies have reached the point at which they may be successfully applied to problems outside of that field.

Pedagogical methods developed by teachers in women's studies and ethnic studies may help create a classroom climate which is more conducive to learning for women and people of color. Some research has shown that women experience a decrease in self-esteem and a decline in academic and career aspirations during their college years (Alexander Astin, 1977). The higher dropout rate for people of color, particularly black men and Hispanics, has been documented (Peter Nulty, 1989). Although most teachers in institutions of higher education strive to create an environment conducive to learning, their efforts may be undercut if they fail to be sensitive to factors such as sexism and racism, which are an obstacle to learning.

LANGUAGE

One obstacle to learning may be inherent in language. A substantial amount of early research in women's studies has shown how both written and spoken language may transmit bias regarding roles and stereotypes of gender, class, and race. Wendy Martyna (1978) demonstrated that when generic terms such as *he* and *man* are used, people rarely visualize women. Generic use of masculine terminology also implies that the male is the norm in society. Using masculine nouns and pronouns to refer to all people excludes more than half the population. Several solutions to the generic male pronoun problem are possible. Using plural nouns and pronouns ("help children to develop their table manners", rather than "help the child to develop his table manners"), replacing pronouns with articles ("every doctor has a preferred method of treatment" for "every doctor has his preferred method of treatment"), and simply eliminating the pronoun ("each social worker determines the best way to handle difficult clients" instead of "each social worker determines the best way that she can handle difficult clients") are effective alternatives. They are usually less awkward than using both pronouns and varying their order ("each student should have her or his assignment completed before the end of class to insure that he or she can take full advantage of the laboratory materials"). Specific genderless nouns ("the average citizen" rather than "the man on the street") and precise job titles and descriptions ("the professor will not respect students who do not work" or "she will not respect students who do not work") usually provide clarity and precision to writing and speaking, as well as eliminating the problem of the generic male pronoun.

Sexism in language takes a variety of forms beyond usage of the generic pronoun. Gender referencing ("the doctor gives his patient", "the nurse gives her patient") permeates classroom language and writing and transmits stereotypes of occupational, social, and gender roles. Labeling has often been used as a subtle form of discrimination against women and people of color ("boy" or "girl" for an adult; "credit to your race"). Nonparallel terminology ("men and ladies" or "the dentist and his doctor wife were in Hawaii") also conveys differential status.

Stereotyping encompasses a broad range of issues including age, gender, and race. It includes stereotypes of roles (all women as housewives), occupations (all truckdrivers as men), personality characteristics (stoic men, passive women), and physical, mental, and emotional characteristics (mathematical men and verbal women). It is not difficult to replace language stereotyping men or women with words appropriate for both men and women in an occupation ("fire fighter" rather than "fireman"; "salesperson" for "salesman"; "student" instead of "coed"; "secretary" or "assistant" for "gal" or "Girl Friday").

Paternalism is a subtle form of stereotyping as is racism that conveys surprise that a woman or person of color succeeded in a certain situation ("Dr. Jane Wright, a black woman who rose to the position of Associate Dean of the New York Medical College"). Behaviors have changed with the changing roles and occupations that men and women are assuming in our society. Language needs to reflect this change by replacing stereotypical adjectives and expressions ("nature" and "time" rather than "Mother Nature" and "Father Time;" "chauvinist" for "male chauvinist").

Teachers in women's studies and ethnic studies are sensitive to eliminating the barriers to learning raised by language that is stereotypical, sexist, or racist. However, because of varied backgrounds and experiences, some teachers in science and engineering have difficulty in recognizing language that is biased. In their publication, A Guide to Nonsexist Language, the Association of American Colleges suggests "two abbreviated rules to check material for bias: Would you say the same thing about a person of the opposite sex? Would you like it said about you? That's the bottom line. Use your own good sense on whether a joke, comment or image is funny—or whether it unfairly expoits people and perpetuates stereotypes" (AAC, 1986, p. 1).

Publications in education (U.S. Department of Health, Education, and Welfare, Office of Education, 1978) and social sciences (Mercilee M. Jenkins, 1983) include excellent guidelines for student–faculty communication. Most of these guidelines are also appropriate for health and science courses. However, I would like to discuss a couple of problems or special adaptations that might be more appropriate for the natural sciences. Because the sciences have fewer women and people of color (NSF, 1988) than either the social sciences or humanities, I think that it may be advisable to employ particular techniques to break stereotypes and emphasize contributions of women and people of color. The usual custom is to refer to scientists who have made important discoveries or carried out significant experiments by their last names ("Watson and Franklin's work on DNA"). Use of last names only in referring to work of both men and women scientists is parallel treatment. However, the picture in most people's minds upon hearing a last name is that of a male scientist, because most scientists in our society are men. Similarly, the use of initials rather than forenames in lists of references provides parallel treatment for both men and women. Nevertheless, Virginia Johnson-Gazzam (personal communication, fall, 1984) found that the overwhelming majority of students in education classes assumed that when initials were used, they stood for a male forename. Therefore, the parallel treatment that may be more helpful in breaking the stereotype of all scientists as male is the use of full forenames and surnames for all experimenters ("James Watson and Rosalind Franklin").

It is unparallel treatment to compare the work done by "black scientist E.E. Just and scientist R. M. Auerbach" (Kenneth R. Manning, 1983). Prefacing Just's name with "black scientist" while not using "white scientist" before Auerbach's name assumes white as the racial norm. It may be effective and parallel to mention everyone's race and gender when talking about individual contributions: "The black female physician Susan McKinney Steward and the white male physicist Albert Einstein." This technique emphasizes the contributions of women and people of color while placing parallel prefixes before the names of white male scientists. Students inevitably begin to think about why most scientists are white men. The use of language provides a subtle, yet powerful form of breaking biases and stereotypes of gender, class, and race so that the dominant cultural environment is not replicated in classroom interactions.

CLASSROOM BEHAVIORS

Other differences in verbal behavior between men and women may be carried over into the classroom. Studies in formal groups containing both men and women have demonstrated that men talk more than women and exert more control over the topic of conversation (Cheris Kramarae, 1980). White men also interrupt women much more frequently than women interrupt men and their interruptions more often introduce trivial comments or statements that end or change the focus of the women's discussion (Don H. Zimmerman & Candace West, 1975). Further, the more frequent use by women of "tag" questions ("This is true, don't you think?"), excessive use of qualifiers, and excessively polite and deferential speech forms may make women's comments more easily ignored or seem to carry less weight in the classroom. In a science classroom, where women students are more frequently the statistical minority, their comments can be even more easily interrupted or ignored.

Forms of verbal interaction, such as knowing and addressing the male students more frequently by name and interrupting female students more frequently than males, may be unconscious behaviors on the part of faculty that discourage female participation. Humorous or teasing references to physical or sexual characteristics (more frequently applied to females) or humorous treatment of serious topics such as rape, lesbianism, or depression are likely to be offensive to women and make them feel uncomfortable in the classroom interaction.

In addition to written and spoken language, sexism in nonverbal behavior and interaction with students may provide differential encouragement to learn to males compared to females. Studies have indicated that some faculty make eye contact more often with men than women (Barrie Thorne, 1979), nod and gesture more often in response to men's questions and comments than to women's, and wait longer for men than for women to answer a question before going on to another student (Myra Sadker & David Sadker, 1979). In certain situations women may be "squeezed out" from viewing a laboratory assignment or demonstration, may be asked lower order questions than men ("How many chambers does the heart have?" versus "What is the function of macrophages in the immune system?"), or may not be favored by being chosen as student assistants (Roberta M. Hall & Bernice R. Sandler, 1982).

Other studies have demonstrated that Asian and black students feel ignored or put down by faculty (John Noonan, 1980). Clearly, these types of behaviors by the faculty, although often unconscious or unintentional, do not create an atmosphere of mutual trust and respect between faculty and students. In science classes, where women and people of color generally comprise a small percentage of the class, these behaviors create further barriers to participation and increase the chances of being ignored. The facts that most faculty in science departments are white men and that science fields are perceived as "masculine" disciplines further exacerbate the problem and alienate women and men of color.

Science faculty need to evaluate their verbal and nonverbal communication with students, to ascertain whether their classroom behavior discriminates on the basis of gender or race. Because most of us are relatively blind to our own behaviors, it might be helpful to ask a colleague from another department—women's studies of ethnic studies would be ideal—to evaluate several classes solely from the perspective of faculty-student interaction. Videotaping class sessions provides another approach to examining these behaviors.

CURRICULUM

The education reports dismiss women's studies without a serious examination of what it entails and the effect that it is having on the curriculum. Ironically, women's studies provides the solutions for many of the problems that Bloom pinpoints in higher education. In some institutions (Liz McMillen, 1987) women's studies has pioneered revitalization of the curricula and made connections among students, faculty, and the curricula.

If Bloom had taken the time to ask the question "What is women's studies?" he would have discovered how the new scholarship on women is transforming curricula nationally. Women's studies began almost two decades ago when the first courses that focused on women were initiated on college campuses. Since that time about 40,000 women's studies courses (Hoffman, 1987) have been taught. In its latest directory, the National Women's Studies Association (1988) lists programs at over 500 institutions of higher education including 64 masters programs and 25 doctoral level programs. In addition, several refereed journals publish the papers of feminist scholars working in women's studies programs and in the 51 academic centers for research on women.

Beginning in 1980, several projects funded by the federal government and private foundations for integrating the new scholarship on women were initiated at a variety of four year colleges and universities in different regions throughout the country. By 1984, 60 curriculum integration projects had been undertaken (AAC, 1984) in institutions ranging from former men's colleges (Yale and Dartmouth) to women's colleges (Smith and Stephens), as well as large state universities (Kansas State and Indiana University at Bloomington), medium-sized state institutions (Mankato State and Old Dominion), and small liberal arts colleges (Guilford and Claremont Colleges). More recently, in addition to curriculum transformation efforts at over 100 institutions, integration efforts have moved to the state-wide level. The New Jersey Department of Higher Education has given $362,500 to support the endeavor at the state's 56 public and private colleges for the "inaugural year of integrating the scholarship on women" (McMillen, 1987).

Several models have been developed by individuals who have studied the institutions with projects for transforming the curriculum (Peggy McIntosh, 1984; Marilyn R. Schuster & Susan Van Dyne, 1985; Mary K. Tetreault, 1985). All the models reflect the idea that integrating information about women into the curriculum is a process that occurs in phases. The first phase constitutes the situation in which women are absent from the curriculum; the final phase is the gender-balanced curriculum. The model developed by McIntosh (1984) of the Wellesley Center for Research on Women will be elaborated and expanded here to illustrate the process of transforming the curriculum, using examples from five disciplines.

McIntosh Model

Phase I

The Womanless Curriculum. This is the traditional curricular approach taken by Bloom in which the absence of women is not noted. It provides a very traditional approach to history, deeming only great events and men worthy of consideration (i.e., Presidents and battles are emphasized). Art history courses taught on many campuses exemplify this phase. The most widely used art history text, by Janson, a very thick volume of 750 pages included no women artists until the 1986 version (Harriet McNamee & Dorothy Fix, 1986). English courses at this stage include no or very few women authors. In my opinion, Bloom's idea of a curriculum based on the Great Books would probably include no women authors. Much psychological research and many psychology courses are also at this stage. For example, many theories of human development are really based on male development. The model of adult development by Daniel J. Levinson, Charlotte Darrow, Edward Klein, Maria Levinson, and Braxton McKee (1974), the model by Erik H. Erikson (1963), and, of course the work by Freud all assumed a male norm. In most biology and other science courses, gender is not even considered to be an issue because science is supposedly objective. However, many experiments are run on male animal subjects only. Certain subjects of particular interest to women such as childbirth and other women's health concerns have received less funding for research except in instances such as the new reproductive technologies where women have become the funders and subjects for basic research (Gena Corea, et al. 1987). Responding to this problem, the National Institutes of Health issued new guidelines in December, 1986 ("NIH Urges Inclusion," 1986) suggesting that proposals should include both male and female experimental subjects and include topics of interest to women.

Phase II

Women as an Addition to the Curriculum. Heroines, exceptional women or an elite few who are seen to have been of benefit to culture as defined by the traditional standards of the discipline, are included in the curriculum. Hirsch's (1987) list of names and terms that all educated individuals should know would fall in this category. Bennett's (1984) list of fifty books to be read—including only two female authors, Jane Austen and George Eliot—constitutes another example of phase II. History courses taught in this phase might include women such as Joan of Arc, Abigail Adams, or Betsy Ross. An art history course in phase II might include a few slides of work by Berthe Morisot or Mary Cassatt or a handout about them used with the Janson text. The traditional Norton Anthology in English provides an evolving model of this phase. The first edition included only two women, Jane Austen and Emily Dickinson. Now in its fifth edition, due to the new scholarship on women, the Norton Anthology includes twenty-eight female authors. In psychology, the work of Melanie Klein, Karen Horney, or even Anna Freud, who modified Freud's ideas about women, might be included in a course at this stage. Science courses that emphasize the nine women who have won the Nobel Prize in medicine or science would certainly be categorized here. Phase II is characterized by adding women on without changing the basic syllabus or traditional framework of the course.

Phase III

Women as a Problem, Anomaly, or Absence from the Curriculum. Women are studied in this phase as victims, as deprived or defective variants of men, or as protestors, with critical issues. At this phase, historians may begin to ask why there have been no women presidents, but the categories of historical analysis are still derived from those who had the most power.

People considering art history at this phase begin to ask questions such as, why aren't there more women artists and what is art anyway? In English the question becomes, why aren't there any female Shakespeares? In psychology the question centers on why women's development doesn't fit the model of human development. This soon leads to the overarching question of what must be wrong with models that don't fit the development of half of the people in the world. Many biologists at this stage point out some of the flaws in experimental design in some of the studies which have supposedly "proven" superior mathematical ability in males, or the circularity of logic involved in some sociobiology research in which human language and frameworks are used to describe certain animal behaviors, such as aggression, which then "proves" that certain human behavior is biologically determined—because it has also been found in animals.

Phase IV

Women as the Focus for Studies. This is the arena of women's studies where women become the center of research and teaching. In this phase the categories for analysis shift and become racially inclusive, multifaceted, and filled with variety; they demonstrate and validate plural versions of reality.

This phase takes account of the fact that because women have had half of the world's lived experience, we need to ask what that experience has been and to consider it as half of history. This causes faculty to use all kinds of evidence and source materials which they are not in the habit of using. People doing art history research at this phase may begin to look at certain types of crafts, quilts, and stitchery work (much of which has traditionally been work done by women) as art. In English people look at what women have written—diaries, letters, novels. They look at women's writing for what it is and examine how it differs from that of men. Psychologists such as Carol Gilligan working at this stage have begun to explore female models of development which emphasize different methods of ethical and moral decision making practiced by girls and women.

In biology, the work of Barbara McClintock may serve as an example of this stage of research. McClintock is an achieving scientist who is not a feminist. However, in her approach toward studying maize, she indicates a shortening of the distance between the observer and the object being studied and a consideration of the complex interaction between the organism and its environment (Evelyn Fox Keller, 1983).

Phase V

The Curriculum Redefined and Reconstructed to Include Us All. This is the ultimate goal of the transformed curriculum. Although this curriculum will be a long time in the making, it will help students to sense that women are both part of and alien to the dominant culture. It will create more useable and inclusive constructs which validate a wider sample of life.

Obviously Phase V has not yet been reached in the work of scholars in women's studies. However, it is a goal toward which women's studies strives. In this final phase women are present in all disciplines. The idea is not to replace the womanless curriculum with the manless curriculum; the ideal is to have the knowledge about women present in all introductory and advanced courses in the curriculum. Only when the curriculum reflects the diversity of experiences, roles, and achievements present in our population will it begin to prepare students for the diversity in the world. Transforming the curriculum is one important step towards increasing that diversity and connecting students with the curriculum.

The phase theory for integrating information on women into the curriculum provides a model linking the content of the curriculum to the female majority of students. In this way it is very different from the disconnected Great Books curriculum envisioned by Bloom in which little or no curricular content includes the experiences of the majority of students who are women and people of color.

Women's studies also provides models for overcoming four of the other disconnections that Bloom suggests exists in higher education:

1. Fragmentation of knowledge into specialized areas—Bloom deplores the fragmentation of knowledge into specialized areas compared to the early days when philosophy and natural science included the study of all knowledge. He suggests that the departments compete with and contradict each other making no attempt to demonstrate to the students how their discipline relates to others in the university. "So the student must navigate among a collection of carnival barkers, each trying to lure him to a particular sideshow" (1987, p. 339).

Women's studies is interdisciplinary. Gender is the lens which focuses the questions asked in women's studies; interdisciplinary approaches are needed to investigate the questions raised when women are brought to the center of the study. For example, when considering questions such as the role of women in revolutionary movements, the economics of the family, or changes during menopause, the methods from only one discipline are inadequate. The interdisciplinary approach in women's studies overcomes the problems of fragmentation resulting from overspecialization.

2. Depersonalization of knowledge—As a result of overspecialization, students are unable to relate the details they learn in a course to their own lives. Learning in courses becomes abstract and separate from the everyday personal experiences of the students. Bloom (1987) simultaneously laments this and encourages it with his call for the return to the Great Books.

    Programs based upon judicious use of great texts provide the royal road to students' hearts. Their gratitude at learning of Achilles or the categorical imperative is boundless. (p. 334)

Women's studies takes an entirely different approach. Because of the extent to which women's experiences have been excluded from the canon and traditional curriculum, early women's studies teaching and research was grounded in women's experience. Women's personal experiences provided the origins for much initial information in women's health, psychology, and sociology because the experts and classic texts had not investigated those realms. Women's studies continues to encourage students to consider the validity of material they are learning in light of their own experiences.

3. Separation of the academy from the polity—Bloom (1987) deplores the discontinuity between what is taught in the academy, particularly in the liberal arts, and its effects upon the lives of people in the real world.

    The greatest of thoughts were in our political principles but were never embodied, hence not living, in a class of men. Their home in America was the university, and the violation of that home was the crime of the sixties. (p. 344)

Women's studies arose as the academic arm of the women's movement. Its connection with politics is still evident in many of the questions studied: What is the source of women's oppression? Do women fare better economically under communism or capitalism? Is there anthropological evidence that patriarchy has always been universal? Has the funding of scientific research led to inadequate study of women's major health problems?[1]

---

[1]Although women's studies became the academic arm of the women's movement, this does not imply that women's studies scholarship or teaching advocates a uniform political stance on questions or issues. Moving women to the center of study does not necessarily imply that all information discovered will be positive and reflect women in a good light or that diversity of interpretation on issues will not be accepted. Critics of women's studies have often interpreted its connection to the women's movement to imply one or both of these political approaches to research.

4. Elitism and racism within the curriculum—Bloom traces the current crisis of higher education to the decomposition of the university which began in the sixties with the demands of students to eliminate elitism, racism, and sexism. Although he praises the natural sciences as the area
   within the university that has maintained its standards because it is the
   sole preserve of white males, this status must change to alleviate the
   dearth of scientists.

The early research and teaching in women's studies suffered from the
limited perspective of the white, middle class females who provided the
bulk of individuals initiating the early developments in the field (Bonnie T.
Dill, 1983). Increasingly, women's studies has labored to include the diversity of women's experience and to provide analyses of the intersection of
race, class, and gender. These more complex analyses are likely to be more
appropriate in the 1980s and 1990s to attract women and minorities to science than the 1950s white, male, elitist approach lauded by Bloom.

The presence of sexism in language and classroom behaviors combined
with the absence of information about the achievements, roles, and experiences of women from most curricular content leave many female students
and people of color feeling somewhat distant, different, and alienated from
what they are learning. Sexism may be particularly severe in cases where
women are attempting to enter fields in science and engineering which are
not perceived as traditional arenas for women. The work of Hall and Sandler
from the AAC Project on the Status and Education of Women "The Classroom Climate: A Chilly One for Women?" (1982) documents the ways in
which small inequities in the classroom may have cumulative negative effects upon a female student's self-esteem, choice of major, and career plans.

Women students in traditionally masculine fields such as science and
engineering are likely to face difficulties for the following reasons:

- they comprise a distinct minority in a given class or department;
- they have little contact with other women pursuing the same major because of the vertical progression of required courses;
- they find few female teachers who might serve as role models; and
- they work with many professors who are not accustomed to having
  women students in their classes. (Hall & Sandler, 1982)

In the United States we have made a commitment as a nation to mass
education. Although Bloom may wish to return to the Greek model in which
education was for a small group of propertied men, such a model is no
longer appropriate for the United States. It is questionable whether it was
ever appropriate. When the majority of students is female and/or a minority
member, as it is in the 1980s and will continue to be in the 1990s, that
model most surely is not suitable and will not attract them to science.

Scholars in women's studies and ethnic studies are retrieving information and developing new theories about the roles, accomplishments, and experiences of women and people of color. This new scholarship needs to be integrated into the traditional curriculum to connect students with the appropriately diverse and complex educational background they will need for functioning in the world. A curriculum that includes the history, literature, and cultural heritage of all—men, women, rich, poor, people of color, and whites—provides the complex background needed by students for the twenty-first century.

Extension of these theories and adaptation of pedagogical techniques leads to specific changes in curricular content and teaching methods used in science courses that will attract more women and people of color to the study of science. Specific guidelines for textbook selection and exercises for faculty to raise their sensitivity to avoid gendered and racist language, sexist behaviors, and sexual harassment, help create a classroom climate that is more conducive to learning. The ultimate effect of these changed, inclusionary theories and methods may reach beyond their original aims. Not only are more women and people of color likely to become scientists, but also more men may choose careers in science, since these improved methods have been shown to also be attractive to white males (Jane B. Kahle, 1985). More importantly, however, these theories and methods may help to change science to be more accessible, varied, and humane. As more people from differing races, classes, ethnic backgrounds, and genders become scientists, the science they evolve is likely to reflect their rich diversity of perspective.

Chapter 3

The M. Butterfly Dilemma

*Similarities and Differences Between the
African-American, Marxist, Non-Western, and
Feminist Critiques of Science*

The basis of the popular Broadway play "M. Butterfly" is a most surprising event: A white, upper middle class Western male has a sexual relationship with his Oriental mistress for twenty years without ever recognizing that "she" is a biological male. The likelihood of this event seems so remote that the public probably would not have accepted it as the basis for a play, had it not in fact been based on a true story.

> From Gallimard's intimate tale, which is based on an actual French espionage case uncovered in this decade, Mr. Hwang has erected a sweeping (if at times discursive and didactic) meditation not only on the gulf between men and women and West and East but also on imperialism and Maoism. (Frank Rich, 1988, p. 17)

The duped lover asks his mistress how "she" hid her true biological identity from him for all these years. "Her" answer reveals much about the overlapping biases of sexism, racism, classism, and non-Westernism that led to the duping and downfall of this white, upper middle class Western male. "She" suggests that he confused being from a different race and culture with being female.

A similar question arises when one considers attracting women and people of color to science. Will the same methods and approaches attract both women and people of color to science or are different methods needed to attract each group? A related, and perhaps more significant question, arises when one considers the result of having more women and people of color in science: Will science itself—its questions asked, approaches and experimental subjects used, and theories and conclusions drawn from the data—

change if the pool of scientists becomes more heterogeneous with regard to race, gender, class, and ethnicity? In other words, to what extent has the pool of scientists, which is white, middle to upper class, Western, and male, created a science that reflects their perspective and approaches to the world? Is the developed science a reflection of the standpoint from which the scientist views the world or does the positivist view of a truly objective standpoint free from bias still hold?

A controversy has recently surfaced in feminist circles, and possibly in scientific circles, surrounding these questions. Feminists anticipated that our critiques of science might be dismissed by the traditional scientists upon the bases of the objectivity and value-free nature of good science. However, some of the feminists (Vivian Gornick, 1983; Evelyn Fox Keller, 1984) who have developed these critiques have implied recently that good scientific research is not conducted differently by men and women and that the theories derived from such research might be free from gender constraints.

> My exploration of McClintock's life has also sharpened my thinking on a subject I have written about elsewhere: the relation of gender to science. In her adamant rejection of female stereotypes, McClintock poses a challenge to any simple notions of a "feminine" science. Her pursuit of a life in which "the matter of gender drops away" provides us instead with a glimpse of what a "gender-free" science might look like. (Keller, 1983, p. xvii)

I believe that scientific research and theories cannot be gender (or class, race, or sexual preference) neutral as long as our society is not neutral on these issues. Elizabeth Fee (1982) states that a sexist society should be expected to develop a sexist science; conceptualizing a feminist science from within our society is "like asking a medieval peasant to imagine the theory of genetics or the production of a space capsule" (p. 31). In this Chapter, I further develop the reasons why I think science cannot be free from the values of the society in which it is developed.

FEMINIST CRITIQUES OF TRADITIONAL SCIENTIFIC APPROACHES AND THEORIES

The critiques made by feminists in science of specific studies and general theories in animal behavior, the neurosciences, and endocrinology are often dismissed as correct but obvious: corrections of poorly designed experiments or conclusions drawn from overgeneralizations of data. The implication of these dismissals is that any "good" scientist would not have designed or accepted the results of the experiments and could certainly have made the critique him or herself without the benefit of the feminist perspective.

To illustrate the feminist critiques and their dismissals, I have chosen three examples from different areas within the natural sciences.

Animal Behavior

Some researchers have observed behavior in lower animals in a search for universal behavior patterns that occur in males of all species or in all males of a particular order or class such as primates or mammals. This behavior is then extrapolated to humans in an attempt to demonstrate a biological or innate basis for the behavior. Sociobiologists, such as David Barash (1977), Richard Dawkins (1976), and Edward O. Wilson (1975) have based their new discipline on biological determinism in stating that behavior is genetically determined and that differences between males and females in role, status, and performance are biologically based.

Feminist critiques of sociobiology have centered around criticisms of the assumption that behaviors such as aggression, homosexuality, promiscuity, selfishness, and altruism are biologically determined and around the problems involved with anthropomorphosis in animal behavior studies. The anthropomorphosis occurs in at least two forms: a) the use of human language and frameworks to describe animal behavior which is then used to "prove" certain human behaviors are innate because they are also found in animals, b) the selective choice of species for study that mirror human society. The data from those selected species are then assumed to be the universal behavior of all species. Some scientists have suggested that these feminist critiques are obvious. However, the most renowned sociobiologists (Richard D. Alexander, 1987; Dawkins, 1976; Robert L. Trivers, 1972; Edward O. Wilson, 1978) have continued to assume genes do determine behavior and the behaviors described as aggression, homosexuality, rape, selfishness, and altruism in animals are equivalent to those behaviors in humans, even though almost one decade of criticism by feminists (Ruth Bleier, 1976; Ruth Hubbard & Marian Lowe, 1979; Marian Lowe, 1978) has been leveled against the "obvious" flaws in the sociobiological theories and assumptions.

Similarly, although it was clear in the early primatology work (R. M. Yerkes, 1943) that particular primate species, such as the baboon and chimpanzee, were chosen for study primarily because their social organization was seen by the observers as closely resembling that of human primates, subsequent researchers forgot the "obvious" limitations imposed by such selection of species and proceeded to generalize the data to universal behavior patterns for all primates. It was not until a significant number of women entered primatology that the concepts of the universality and male leadership of dominance hierarchies among primates (Jane Lancaster, 1975; Ruth R. Leavitt, 1975; Lila Leibowitz, 1975; Thelma Rowell, 1974) were questioned and shown to be inaccurate for many primate species. The "evident" problems discussed by feminist critics (Ruth Bleier, 1984) of studying nonhuman primates in an attempt to discover what the true nature of humans would be without the overlay of culture, have also been largely ignored by many of the sociobiologists and scientists studying animal behavior.

Neurosciences

In the neurosciences, a substantial amount of work has been done relating to sex differences in the brains of men and women. The studies on brain lateralization, genes, brain structure, and effects of prenatal and postpubertal androgens and estrogens on the nervous system have been carried out in an attempt to discern biological bases for differences between males and females in behavioral or performance characteristics such as aggression, and verbal, visuo-spatial, and mathematical abilities. Excellent critiques have been made by feminists of the faulty experimental designs and unfounded extrapolations beyond the data of the work in brain lateralization (Susan Leigh Star, 1979), hormones (Bleier, 1984), genes (Elizabeth Fennema & Julie Sherman, 1977), and brain structure (Bleier, 1986). Although most scientists accept the validity of the critiques, reputable scientific journals (see Ruth Bleier, 1988 for an account of her encounters with *Science* over this matter), textbooks, and the popular press continue to publish studies biased by similar methodological inconsistencies, extrapolations of data from one species to another and overgeneralizations of data.

Endocrinology

Overlapping both the fields of animal behavior and the neurosciences, some of the work in endocrinology has assumed that the cyclical nature of the female reproductive pattern made female rodents and primates unsuitable as experimental subjects for tests of hormones or other chemicals, or for use as a model system of hormone action. Other work has centered on qualitative and quantitative differences in androgen and estrogen hormone levels and their relationship to behavioral and achievement manifestations. Feminists in science have again pointed out the problems of hormonal and drug tests (including those for human consumption) run only on male subjects which may yield "cleaner" but limited data (Bleier, 1984). The work of Joan C. Hoffman in particular (1982) suggests the female body with its cyclic reproductive hormone levels provides a more accurate model for most hormones. Ruth Bleier (1979) has discussed at length the subtle problems that occur with biochemical conversions of hormones in the body so an injection of testosterone may be converted to estrogen or another biochemically-related derivative before it reaches the brain. She and others (Ruth Hubbard, 1983; Marian Lowe, 1983) have also repeatedly warned against extrapolating from one species to another in biochemical traits and from assuming that changes in hormone levels necessarily are the cause of behavioral or performance differences between the sexes. Again, the validity of these critiques is usually acknowledged. However, some scientists ignore the critiques and continue to publish experiments bearing the same errors, using only male subjects and confounding correlation of changing hormone levels and behavioral manifestations with cause and effect in their conclusions. Other scientists accept the critiques, but suggest it is merely coincidence that a feminist happened to point out yet another incidence of bad science.

NATURE/NURTURE: A FALSE DICHOTOMY

What do the feminist critiques of these three fields of natural science have in common? And perhaps more importantly, what do they have in common with the controversy surrounding the possibility of a feminist science versus the idea that good science is gender free or gender neutral?

It is my opinion that the basis of the feminist critique common to the fields of animal behavior, neuroscience, and endocrinology is a rejection of the nature/nurture dichotomy implicit in the traditional approaches to research in each field. The feminist critique of animal behavior and sociobiology attacks the assumption of biological determinism: that biology (genes) determine behavior and that biological effects may be measured separately from those of culture. Ruth Hubbard (1985) in reviewing *Not In Our Genes: Biology, Ideology, and Human Nature* by Richard C. Lewontin, Steven Rose, and Leon J. Kamin (1984) presents an excellent critique of the problems with the nature/nurture dichotomy:

> Reductionist thinking about organisms would have us believe that an organism can be looked at in isolation, untouched by what we, for convenience, separate off as its environment. But organisms and their environments are quite literally parts of each other. We continuously incorporate portions of what we call our environment and continuously change it by breathing, excreting, and other activities. Similarly, our biological functions and the ways society affects us are inseparable: Their conjunction makes us who we are. Anti-reductionists, myself included, have sometimes proposed "interactive" models to describe the relationships between organism and environment, biology and society. Lewontin, Rose and Kamin object that this does not go far enough because the notion of interaction implies the existence of separate units that "interact." Far better, they say, to insist on the essential oneness of the organism-in-its-environment. I agree. (pp. 7–8)

The feminist critique of the neurosciences again has the same basis: Genetic, hormonal, and structural effects of the brain on behavior cannot be separated from the effects of learning and socialization in the environment on behavior. Indeed, the two are so interrelated that the environment can actually affect the prenatal structure of the brain which can then affect learning abilities. As Bleier (1984) points out:

Even though genes are involved in the embryonic differentiation of the various nerve cell types and in the spatial organization of nerve cells (neurons) within the fetal brain, the final form, size, and connections between different neurons and therefore the brain's proper functioning also depend on maternal environmental milieu and on input from the external world. . . . It has been found that malnutrition throughout the period of postnatal development of rat pups results in a decrease in both the number and the size of neurons in the brain. If the pups were also malnourished *in utero,* they can suffer as much as a 60 percent reduction in brain cell number, as compared with controls, by the time of weaning. Human infants dying of malnutrition during the first year of life also have smaller than normal brains with a reduced number and size of neurons. (M. Winick, 1975 quoted in Bleier, 1984, p. 44)

In endocrinology, feminists have stressed the importance of the inseparability of biological and behavioral factors. Environmental physical or psychological stress factors such as position in the dominance hierarchy have been shown to be both the cause and the effect of higher or lower levels of testosterone in primates (R. M. Rose, J. W. Holady & I. S. Bernstein, 1971). In addition, Sarah Hrdy (1981) discusses the interrelationships between hormone levels, reproductive inhibition, and dominance in female primates.

Rejection of the biology/environment or nature/nurture dichotomy unites the feminist critique of all of these fields. But how is this common theme related to the question of the gender neutrality of science and the possibility of a feminist (or a black, homosexual, and/or Marxist) science? Even some of the feminists in science (Gornick, 1983; Keller, 1983, 1984) who have made critiques of the traditional approaches to animal behavior, the neurosciences, and endocrinology precisely because these approaches assume a false dichotomy between biology and the environment, maintain that good science is gender neutral or gender free. However, I find that they are accepting precisely the same false dichotomy between nature and nurture when they claim that good science is gender free or free from constraints of class, race, or sexual preference. Suggesting that good science can be gender free is tantamount to accepting a positivist position. Jaggar (1983) describes this positivist assumption as the downfall or flaw of liberal feminism. Liberal feminism fails to acknowledge the social construction of knowledge, particularly scientific knowledge. Liberal feminism suggests that science is somehow different from the other intellectual constructs, theories, models, and endeavors pursued by humans. This possibility assumes that science really is objective and value free and that scientific experiments are designed, run, and interpreted without bias derived from gender, class, race, historical period, and/or sexual preference.

Beginning with the work of Thomas S. Kuhn (1970) and his followers, historians and philosophers of science have pointed out that scientific theories and practice may not be dichotomized from the other human values which the scientist holds. The scientific paradigms acceptable to the mainstream of the practicing scientists are convincing precisely because they reinforce or support the historical, economic, social, racial, political, and gender policies of the majority of scientists at that particular time. Hilary Rose and Steven Rose (1980) underline the fact that Darwin's theory of natural selection was acceptable to nineteenth century England because it was laden with the values of the upper classes of that Victorian period:

> its central metaphors drawn from society and in their turn interacting with society were of the competition of species, the struggle for existence, the ecological niche, and the survival of the fittest. (p. 28)

These metaphors reflect Victorian society and were acceptable to it because they, and the social Darwinism quickly derived from the theory of natural selection, seemed to ground its norms solidly in a biological foundation. The use of craniometry provides a nineteenth century example of the acceptance of incorrect biological measurements and false conclusions drawn from accurate measurements because the biological "facts" initially permitted a justification for the inferior social position of colonials (especially blacks) and eventually for women (Gould, 1981).

Contemporary feminist critics (Lynda Birke, 1986; Bleier, 1984, 1986; Fee, 1982; Donna Haraway 1978; Hilde Hein, 1981; Hubbard, 1983) have discussed the extent to which the emphasis on sex differences research (when in fact for most traits there are no differences or only very small mean differences characterized by a large range of overlap between the sexes), in the neurosciences and endocrinology and in the search for genetic bases to justify sex role specialization and the division of labor, comes from the desire to find a biological basis for the social inequality between the sexes. The measurement of hormone levels in homosexuals compared to heterosexuals and the search for a "gene" for homosexuality provide other examples of an attempt to separate biological from environmental determinants and to seek biological bases for the discriminatory treatment against homosexuals (Birke, 1986). One can imagine that a society free from inequality between the sexes and lacking homophobia would not view sex differences and sexual preferences differences research as valid scientific endeavors. The fact that our society supports such research indicates the extent to which the values of the society and the scientists influence scientific inquiry and supposed objectivity.

Hubbard (1983), a feminist scientist, states that science and scientists reflect the bias of the powerful within the society.

> Oppressive ideas and explanations that derive women's roles from women's "nature" are grounded in the material conditions in which the scientists who generate them live. These scientists are predominantly university-educated, economically privileged white men, who either belong to the hegemonic group or identify with its interests. (The few women and Third World men who have recently gained access to the scientific elite generally have the same economic and educational backgrounds as the traditional, white male members and often identify with the same interests.) It is therefore not an accident

that scientists' perceptions of reality, as well as their descriptions of it, often serve to perpetuate and bolster the privileges of that disproportionately small group of people who have economic and social power in society. (pp. 1–2)

CRITIQUES FROM STANDPOINTS OTHER THAN FEMINIST

Critiques from other standpoints outside of the mainstream scientists overlap with feminist critiques, viewing scientific knowledge as being socially constructed. In discussing scientific colonialism, McLeod (1987) suggests that "national science is a process by which a vernacular language is used by the powerful to structure national science policy in their own interest" (p. 218). This sounds surprisingly similar to the position put forward by Bill Zimmerman et al. (1980) who critique science from a Marxist perspective:

> In this society, at this time, it is not possible to escape the political implications of scientific work. The U.S. ruling class has long had a commitment to science, not merely limited to shortrange practical applications, but based on the belief that science is good for the long-term welfare of U.S. capitalism, and that what is good for U.S. capitalism is good for humanity. This outlook is shared by the trustees of universities, the official leaders of U.S. science, the administrators of government and private funding agencies. Further, they see this viewpoint as representing a mature social responsibility, morally superior to the "pure search of truth" attitudes of some of the scientists. But they tolerate the ideology since it furthers their own aims and does not challenge their uses of science.
>
> We find the alternatives of "science for science's sake" and "science for progress of capitalism" equally unacceptable. We can no longer identify the cause of humanity with that of U.S. capitalism. (p. 311)

Traditional Marxist critiques of science object that the particular problems any given community of scientists chooses for investigation and the content of the formulated theories reflect class-specific interests and cognitive limitations. Neo-Marxists extend this critique to suggest that the entire scientific enterprise is a function of context and class-specific interests and that scientific methodology is itself constituted by these interests.

African–American critiques show considerable overlap with feminist critiques. Sandra Harding (1986) discusses this "curious coincidence" in her book *The Science Question in Feminism*.

> Observers of social hierarchies other than that of masculine dominance have pointed to these very same dichotomies as the conceptual scheme that permits these other kinds of subjugation: Russell Means contrasts Native American and Eurocentric attitudes toward nature in these terms: Joseph Needham similarly contrasts Chinese and Western concepts of nature. As we shall see, some

observers of both African and Afro-American social life contrast African and European thought in these terms; they posit an African world view which, they imply, could be the origin of a successor science and epistemology. What they call the African world view is suspiciously similar to what in the feminist literature is identified as a distinctively feminine world view. What they label European or Eurocentric shares significant similarity with what feminists label masculine or androcentric. Thus on these separate accounts, people (men?) of African descent and women (Western?) appear to have very similar ontologies, epistemologies, and ethics, and the world views of their respective rulers also appear to be similar.

It is no surprise to be able to infer that Western men hold a distinctively European world view or that the easily detectable expressions of a European consciousness are masculine. But it is startling to be led to the inference that Africans hold what in the West is characterized as a feminist world view and that, correlatively, women in the West hold what Africans characterize as an African world view. (pp. 165–166)

To the extent that science reflects the interests of the white, middle and upper class Western male and that most scientists are also personal representatives of that elite, critiques from groups outside the scientific mainstream might be expected to show considerable overlap. Most likely the overlap among feminist, African–American and Marxist critiques is due to what Harding calls "the return of the repressed."

For the purposes of the NSF and the AAAS—whose missions now include attracting women, minorities, and people from diverse socioeconomic classes to science and engineering—emphasizing the congruence among the critiques of nonmainstream scientists may be ideal. Finding the broadest base possible for theories and teaching techniques to attract individuals from many diverse backgrounds previously underrepresented in science should be a goal. Only a scientific community composed of individuals from very heterogeneous backgrounds will be likely to begin to reveal some of the values associated with race, class, gender, ethnic, and religious affiliation that may be biasing data gathering, interpretation, and theorizing.

DIFFERENCES AMONG THE CRITIQUES

For individuals interested in attracting women and men of color to science and particularly for scholars interested in feminism, racism, classism, and science, examining the similarities is important, but not sufficient. It is necessary to examine how female approaches to science differ from that of other nonmainstream groups. Further gradations among approaches taken by scientists who are women and male-identified, women and female-identified, and feminists must be delineated, particularly to explore what might constitute a feminist science.[1]

Frequently in the dualistic approach to knowledge that permeates our society, feminine has been identified with the latter half of the following dichotomies: culture/nature; rational/feeling; objective/subjective; quantitative/qualitative; active/passive; focused/diffuse; independent/dependent; mind/body; self/others; knowing/being. In addition, as many authors have pointed out, the same half of these dichotomies has been used in other nonmainstream critiques of science, accounting for much of the overlap previously discussed. Clear dangers exist in overemphasizing the congruence among the critiques of the nonmainstream groups. One danger is that it obscures significant differences that exist among the critiques by lumping them all as "other" compared to the mainstream group. More fruitful information about feminist approaches might be obtained by examining the differences among the critiques.

Exploring differences among the critiques necessitates delineating the major defining characteristics of each of the nonmainstream critiques. This raises a second danger of the lumping of strategy. Within each of the nonmainstream critiques exists considerable diversity; there is not one feminist critique, one Marxist critique, one African-American critique, nor one non-Western critique. Only the mainstream scientist and/or an individual unfamiliar with the complexities and varieties of perspectives within each critique would assume each of these groups espouses a singular critique. The diversity in a group opens the possibility that a different type of overlap may exist between parts of the nonmainstream groups. For example, Marxist–feminists have developed a critique of science that would not be accepted by many Marxists or feminists; similarly black feminists could develop a critique separate from that of blacks who are not feminists or feminists who are not black.

Reducing each critique to its major defining characteristics does obscure the real plurality and diversity of perspective in each group. However, such a reduction may contribute valuable insight into differences among the groups. Although considerable debate has centered around what constitutes defining approaches of each group, much of the literature would support the following basic definitions: In feminism and feminist inquiry, women

---

[1] It is also crucial to specify that no necessary connection exists between biological sex and the terms female, feminine, or feminist approach to science. Due to the processes of socialization in our gender polarized society, most feminists are more likely to be biological females. However, it would not be impossible for a biological male to take a feminine or even feminist approach to science. Most current scientists who are biologically female probably take a masculine approach which has been identified as synonymous with the "objective, rational" approach to science.

are the central or primary focus, gender providing the major source for patriarchal domination in society; equality for women will begin the end of all
oppression. In Marxism and Marxist inquiry, class is the organizing princi-
ple around which the struggle for power exists; with the redistribution of
wealth and goods, other oppressions will cease. African-American and
other ethnic studies inquiries posit race as the primary oppression; overcoming racist oppression is the beginning of the solution for oppression based
on gender and class.

Each critique differs in its assessment of whether the primary oppression
in society is gender, class, or race. However, all critiques are united in their
recognition that knowledge is socially constructed. Members of the groups
proposing each critique have also begun to recognize that gender, class,
and race are interlocking political phenomena determining the standpoint
from which everyone views the world.

CONCLUSION

In our society there are certainly differences in the social treatment and
learning of girls and boys, men and women, and of different races, classes,
and sexual preferences. There are also biological differences and possible
psychological differences between girls and boys and men and women. If
one accepts the biopsychosocial unit as fundamentally indivisible and accepts science as an intellectual human endeavor which is affected by the
values and experiences of the scientist, then one accepts that a woman and/
or a feminist, an African-American, Marxist, and/or homosexual in science
would develop different approaches, questions to be asked, and interpretations of data from that of the traditional science. This is particularly likely to
be the case when most of the current traditional science has been developed
primarily by white middle and upper class Western males who would be
expected to have had relatively homogeneous (compared to women,
blacks, homosexuals, and individuals of other classes) biological, psychological, and social experiences. Perhaps this is why people have viewed the
work of Barbara McClintock as somehow qualitatively different from that of
traditional male science, despite the facts that she denies she is a feminist
and that she views science as gender neutral. Perhaps this is also the reason
that the "obvious" critiques by feminists in science were not seen by other
scientists until they were pointed out.

The standpoint (as influenced by gender, race, class, and sexual preference) determines the reality seen by the observer. By rejecting the positivist
stance of the possibility of a neutral observer, the standpoint theorist is left
in a quandry regarding obtaining an accurate picture of the physical, natural
world necessary for science. Some standpoint epistemologies posit that the
least powerful or most oppressed individual has the most accurate or least

biased view. According to this stance black lesbian women from the working class would be expected to be the least biased scientists. Precisely because of the current social structure it seems unlikely that the majority of scientists will come from this group any time in the near future. However, perhaps elimination of some bias can be achieved by attracting as many individuals from as diverse backgrounds (with regard to gender, race, class, and sexual preference) as possible to become scientists. According to this scheme, no one individual would have an unbiased view. However, the diversity within the group of scientists might lead to a less biased world view if each individual's ideas were heard. If science is socially constructed, then attracting a more heterogeneous group of scientists would result in different questions being asked, approaches and experimental subjects used, and theories and conclusions drawn from the data.

Chapter 4

Women's Ways of Knowing

*Research by Women Scientists Reflecting
Women's Studies Scholarship*

If women and minorities hold differing standpoints from the white middle to upper class males, who are the traditional practitioners of science, it will be useful to examine any differences between ways women have approached science compared to men.

During July 29–31, 1987 the American Association for the Advancement of Science (AAAS), the largest, most prestigious of the professional scientific societies, sponsored the conference "Women in Science and Engineering: Changing Vision to Reality." This conference overlapped with fourth international conference "Girls and Science and Technology" (GASAT). For the first time at a scientific meeting I heard substantial discussion of the idea that perhaps the scientific community—in its questions asked, approaches taken, experimental subjects used, interpretation of data, and theories and conclusions drawn—might need to change to take into account the critiques and concerns of women. Although ways that women themselves might have to change to be accepted as scientists still figured as a substantial part of the discussion, the accommodation of science, as it is currently practiced, to suit women's needs was considered during several conference sessions, including major meetings at which the President of AAAS and budget directors from the NSF were present.

Feminist scientists (Bleier, 1984, 1986; Fee, 1982; Haraway, 1978; Hein, 1981; Hubbard, 1983) have critiqued the androcentric bias in the questions studied, choice of experimental subjects, methods of data collection, and conclusions and theories drawn from the data. Some (Birke, 1986; Bleier, 1984) have envisioned the parameters of a feminist science. More recently, some feminists have shifted the focus of interest from forces of socialization, that have caused women to be excluded and to exclude themselves from science, to the realm of metaphor, discourse, and the power of language and models of science (Donna Haraway, 1989; Harding, 1986; Evelyn Fox Keller, 1989).

The mainstream scientists have largely ignored or been oblivious to feminist critiques of science. Although a variety of efforts (Sheila Humphreys, 1982; Kahle, 1985) has been undertaken during the last two decades to attract more women to science; these efforts have concentrated on how women might change to fit in with male scientists and science (Marsha L. Matyas, 1985; Claire E. Max, 1982). Until the 1987 AAAS meeting the scientific community had failed to consider the problem might be approached from the other direction: changing male scientists and science to be more in harmony with women's concerns and female approaches to problem solving.

In 1986 the book *Women's Ways of Knowing,* written by Mary Field Belenkey, Blythe McVicker Clinchy, Nancy Rule Goldberger, and Jill Mattuck Tarule, was published. Some had looked forward to the book for several years, having had their interest piqued by reports heard at national meetings about the research and tidbits gleaned from colleagues at the institutions where the research was taking place. Everyone sensed that this book and the research upon which it was based would have an impact on the academy.

The impact has been felt in numerous and diverse ways on campuses across the nation. Almost immediately large numbers of women heralded it as the story accurately chronicling their experience with teaching and learning. It became required reading for all faculty on some campuses. Almost as quickly, critics emerged who questioned the methods, sample size, and the extent to which the data might be generalized. Some women said it did not represent their experience; some men wondered why it was called *Women's Ways of Knowing* when it seemed to reflect the way they know too.

Based upon their research, Belenky et al. examined women's ways of knowing and described "five different perspectives from which women view reality and draw conclusions about truth, knowledge, and authority" (p. 3):

> *silence,* a position in which women experience themselves as mindless and voiceless and subject to the whims of external authority; *received knowledge,* a perspective from which women conceive of themselves as capable of receiving, even reproducing, knowledge from the all-knowing external authorities but not capable of creating knowledge on their own; *subjective knowledge,* a perspective from which truth and knowledge are conceived of as personal, private, and subjectively known or intuited; *procedural knowledge,* a position in which women are invested in learning and applying objective procedures

for obtaining and communicating knowledge; and *constructed knowledge,* a
position in which women view all knowledge as contextual, experience themselves as creators of knowledge, and value both subjective and objective strategies for knowing. (p. 15)

They also distinguish two types of procedural knowing—separate and
connected: "When we speak of separate and connected-knowing, we refer
not to any sort of relationship between the self and another person but with
relationships between knowers and the objects (or subjects) of knowing
(which may or may not be persons)" (p. 102). Does the work of Belenky et
al. offer any insight into the issue of attracting more women and minorities
to science?

In terms of knowing science, the majority of the American population,
both male and female, falls in the first three perspectives on knowledge
described by Belenky et al.: silent, received, and subjective knowers. Between 45% and 50% of Americans (Georgina M. Pion & Mark W. Lipsey,
1981) think that science and technology have caused some of our problems.
A substantial fraction of the population is overwhelmed by science and its
methods and feels deaf and dumb in the face of scientific knowledge. For
example, an OTA survey (1987) revealed that only 16% of the U.S. population rates their "own basic understanding of science and technology" as
very good; 28% of the U.S. population rates their own understanding of
science and technology as poor (OTA, 1987): While only 20% of males rate
their understanding as poor, 35% of females rate themselves as having poor
understanding of science and technology. The jargon of science may have
kept those with poor understanding in their place and made them fear questioning anything they hear that is scientific. The extent to which most students, regardless of grades, attempt to avoid science courses represents their
silence towards and fear of science.

Another considerable fraction of individuals, both male and female, appears to be received knowers. They accept without question and may repeat
the information provided by the latest scientific research findings presented
by the scientist or surrogate authority for the scientist. Received knowers
may change their life habits (what they eat, medications they give their children, the level of exercise they strive to achieve) without question depending on the latest scientific findings reported on the evening news.

Subjective knowers distrust and may even reject science, its methods,
and its findings. No one really knows what percentage of the American
population, both male and female, might fall in this camp. However, 29%
of the population rates itself as rather uninterested (11%) or not interested
at all (18%) in scientific and technological matters (OTA, 1987). Again more
women (33%) than men (23%) report this lower interest in science (OTA,
1987). Other surveys indicate 44% of the population believes in creationism

and 38% believes in evolution guided by God (George H. Gallup, 1983); one could infer from these that a substantial number of people are subjective knowers with regard to science. Given the status and authority that science and scientists hold in our society, it is possible that an even larger percentage of people in fact do not rely on scientists or scientific knowledge but refuse publicly to admit this rejection.

Some feminists in this current phase of the women's movement have sought to reject science. They recognize scientific theories have often been used to provide a biological justification for the socially inferior positions of women and people of color in our society. They note the application of chemistry and physics for militaristic and destructive technologies which maim people and the environment (Birke, 1986).

According to Belenky et al., the scientific method with its emphasis upon objectivity and distance between observer and object of study is an example of separate, procedural knowing. As the data collected for *Women's Ways of Knowing* suggest, most college curricula and professors strive for their students to obtain the critical thinking skills, logical reasoning, and abstract analysis that characterize separate, procedural knowing.

Science as it is taught and practiced in the United States exemplifies this type of knowing. The discomfort of larger numbers of women than men with separate, procedural knowledge may signify one of the many reasons why fewer women than men are scientists. Even before the publication of *Women's Ways of Knowing*, feminist philosophers, historians, and scientists considered the extent to which the mechanistic, objective approach to science, that supplanted the hermetic, organic approach in the seventeenth century, might be synonymous with a masculine world view (Evelyn Fox Keller, 1985; Carolyn Merchant, 1979). They (Keller, 1985) applied feminist theories from psychology, such as the work of Nancy Chodorow (1978) and Carol Gilligan (1982), to further explain that scientific individuals who value autonomy, distance, and masculinity then develop scientific theories and methods that embody those same characteristics.

Probably most women scientists, as well as men scientists, approach science as separate procedural knowers. However, I decided to explore the work of some women scientists to see if any of it might be characterized as other than separate, procedural knowing. Specifically, I was curious to learn whether the work of women scientists might represent either of the other two categories: connected procedural knowledge or constructed knowledge. Using examples from the work of women scientists, I explore the ways some women in science have provided evidence of differences in observations and types of problems chosen for study, the way hypotheses are formulated, methods of data collecting and testing, conclusions and theories drawn, and use of scientific information compared to traditional male approaches to science. However different their approach, none of them violated or changed the basic approach to science known as the scientific method.

I have used the steps of the scientific method as a mechanism for arranging the examples of women's approach to science. In addition to observations, methods of data gathering, and conclusions and theories drawn from data gathered, I also include use of scientific information and practice of science as a heading under which examples of women's approach may differ from the separate, procedural approach to science.

OBSERVATIONS

Women scientists have demonstrated the following differences in observation:

1. Expansion of the kinds of observations beyond those traditionally carried out in scientific research to include various interactions, relationships, or events not seen or considered worthy of observation by traditional scientists operating from an androcentric perspective.

Ellen Swallow Richards was trained as a chemist and practiced analytical chemistry throughout her life. She had been sensitized to the issues of food product purity and air and water contamination while working in her father's store. (Marilyn B. Ogilvie, 1986). She believed the home should be an ideal environment and developed methods to insure food purity, nutrition, and purity of air and water in the home; hence she is known historically as the founder of home economics. However, she applied similar methods on a broader scale out-of-doors. Following her tenure as head of the Woman's Laboratory at MIT, she became an instructor in sanitary chemistry in the MIT laboratory for the study of sanitation.

> From 1887 to 1889 she supervised a highly influential survey of Massachusetts inland waters; for many years she taught techniques of water, air, and sewage analysis to students in the MIT sanitary engineering program. Throughout her years in the Woman's Laboratory and in the sanitary chemistry laboratory, Richards also took on consulting work for government and industry, testing commercial products as well as the air, water, and soil for harmful substances. (Ogilvie, 1986, p. 151)

It seems unlikely that a male scientist would have initially developed such methods to insure sanitation and purity for the home and then extended them to the surrounding outdoor environment.

Female primatologists such as Sarah Hrdy, (1977, 1979, 1981, 1984), Lancaster (1975), Jane Goodall (1971), and Dian Fossey (1983) transformed theories of dominance, subordination, and hierarchy regarding primate group interaction because they observed female–female interaction which

had not been seen or considered worthy of observation by most male primatologists.

> For over three decades, a handful of partially true assumptions were permitted
> to shape the construction of general evolutionary theories about sexual selec-
> tion. These theories of sexual selection presupposed the existence of a highly
> discriminating, sexually "coy," female who was courted by sexually undis-
> criminating males. Assumptions underlying these stereotypes included, first,
> the idea that relative male contribution to offspring was small, second, that
> little variance exists in female reproductive success compared to the very great
> variance among males, and third, that fertilization was the only reason for
> females to mate. While appropriate in some contexts, these conditions are far
> from universal. Uncritical acceptance of such assumptions has greatly ham-
> pered our understanding of animal breeding systems particularly, perhaps,
> those of primates.

> These assumptions have only begun to be revised in the last decade, as re-
> searchers began to consider the way Darwinian selection operates on females
> as well as males. This paper traces the shift away from the stereotype of fe-
> males as sexually passive and discriminating to current models in which fe-
> males are seen to play an active role in managing sexual consortships that go
> beyond traditional "mate choice." It is impossible to understand this history
> without taking into account the background, including the gender, of the re-
> searchers involved. Serious consideration is given to the possibility that the
> empathy for other females subjectively felt by women researchers may have
> been instrumental in expanding the scope of sexual selection theory. (Sarah
> Hrdy, 1986, pp. 119–120)

2. Increasing the numbers of observations and remaining longer in the observational stage of the scientific method.

Some women scientists have suggested to me that they and some of their
female colleagues spend more time than most of their male colleagues observing before developing a hypothesis. The work of Gilligan (1982) suggests that females are less likely to approach decision making and problem-
solving from a hierarchical or abstract mode. The group of adolescent girls
Gilligan (1982) studied spent more time with details and the relationships
among those details before considering an abstract or hierarchical framework into which the details could fit than did a comparable group of adolescent boys. The unique contributions of women primatologists, biologists,
and astronomers support this idea.

Female primatologists such as Goodall (1971) and Fossey (1983) have
dramatically increased the amount of information as well as the quality of
observation of chimpanzees and gorillas. Their willingness to devote decades of their lives in daily observation of primates in their natural habitats
tremendously expanded the data base provided by observation of laboratory
animals or brief periods of observation of animals in the wild.

Dr. Rena Sabin's painstaking observations while she stayed up all night watching "the birth of a bloodstream" from a live chick embryo during her research at John's Hopkins University (1901–1925) was the breakthrough necessary for the understanding of the origin of blood vessels and the development of blood cells (Ogilvie, 1986). She discovered that blood plasma is developed by liquefaction of the cells forming the walls of the first blood vessels.

Her previous work, based on careful observation of the lymphatic system, overturned the medical theory of the time. By extremely precise and detailed work, she traced the origin of the lymphatic system in embryos.

> Sabin's conclusions, at first highly controversial and eventually proved correct, were that the lymphatics represented a one-way system—that they were closed at their collecting ends, where the fluids entered by seepage, and that they arose from pre-existing veins instead of independently. (Ogilvie, 1986, p. 155)

Historical examples from an entirely different field, astronomy, also support the idea that women spend increased amounts of time in observation. Because of sexist attitudes, women astronomers were often relegated to calculating the positions and analyzing other information from the photographic plates (Vera Rubin, 1986). The calculating was considered tedious and menial, therefore worthy of women's work; planning and directing the projects were men's work. While relegated to this menial role and forbidden to use the giant telescopes until the mid-1960s (Rubin, 1986), women astronomers helped develop systems and discoveries that laid the groundwork for modern astronomy. For example, in the early twentieth century Annie Jump Cannon established the classification spectrum for arranging spectral stars in order of decreasing temperature. Henrietta Swan Leavitt's discovery of the Cepheids in 1910 led to the most fundamental method of calculating distances in the universe (Rubin, 1986). Based on her own calculations, Caroline Herschel discovered light comets and planned the next day's research, including the direction in which her brother, Sir William Herschel, should point the telescope for his observations. This led to his designation as the "pioneer of modern physical astronomy" (H. J. Mozans, 1974, p. 182).

3. Acceptance of the personal experience of women as a valid component of experimental observations.

In the health care area, women have often reported (and accepted among themselves) experiences that could not be documented by scientific experiments or were not accepted as valid by the researchers of the day. Cases of toxic shock syndrome were reported by the women on whom the Rely tampon was tested. The Proctor and Gamble Company chose not to reveal these data until litigation ensued (C. Marwick, 1983).

In "A case of corporate malpractice and the Dalkon shield" Mark Dowie and Tracy Johnson (1977) document that many of the problems with the Dalkon shield had been uncovered during the testing and early marketing phases of the development of the IUD (intrauterine device). The A. H. Robins Company and the developers of the shield chose to ignore that data. The company continued the coverup even when reports accumulated of severe complications and deaths from the Dalkon shield due to problems similar to those reported during development. Only legal action from women harmed by this shield brought the initial test results to light and resulted in the removal of the shield from the market.

For decades, dysmenorrhea was attributed by most health care researchers and practitioners to psychological or social factors despite the reports of an overwhelming number of women that these were monthly experiences in their lives. Only after prostaglandins were "discovered" was there widespread acceptance among the male medical establishment that this experience reported by women had a biological component (Ruth L. Kirschstein, 1985).

4. Unwillingness to undertake research likely to have applications of direct benefit to the military and more likely to propose hypotheses to explore problems of social concern.

Men and woman consistently show the most differences in the so-called "gender-gap" polls on the issues of guns versus butter. Women consistently register their preference for having more money spent for health, education, and social welfare programs and less money spent on defense and the military (Ethel Klein, 1984). Based on this finding one might assume that large numbers of women scientists would reflect this preference in both their individual research hypotheses and in their policies and recommendations for national priorities for funding scientific research.

Because of the importance women attach to relationship compared to hierarchy as an approach to problem-solving, many women scientists are unwilling to consider separating basic research from the social consequences and potential practical applications of that research. Some women scientists (Bleier, 1986; Ruth Hubbard, 1979) do not draw the sharp distinction, which many male scientists have drawn, between the work they do as scientists and the uses society makes of that work.

Most of the prominent male physicists and many of the outstanding chemists and engineers were eager to apply their basic research to build the atomic bomb and to produce other war technology.

> The physicists engaged on the atomic bomb problem were to be grouped under three program chiefs, Compton, Lawrence, and H. C. Urey, all Nobel Prize Winners. Contracts relating to the diffusion and centrifuge processes were to be recommended to Bush by a group of eminent chemical engineers to be called the Planning Board, which included E. V. Murphee of the Standard Oil Development Company as chairman, W. K. Lewis, L. W. Chubb, G. O. Curme, Jr., and P. C. Keith. (James Phinney Baxter, 1946, p. 428)

The "Manhattan Project" (the secret program for the development of the atomic bomb) came directly under the control of the army.

> With them came an extraordinary group of scientists. From 1940 on a large and increasing proportion of the best scientific minds in the country had been engaged on the problem of the atomic bomb under one or more of the 102 NDRC and OSRD S–1 contracts. Most of these men were still at work when success was finally attained in July 1945, and by that time they had been joined by scores of others, who had "taken the veil" and vanished from the groups working on other problems. Their chief was J. R. Oppenheimer, a 41-year-old theoretical physicist on the staff of the University of California who had taken part earlier in the extraordinary advances made there and at Chicago. (Baxter, 1946, p. 444)

In contrast, Lise Meitner, who first described the splitting of the uranium atom with its concurrent release of tremendous amounts of energy as nuclear fission, was horrified by the use to which her discovery was put (Louis Haber, 1979). She opposed the use of her discovery to make the atomic bomb, refused, although invited, to have anything to do with its development and worked instead towards international cooperation to prevent the destructive use of atomic weapons (Haber, 1979). She made the following comment after the bombs were dropped on Hiroshima and Nagasaki: "Women have a great responsibility and they are obliged to try so far as they can to prevent another war" (Haber, 1979, p. 50).

Current feminist scientists (Birke, 1986; Bleier, 1984; Anne Fausto-Sterling, 1985) have repeatedly stressed the importance of changing science to consider the effects of its application on a global scale. As Bleier states, "it *would* aim to eliminate research that leads to the exploitation and destruction of nature, the destruction of the human race and other species, and that justifies the oppression of people because of race, gender, class, sexuality, or nationality" (Bleier, 1986, p. 16).

An extension of women's desire to make the connection between basic research and its practical application is likely to result in individual scientists developing hypotheses to examine issues they see as having beneficial social applications. Karen Messing (1983) suggests several topics including "the occupational exposures that present a risk to the nursing mother, alternate (non-hormonal) treatments for the discomforts of menopause, how a woman can give herself a safe (and, where necessary, secret) abortion, what work postures increase the likelihood of menstrual cramps, and how a low-income family can provide itself with nutritious meals" (p. 78) that would be suitable issues for hypotheses.

5. Consideration of problems that have not been deemed worthy of scientific investigation because of the field with which the problem has been traditionally associated.

Because science is considered a masculine pursuit in our culture (Fee, 1982; Harding, 1986; Evelyn Fox Keller, 1982), science performed by women is often defined as nonscience. H. Patricia Hynes (1984) documents the redefinition of Ellen Swallow Richard's experiments in water chemistry, toxicity, and food purity out of the science of chemistry and into home economics. Her work was considered unscientific because it was interdisciplinary research done by a woman (Hynes, 1984).

In *For Her Own Good* Barbara Ehrenreich and Deirdre English (1978) explore the ways in which methods to aid birthing are considered to be science or nonscience depending upon who is practicing them. Midwifery is not usually considered a science because it is practiced by women, although obstetrics is a science because it is a medical field dominated by men. A majority of women scientists is likely to end the stereotyping of certain kinds of research (carried out using the scientific method) as nonscience simply because the research is done by women or is related to home economics, childbirth, environmental, or other issues frequently viewed as part of female-dominated fields.

6. Formulation of hypotheses focusing on gender as a crucial part of the question being asked.

Recognition of the importance of gender is crucial for the definition of the problem studied and the wording of the hypothesis. Frequently data have been collected from only one gender because the disease has been stereotyped as a "man's disease" or a "woman's disease." The designation "man's disease" for heart disease is based upon the fact that heart disease occurs more frequently in men than women. However, it does not automatically mean "that heart disease is either less important, or unimportant, in women. In fact, women live longer than men, and heart disease is a leading cause of death in older women" (Jean Hamilton, 1985, p. IV-55). As Messing (1983) states: "Articulating the hypothesis is crucial to the scientific method. Research is done in order to find an answer to a specific question, and the way the question is posed often determines the way the research will be carried out and how the eventual data will be interpreted" (p. 78).

Part of the focus on gender might be demonstrated in research topics of particular concern to women. Effects of exercise level and duration upon alleviation of menstrual discomfort, or the length and amount of exposure to Video Display Terminals that have resulted in the "cluster pregnancies" of women giving birth to deformed babies in certain industries would be examples of this focus.

In addition, one might anticipate that women scientists are more likely to routinely consider and test for differences or lack of differences based on gender in any hypothesis which they are testing. In short, gender becomes a category of analysis. For example, when exploring the metabolism of a particular drug, a null hypothesis routinely investigated should be: This drug is metabolized differently in males than it is in females.

7. Investigation of problems of more holistic, global scope than the more reduced and limited scale problems traditionally considered.

Based on the work of Gilligan (1982), and Chodorow (1978), it appears women are more likely to consider relationship and interdependence in their definition and conception of what constitutes the problem. Traditional male scientists are more likely to use a deductive approach to isolate and sever connections and interrelationships thereby resulting in a reduced definition of what the problem is.

The work of environmentalists, pioneered by women such as Rachel Carson (1962), contrasted with that of a more quantitative approach to ecology, pioneered by men such as H. T. Odum (1957), provides an example of the difference in level of definition of the problem. Carson emphasized the extreme extent to which pesticides were likely to damage all aspects of the environment. Although she turned out to be correct, she extrapolated beyond the available data to underline the fact that pesticides might be carcinogenic and cause chromosomal damage. "She specifically cites 2, 4–D and 2, 4, 5–T—the mixture known since the Vietnam war as Agent Orange— as compounds which may cause serious chromosomal and other subtle physiological effects" (Hynes, 1984, p. 297). In her book *Silent Spring* she painted a picture of contamination, mutation, and possible death for all forms of life—from nitrogen-fixing bacteria up to people—from contamination of ground water due to insecticide runoff from forests and crops into nearby lakes and streams (H. Patricia Hynes, 1989). In contrast to Carson's definition of the problem on a global level, quantitative ecologists typically seek to demonstrate harmful or potentially harmful effects by a quantitative examination of change in the micro-environment.

METHODS OF DATA GATHERING

Women scientists may use the following approaches for collection of data:

1. Use of a combination of qualitative and quantitative methods.

Because women may be likely to examine more holistic hypotheses in which relationships and interdependencies are explored, both quantitative and qualitative methods may be necessary to obtain the needed data. For example, the hypothesis that decreasing stress level will decrease the production by the body of a certain chemical (such as prostaglandins) is best tested using both quantitative and qualitative methods. Direct quantitative methods could be used to measure prostaglandin levels and physical stressors. However, psychological stressors will have to be determined in part by qualitative means because what is stressful to one person may not be equally stressful to another. The qualitative measures can be converted to a quantitative scale for purposes of statistical analysis.

2. Use of methods from a variety of fields or interdisciplinary approaches to problem-solving.

Because the scope of problems explored by women tends to be broader, methods which cross disciplinary boundaries or include combinations of methods traditionally used in separate fields may provide more appropriate approaches. For example, if the topic of research is exploring occupational exposures that present a risk to the pregnant woman working in a plant where toxic chemicals are manufactured, a combination of methods traditionally used in social science research combined with traditional methods frequently used in biology and chemistry could be the best approach.

Methods such as karyotyping chromosomes of any miscarried fetuses, chemical analyses of placentae after birth, and blood samples of the newborns to determine trace amounts of the toxic chemicals would be appropriate biological and chemical methods used to gather data about the problem. In-depth interviews with women to discuss how they are feeling and any irregularities they detect during each month of the pregnancy, Apgar Scores of the babies at birth, and evaluations using weekly written questionnaires regarding the pregnancy progress include appropriate methods more traditionally used in the social sciences for approaching this sort of problem.

In her insightful commissioned paper for the Report of the Public Health Service Task Force on Women's Health Issues, Jean Hamilton (1985) calls for interactive models to draw on both the social and natural sciences to explain complex problems.

> Particularly for understanding human, gender-related health, we need more interactive and contextual models that address the actual complexity of the phenomena that is the subject of explanation. One example is the need for more phenomenological definitions of symptoms, along with increased recognition that psychology, behavioral studies, and sociology are among the "basic sciences" for health research. Research on heart disease is one example of a field where it is recognized that both psychological stress and behaviors such as eating and cigarette smoking influence the onset and natural course of a disease process. (pp. IV-62, IV-56)

3. Inclusion of females as experimental subjects in research design.

Recognizing gender as an important factor in formulating hypotheses makes women scientists cognizant of the importance of using females, whether they be rodents or primates, as experimental subjects. This recognition should lead to fewer experiments such as one recently done in which the usefulness of cholesterol-lowering drugs was tested on 3,806 men and no women (Hamilton, 1985, p. IV-56). Women are likely to recognize the flaw in an experiment in which data are collected solely from male subjects but in which the conclusions are generalized to include both sexes of the species.

Models which more accurately simulate functioning complex biological systems may be derived from using female rats as subjects in experiments. Women scientists such as Hoffman (1982) have questioned the tradition of using male rats or primates as subjects. With the exception of insulin and the hormones of the female reproductive cycle, traditional endocrinological theory predicted that most hormones are kept constant in level in both males and females. Thus, the male of the species, whether rodent or primate, was chosen as the experimental subject because of his noncyclicity. However, new techniques of measuring blood hormone levels have demonstrated episodic, rather than steady, patterns of secretion of hormones in both males and females. As Hoffman (1982) points out, the rhythmic cycle of hormone secretion as portrayed in the cycling female rat, appears to be a more accurate model for the secretion of most hormones than the male rat (Hoffman, 1982).

4. Use of more interactive methods, thereby shortening the distance between observer and the object being studied.

The work of Barbara McClintock as described by Evelyn Fox Keller (1983) is frequently cited as an example of this shortened distance. In her approach to studying maize, she indicates a shortening of the distance between the observer and the object being studied and a consideration of the complex interaction between the organism and its environment. Her statement upon receiving the Nobel Prize was that "it might seem unfair to reward a person for having so much pleasure over the years, asking the maize plant to solve specific problems and then watching its responses" (Keller, 1984, p. 44). This statement suggests a closer, more intimate relationship with the subject of her research than typically is expressed by the male "objective" scientist. One does not normally associate words such as "a feeling for the organism" (Keller, 1983, p. 44) with the rational, masculine approach to science. McClintock also did not accept the predominant hierarchical theory of genetic DNA as the "Master Molecule" that controls gene action but focused on the interaction between the organism and its environment as the locus of control (Keller, 1983).

A different method of interaction between observer and subjects and of overcoming the distance between subjectivity and objectivity is suggested by Elizabeth Fee (1983) in her account of occupational health research in an Italian factory.

> Prior to 1969, occupational health research was done by specialists who would be asked by management to investigate a potential problem in the factory. The expert collected individual, quantifiable information from each worker by means of questionnaires, interviews, and medical records, and then statistically combined and manipulated the data to test hypotheses about the

causes of the problem. The procedure was rigorously objective; the results were submitted to management. The workers were the individualized and passive objects of this kind of research.

In 1969, however, when workers' committees were established in the factories, they refused to allow this type of investigation. The new structures of direct democracy in the workplace forced a transformation in the methods of occupational health research. Now workers would collectively produce the information needed to define and solve a problem; the generation of hypotheses would be a collective, not an individual, activity. Occupational health specialists had to discuss the ideas and procedures of research with workers' assemblies and see their "objective" expertise measured against the "subjective" experience of the workers. The mutual validation of data took place by testing in terms of the workers' experience of reality and not simply by statistical methods; the subjectivity of the workers' experience was involved at each level in the definition of the problem, the method of research, and the evaluation solutions. Their collective experience was understood to be much more than the statistical combination of individual data; the workers had become the active subjects of research, involved in the production, evaluation, and uses of the knowledge relating to their own experience. (p. 24)

CONCLUSIONS AND THEORIES DRAWN FROM DATA GATHERED

Women scientists have demonstrated the following differences in conclusions and theories:

1. Use of precise, gender neutral language in describing their data and presenting their theories.

A great deal of feminist scholarship has focused on problems of sexism in language (Robin Lakoff, 1975; Barrie Thorne & Nancy Henley, 1975) and the extent to which patriarchal language has excluded and limited women (Cheris Kramarae & Paula Treichler, 1986). Our language shapes our conceptualizations and provides the framework through which we may express our ideas. The awareness of sexism and of the limitations of a patriarchal language in science can allow feminist scientists to describe their observations in less gender-biased terms.

As more women have entered primate research, they have begun to challenge the language used to describe primate behavior and the patriarchal assumptions inherent in searches for dominance hierarchies in primates. Lancaster describes a single–male troop of animals as follows:

For a female, males are a resource in her environment which she may use to further the survival of herself and her offspring. If environmental conditions are such that the male role can be minimal, a one–male group is likely. Only one male is necessary for a group of females if his only role is to impregnate them. (1975, p. 34)

Her work points out the androcentric bias of primate behavior theories which would describe the above group as a "harem" and consider dominance and subordination in the description of behavior. One might imagine a gynocentric bias in which the male in the group would be called a "stud." "One–male group" certainly seems like less biased terminology.

An awareness of language should aid experimenters to avoid the use of terms such as "tomboyism" (John Money & Anke A. Erhardt, 1972) and "hysteria" which reflect assumptions about sex-appropriate behavior (Hamilton, 1985) in behavioral descriptions. Once the bias in the terminology is exposed, the next step is to ask whether that terminology leads to a constraint, or bias, in the theory and the way it is conceived or expressed.

2. Critique of observations, conclusions drawn, and theories generated differing from those drawn by the traditional scientist from the same observations.

Because of different socialization and psychological processes (Gilligan, 1982) and because science has traditionally been a masculine province (Fee, 1982; Haraway, 1978; Keller, 1982) women scientists are likely to approach science from a different perspective than that of their male colleagues. As Margaret W. Rossiter (1982) states, "As scientists they were atypical women; as women they were unusual scientists" (p. xv).

Building on their awareness of the bias possible from language and societal discrimination against women, women scientists (Birke, 1986; Bleier, 1984; Hubbard, 1983) have critiqued the studies in sociobiology, brain–hormone interaction, and sex differences research for their underlying commonality of biological determinism used to justify women's socially inferior position.

Feminist scientists of today refute the biologically deterministic theories by pointing out their scientific flaws (Bleier, 1979; Hubbard, 1979; Lowe, 1978; Sue V. Rosser, 1982). Bleier (1979) has discussed at length the subtle problems occuring with biochemical conversions of hormones within the body and with extrapolating from one species to another in biochemical as well as behavioral traits. Feminist scientists have warned the sociobiologists about the circularity of logic involved with using human language and frameworks to interpret animal behavior which is then used to "prove" that certain human behavior is biologically determined because it has also been found in animals. Perhaps white male scientists are less likely to question biologically deterministic theories that provide scientific justification for men's superior status in society because they as white men gain social power and status from such theories. Scientists from outside the mainstream (women for example) are much more likely to be critical of such theories because they lose power from those theories.

3. Awareness of other biases such as those of race, class, sexual prefer-ence, and religious affiliation which may permeate theories and conclu-sions drawn from experimental observations.

Perception of one bias typically has the effect of arousing an individual's awareness for the potential of other biases.

> Oppressive ideas and explanations that derive women's roles from women's "nature" are grounded in the material conditions in which the scientists who generate them live. These scientists are predominantly university-educated, economically privileged white men, who either belong to the hegemonic group or identify with its interests. (The few women and Third World men who have recently gained access to the scientific elite generally have the same economic and educational backgrounds as the traditional, white male mem-bers and often identify with the same interests.) It is therefore not an accident that scientists' perceptions of reality, as well as their descriptions of it, often serve to perpetuate and bolster the privileges of that disproportionately small group of people who have economic and social power in society. (Hubbard, 1983, pp. 1-2)

Feminist scholarship and the women's movement have been criticized (Dill, 1983) as being biased toward white middle class women. This cer-tainly was a justified critique and in many respects still presents a problem. However, in recent years feminist scholars have made more attempts to examine the connections and separations provided by racism, classism, and sexism and to avoid overgeneralization of data drawn from one group of women. Women aware of sexist bias who use gender as a category of analy-sis should be aware of biases of race, class, sexual preference, and religious affiliation that may be present in some scientific theories.

In *Biological Politics*, Sayers (1982) focuses on the use of theories of bio-logical determinism in both the nineteenth and twentieth centuries to justify women's socially inferior position in society. In her review of the craniome-try research in the nineteenth century she rightly points out that the initial impetus for that research was racism—to justify Western Europe's colonial empire and slavery. However, sexism was a secondary focus of the crani-ometry research; women were grouped with the "other" races and also "measured" as having smaller brains and therefore being inferior to white males. Sayers traces the increasing importance for the justification of wom-en's inferior position based on differences in brain anatomy, as women's demands for coeducation increased throughout the century. Sayer's nine-teenth century example demonstrates how both sexist and racist biases and stereotypes permeate a scientific theory.

Today, sexist bias seems to be primary in the research on brain lateraliza-tion (Bleier, 1988). However, scores on IQ tests and achievement tests of verbal and visuospatial ability are often used to demonstrate superior male ability and therefore justify their higher prestige and paying positions in our gender-stratified labor market. Because these same tests also reveal white superiority over blacks, women scientists should recognize that is likely that the theory may also be used to justify social inequalities based on race.

4. Development of theories that are relational, interdependent, and multicausal rather than hierarchical, reductionistic, and dualistic.

If it is true that women approach problems in terms of relationships rather than hierarchy (Gilligan, 1982) then they are likely to propose theories that indicate dependence and multiple factor causal interactions among the observations they describe. McClintock's lack of acceptance of the predominant hierarchical theory of genetic DNA as the "Master Molecule" that controls gene action provides an example of such a theory. Her theory of genetic transposition focused instead on the interaction between the organism and its environment as the locus of control (Keller, 1983).

In her work in purifying the environment, Richards took an interdisciplinary approach.

> Richards's interdisciplinary approach to the problems of people constituted her scientific vision. Her picture of the relationships between organisms and their physical and social environments accorded with the ideas of the ecology movement then being established by Ernst Haeckel (1834–1919). Along with her perception of the interrelatedness of all forms of life, Richards arrived at the concept of a vehicle for correcting imbalances in the system caused by man's ignorance and greed. (Ogilivie, 1986, p. 152)

Hamilton (1985) suggests a need for more explanatory research designs incorporating an appreciation of context and interactive models of causality.

> When gender-related differences are observed, investigators must consider the full range of hypotheses which might account for differences. For example, genetic sex, sex-related hormones, gender role and orientation (preference of sexual partner), and social expectations, must be distinguished, and the causal factors relevant to their understanding explored.
>
> While scientists must focus their research designs and simplify the hypothesis and conditions of their studies as much as possible, they must avoid oversimplification. The nature versus nurture dichotomy, for example, obscures our understanding of the developmental process and obscures the interaction of innate and learned psychosocial processes. Similarly, biological models derived solely from animal studies, risk neglecting the fact that humans have more plasticity due to cortical inhibition in overriding innate tendencies. That is, much research focuses on models of 100 percent impairment or incapacitation, without an adequate appreciation of the great variety of modifying our compensatory control mechanisms. (pp. IV-61–IV-62)

Feminists (Bleier, 1984; Fee, 1982; Hein, 1981) suggest central ideas to a feminist science could be the rejection of dualisms such as subjectivity/objectivity, rational/feeling, and nature/nurture which focus our thinking about the world. Bleier uses a particularly appropriate example to demonstrate the shortcomings of the nature/nurture dualism in the theory of fetal development.

> Since we tend to take for granted (or ignore) the normal physiological milieu as an essential part of development, it is easier to recognize the influence of environmental milieu on genetic expression if we consider external environmental factors that affect fetal development in humans through their disruptive effects on the maternal milieu. The mother's diet, drug ingestion (for example, thalidomide, DES, alcohol), virus infections (such as herpes and German measles), stress, and other known factors may have serious effects on the physical characteristics of the developing fetus. In some way all of these environmental factors have the capacity to induce abnormalities in the environmental milieu of the fetus, and it is the interactions between genetic factors and disturbed internal environmental factors that result in altered fetal development. There is no way to tease apart genetic and environmental factors in human development or to know where genetic effects end and environmental ones begin; in fact, this is a meaningless way to view the problem since from conception the relationships between the gene's protein synthesizing activity and the fetus' maternal environment are interdependent. As Lappe has said, "Genes and environments do not simply 'add up' to produce a whole. The manner in which nature and nurture interact to cause biological organisms to flourish or decline is an extraordinarily complex problem." (p. 43)

USE OF SCIENTIFIC INFORMATION AND PRACTICE OF SCIENCE

Women scientists have tended to be more sensitive to the following in scientific practice:

1. Use of less competitive models in practicing science.

Research by Matina S. Horner (1969) and Lois Wladis Hoffman (1972, 1974) demonstrates that women function better when they do not perceive the situation as one in which they are competing against others. This, coupled with women's concern about the global effects of science and the importance of relationships (Gilligan, 1982), contributes to women's choice of cooperative rather than competitive models for the practice of science.

Changing the competitive model upon which science is based could significantly change the social structure of science. First, it would be likely to change the hierarchical nature of recognition in science in which one person, usually a white male, heads the laboratory, gains the grant funds, and wins the Nobel Prize. Much more credit and recognition would be given to the team of individuals in the laboratory doing the actual work leading to the discovery.

Second, it should create more cooperation and collaboration among individuals in the same laboratory. All laboratories expect team work and most in fact live up to that expectation. However, the laboratory head often subconsciously, if not consciously, encourages competition for who can get the fastest results, the most grants, and the largest number of published papers among scientists of post-doctoral level, or higher, in the laboratory. This competition in the laboratory is of course a mirror for the microcosmic level of the competition faced by the laboratory head in the larger scientific community.

Third, replacing the competitive model with a more cooperative one should lead to less scientific fraud. Two of the highly publicized cases of discovered scientific fraud in recent years occurred at Harvard University and Sloan-Kettering Institute, two of the most prominent scientific institutions in the country. The young male scientists who perpetrated the fraud were described as "loners" in their work (Alexander Kohn, 1986). Their distinguished laboratory heads who lost their positions over the scandal, cited pressures brought on by scientific competition as important causal factors involved in the fraud (Kohn, 1986). A more cooperative model for science is needed to preserve the integrity necessary for good scientific research.

2. Perception of the role of scientist as only one facet which must be smoothly integrated with other aspects of their lives.

In a world in which a more cooperative approach would be taken towards science, all scientists, both male and female, would be freer to lean on other colleagues during certain periods of their lives when they need to devote slightly less time to science and correspondingly more time to other matters. For example it might be possible for scientists who are parents to work part time while their children are small.

Vivian Gornick (1983) finds in her work *Women in Science: Portraits From a World in Transition* that most women perceive science as incompatible with family life.

> She says, in essence, the only way to be a women in science is to forget about being a woman. It is impossible to live in the world of contemporary professional science, and rise to the top of the profession, and still be a woman in old-fashioned terms (that is, have a family). She says it can't be done, and points out that the majority of women in science are unmarried, or married with no children, or divorced with no intention of remarrying. (pp. 153–154).

Dale Baker (1983) and Jane B. Kahle (1983) both point out that the twenty-four hour per day commitment to science is a serious deterrent for young women considering careers in science. With a less competitive approach, all scientists might work more humane hours without feeling the guilt most feel if they are not in the laboratory every working minute. The work hours lost by each scientist working less would be compensated for by the increased number of individuals attracted to science after it becomes a more humane occupation.

3. Placing increased emphasis on strategies such as teaching and communicating with nonscientists to break down the barriers between science and the lay person.

A much larger percentage of women scientists compared to men scientists choose fields such as teaching and public relations within science. A great deal of this is the result of discrimination which prevents women from entering other occupations in science (NSF, 1988). However, many women prefer these fields because they allow for greater interaction with people.

Women find that teaching and talking with groups of people allows them to feel less isolated and develop the relationships they desire. A research scientist recently confided to me her despair over the fact that she and most of her female colleagues were considering quitting research science: "Despite the fact that I have tenure and am very successful at getting grants, I'm thinking of leaving science. I shouldn't quit because I'm really very good at it. However, I miss relationships with other people, particularly women. Everytime another female colleague opts out of research science I become a bit more isolated. I'm not sure how much longer I can continue to hang in there." (M. H., personal communication, June 26, 1987).

4. Exertion, whenever possible, of positive control over the practical uses of scientific discoveries to place science in its social context.

Women's groups in Europe in the movement known as ecofeminism have taken the lead in making explicit the connection between the potential destruction of the environment and women's bodies by uncontrolled use of science and technology. The women of the Feminist Women's Health Centre in Frankfurt, Germany made the following statements on May 24, 1986 at the Romer Antinuclear demonstration, a month after the Chernobyl disaster.

> Almost everyone in this country felt the whiff of death in these longed for early spring days. We were and still are torn by conflicting feeling: rage, depression and hopelessness before the creeping, invisible destruction potential of nuclear contamination—together with and additional to all the other problems we have anyway: ecological, economic, mental and health. The urge to give up, to resign oneself will constantly assail us—but being resigned also means anticipating death. . . .

> For over two thousand years patriarchy has been exploiting nature: earth, plants, animals and people are subjugated, violated and destroyed. As a refinement and historical further development of the methods this destruction is now being consummated in a totally desensualized and invisible way by nuclear contamination. . . .

> Total dismantling of all life-scorning and life-destroying technologies and machinery is the only solution. . . . (Feminist Women's Health Centre, 1987, pp. 207–208).

Feminists who are scientists have suggested certain research that would no longer be done if we were to have a feminist science:

> Then we, as feminist scientists, in making explicit our own social values and beliefs where they are relevant to the science we practice, may wish to claim a feminist approach to scientific knowledge that in its language, methods, interpretations, and goals, acknowledges its commitments to particular human values and to the solution of particular human problems. This would not eliminate or censor basic scientific investigations done for the sake of knowledge itself, with no known practical, social application, but it would aim to eliminate research that leads to the exploitation and destruction of nature, the destruction of the human race and other species, and that justifies the oppression of people because of race, gender, class, sexuality, or nationality. (Bleier, 1986, p. 16)

Lynda Birke, another feminist scientist, suggests that feminism will change science:

> Perhaps this discussion of creating a feminist science seems hopelessly utopian. Perhaps. But feminism is, above all else, about wanting and working for change, change towards a better society in which women of all kinds are not devalued, or oppressed in any way. Working for change has to include changing science, which not only perpetuates our oppression at present, but threatens also to destroy humanity and all the other species with whom we share this earth. (1986, p. 171)

CONNECTIONS

Most of these examples from the work of women scientists emphasize connection in some way: connection with the practical uses for which the discovery will be used; a chosen connection with the object of study; connection with other related scientific problems; and, most importantly, connection between science and human beings.

Examination of the work of women scientists yields evidence that they are connected knowers. Because almost all of the examples discussed come from the work of successful scientists who obtained degrees from traditional institutions of higher education, most would be classified as constructed knowers. They have the ability to "view all knowledge as contextual, experience themselves as creators of knowledge, and value both subjective and objective strategies for knowing" (Belenky, et al. 1986, p. 15). However, it appears that connected knowing on some level is an important step or portion of the constructed knowledge for these women. It is this connection, identified by Belenky et al. as important to many educated women, that could serve as the link to attract more women, people of color, and those white men not now attracted to science when it is known or taught in the separate, procedural mode.

Chapter 5

Toward Inclusionary Methods

*Connecting to Students by Changing
Approaches in Teaching Science*

In this chapter I explore methods and approaches to teaching science likely to be more attractive to females. These approaches reflect an attempt to convert the connection of women scientists to their work into methods that will connect students to science. These methods are based on years of teaching science to female students and an examination of the ways feminists (Bleier, 1984; Haraway, 1978; Hein, 1981; Keller, 1982) suggest women may approach science differently from men. The likelihood that scientists are now more willing to entertain alternative (and possibly even feminist) approaches to teaching is increased by the predicted need for scientists in the 1990s.

The OTA suggested a solution to the increasing shortage of scientists would include "persuading a greater percentage of college students to major in science and engineering and particularly removing the barriers that prevent women from entering these professions" (OTA, 1986). Although in 1986 women constituted 15% of all scientists and engineers (up from 9% in 1976), this represents a small fraction of the women who could become scientists and engineers. The proportion of women in scientific fields ranges from 12% in environmental science to 45% in psychology. In engineering the range is from 3% in both mechanical and electrical/electronics to 8% in chemical engineering (NSF, 1988). Salaries (College Placement Council Salary Survey, 1979) for individuals who major in science and engineering are significantly higher at all levels than those of students majoring in education, the arts, humanities, and social sciences. Attracting women to the sciences would thus help raise their income as well as fill the demand for scientists.

Research has consistently shown that, in general, girls do not perform as well in science classes as do boys. Between ages nine and fourteen, girls' science achievement declines and their interest in science wanes (J. Hardin & C. J. Dede, 1978; National Assessment of Educational Progress, 1978). During high school, girls do not elect to take science and mathematics courses as often as do their male peers (N. B. Dearman & V. W. Plisko, 1981; NSF, 1982); and, among college-bound senior high school students taking the Scholastic Aptitude Tests (SAT) in 1980, males outscored females by eight points on the verbal portion and forty-eight points on the mathematical portion. In college fewer girls choose science, especially the physical sciences, as their major area of study.

During the last decade a growing body of research has explored possible factors which may deter young women from majoring in science, leading to loss of increased employment opportunities and better paying careers for them, and a valuable source of talent for our increasingly scientific and technological society. A variety of factors such as parental expectations (Patricia Campbell, 1986), experience with scientific observations and instruments (Jane B. Kahle & Marsha Lakes, 1983), peer pressure to conform to traditional sex-role expectations in career choice (Smithers & Collins in Alison Kelly, 1981), and influence of guidance counselors (Helen Remick & Kathy Miller, 1978) contributes to the failure of girls to pursue science. Jane Stallings (1980), Kahle (1985), and Campbell (1986) have described the significant role teachers play in discouraging or attracting girls to the study of science. Donald Freeman et al. (1983) and Jere Brophy (1982) have indicated that most of the methods and content in science teaching may be derived from textbooks. Kahle (1985) indicates that instructional materials such as textbooks should be free of sexism in terms of language and descriptions of science contributions. Jan Harding (1983) and Barbara Smail (1983) in separate studies have indicated that certain activities, particularly laboratories and discussions, may be more appealing to girls in science. Actually many of the techniques particularly attracting girls to science also attract boys (Kahle, 1985).

Several federally funded programs aimed at attracting young women to science have been undertaken at the secondary, undergraduate, and graduate levels at a variety of institutions throughout the nation. Using the research that points to causes for women's choices not to select courses and careers in science, various programs have aimed at addressing different aspects of the problem.

In 1975, Lucy Sells labeled mathematics as the critical filter which prevents women from entering approximately three-quarters of all college majors. In an effort to overcome women's math avoidance, many institutions of higher education developed special programs to encourage and retain women in mathematics. (Lenore Blum & Steven Givant, 1982). Other programs such as the EQUALS program at the Lawrence Hall of Science at the University of California–Berkeley focused on the critical role educators in kindergarten through grade 12 play in encouraging young women in science (Nancy Kreinberg, 1982).

Responding to evidence (Ruth Cronkite & Teri Perl, 1982) that young women are unaware of career opportunities for women in science, several different approaches were initiated to make them more knowledgeable. The support given by the NSF throughout the country to the Expanding Your Horizons Workshops for secondary school-aged girls encouraged many communities, in the absence of federal funding, to continue to provide opportunities for young women to meet women career scientists. Science career conferences were also supported by the NSF, as well as colleges, universities, and the private sector, for college-aged women students. These conferences served as an efficient way to "provide large numbers of women with information about careers and to give them role models and career counseling" (Humphreys, 1982, pp. 165–166). Many members of the women's professional organizations such as the Committee on Women in Physics of the American Physical Society, the women from the American Chemical Society, and the Society of Women Engineers have been willing role models and often actively sought out opportunities to serve as models for students.

Some institutions such as Purdue University under a grant from Women's Educational Equity Act (Jane Daniels & William LeBold, 1982) developed approaches to teaching mathematics and science that would give the young women more hands-on experience with scientific equipment and instrumentation. This was to aid women in compensating for their lack of experience compared to that of many young men—gained from technical hobbies (building stereo equipment, model airplanes, and railroads) and working on mechanical or electrical equipment (car repair).

Traditionally very little research has centered on different methods and approaches to teach science and mathematics to girls and women. Some initial research (Kahle, 1985) examined textbooks for sexism in language, illustrations, citations, and references.

> Those analyses suggested that although progress had been made, it was limited. Women, for example, were pictured in non-traditional careers and were represented in approximately 50 percent of the illustrations. However, their meaningful contributions to science were seldom cited or referenced. (p. 52)

A growing body of literature (Elizabeth Fee, 1981; Hein, 1981; Keller, 1982; Sue V. Rosser, 1988; Rossiter, 1982) substantiates the extent to which science is a masculine province which excludes women and causes women to exclude themselves from it. Science is a masculine province not only in the fact that it is populated mostly by men but also in the choice of experimental topics, use of male subjects for experimentation, interpretation and theorizing from data, as well as the practice and applications of science undertaken by the scientists (Keller, 1982). To attract women to science the masculinity of science must be changed. Several feminists (Haraway, 1978; Harding, 1986; Hein, 1981; Keller, 1982) have written about the ways traditional "objective" science is synonomous with a masculine approach to the world. Some feminist scientists (Birke, 1986; Bleier, 1984; Fausto-Sterling, 1985) have suggested ways in which a feminist science might differ from this traditional approach to science.

The purpose of this chapter is to explore methods and approaches to teaching science likely to be more attractive to females by connecting them to what they are studying. The methods and approaches are arranged under the broad steps of the scientific method. Most of the examples of teaching methods and approaches come from biology and health science courses taught at the college level, because those are the fields and level at which I teach and have had the opportunity to observe the success of those methods. Biology and health science are also the main areas within science on which feminist theory has had an impact.

OBSERVATIONS

1. Expand the kinds of observations beyond those traditionally carried out in scientific research.

Very frequently the expectations of teachers reinforced by experiments in the laboratory manuals convince girls and women that they are not scientific because they do not see or are not interested in observing the "right things" for the experiment. This lack of interest or feeling of inferiority may come from the fact that most scientific investigations have traditionally been undertaken by males who determined what was interesting and important to study.

The expectations and prejudices of the experimenter can bias the observations to such an extent that the data are not perceived correctly. With several thousand years of distance, most scientists admit that Aristotle's experiments in which he counted fewer teeth in the mouths of women than men were biased by his views that women were inferior to men (Rita Arditti, 1980). Having students recreate Kuhn's example (Hubbard & Lowe, 1979) in which an observer still "sees" a black ace of spades which has been in fact changed to red upon being quickly shown a deck of playing cards confirms for them the bias that expectation can have upon observation. The Kuhnian example opens the door for students to recognize that scientists having different expectations can observe different factors in an experiment.

Accurate perceptions of reality are more likely to come from scientists with diverse backgrounds and expectations observing a phenomenon. Because women may have different expectations from men, they may note different factors in their observations. This example may explain why female primatologists (Fossey, 1983; Goodall, 1971; Hrdy, 1977, 1979, 1984) saw "new" data such as female–female interaction when observing primate behaviors. Including this data that had not been previously considered led to substantial changes in the theories of subordinance and domination as the major interactive modes of primate behavior. Women students may see new data that could make a valuable contribution to scientific experiments.

2. Increase the numbers of observations and remain longer in the observational stage of the scientific method.

Data from the NAEP (1976–77) indicate that females at ages nine, thirteen, and seventeen have significantly less science experiences than boys of comparable ages. This disparity in use of scientific equipment (scales, telescopes, thermometers, and compasses), and work with experimental materials (magnets, electricity, and plants) is at least partially due to sex-role stereotyping of toys and extracurricular activities for boys and girls in our society (Kahle, 1985). The lower achievement rate and less positive attitude of girls toward science may be directly related to participation in fewer science activities (Kahle & Lakes, 1983). Girls and young women who lack hands-on experience with laboratory equipment are apt to feel apprehensive about using equipment and instruments in data gathering.

Making young women feel more comfortable and successful in the laboratory could be accomplished by providing more hands-on experience during an increased observational stage of data gathering. In a coeducational environment it is essential that females be paired with females as laboratory partners. Male-female partnerships frequently result in the male working with the equipment while the female writes down the observations. Her clerical skills are improved, but she has gained no more experience with equipment for her next science course.

Because of time constraints, the observational stage of the experiment frequently is shortened and students are simply given the data for analysis. This practice is particularly detrimental to females who have fewer extracurricular opportunities for hands-on experiences. Programs that have been successful in attracting and retaining women in equipment-oriented, nontraditional fields, such as engineering, have included a special component for remedial hands-on experience (Daniels & LeBold, 1982).

3. Incorporate and validate personal experiences women are likely to have had as part of the class discussion or the laboratory exercise.

Most learners, regardless of their learning style, are interested in phenomena and situations with which they have had personal experience. For example, in introductory biology classes students demonstrate more interest in the parts of the course which they perceive to be most directly relevant to human beings. The portion on genetics—in which inheritance of human eye color, blood type, and hair color provides excellent material for examples and problems—generates more questions and interest from a larger fraction of students than parts of the course dealing with the structure of the cell or plant taxonomy.

In 1986, women constituted 25% of employed life scientists; in 1985 they received 47.7% of bachelor degrees awarded in the biological sciences. In contrast only 13% of employed physical scientists are women, and women receive 13.6% of the bachelor degrees in physics (NSF, 1988).

Women may be more attracted to life sciences in preference to the physical sciences because of their experience with more of the equipment and examples used in life sciences than physical sciences (Kahle, 1985). Many of the problems in physics deal with mechanics or electricity which are more likely to be familiar to boys from extracurricular and play activities. Results from NAEP show significant differences, which increase with increasing age, in the experiences of girls and boys in the use of scientific instruments, particularly those geared towards the physical sciences (Matyas, 1985).

Research on science anxiety suggests that experience with an instrument and familiarity with a task ameliorate anxiety (Shirley M. Malcolm, 1983). Beginning the course or individual lesson with examples and equipment with which girls are more likely to be familiar may reduce anxiety for girls. Often the context of a problem can be switched from one that is male gender-role stereotyped to one that is female gender-role typed. Transforming many of the proportions for mixing concrete and measurements for building airplanes to amounts of ingredients for making cookies and dress patterns represents such a switch that has been made in mathematics textbooks.

4. Undertake fewer experiments likely to have applications of direct benefit to the military and propose more experiments to explore problems of social concern.

The gender gap differential of women voting for issues favoring guns over butter (Klein, 1984) might provide a valuable tip for teaching methods to attract females to math and science. Most girls are more likely to understand and be interested in solving problems and learning techniques that do not involve guns, violence, and war. Much of this lack of interest is undoubtedly linked with sex-role socialization.

Some women wish to avoid science, technology, and mathematics because they are disturbed by the destructive ways technology has been used in our society against the environment and human beings. Some feminists during the current wave of feminism reject biology and science altogether (Laurel Holliday, 1978). As Birke (1986) points out, contemporary feminism grew up in a time of considerable antiscience feeling, resulting greatly from the horrors of the Vietnam war. This feeling was enhanced by analyses demonstrating male desire to dominate and control nature through technology might be linked to a desire to use similar means to dominate and control women (Merchant, 1979).

Most girls and young women are neither adamant nor articulate in voicing their feelings about the uses of science and their resulting avoidance of science. However, many are uncomfortable with engaging in experiments that appear to hurt animals for no reason at all or that seem useful only for calculating a rocket or bomb trajectory.

Teachers may confront this issue rather than assuming the "objectivity" of science protects the scientist from the social concerns about applications of theory and basic research. A strong argument for convincing females they should become scientists is that they can have more direct influence over policies and decisions controlling the uses of technology. Avoiding science and not acquiring the mathematical and scientific skills to understand complex decisions surrounding the use of technology insures the exclusion of women from the decision making process.

A second, related argument to induce women to stay in math and science revolves around potential earnings and career options. By avoiding science and mathematics, women exclude themselves from approximately 75% of all college majors (Sells, 1975). These are the majors leading to many of the higher paying jobs in our technological society. Women's avoidance of science and math therefore perpetuates the gender-stratified labor market, in which women are relegated to the lower paying human service positions, and simultaneously prevents them from influencing decisions on uses of technology.

5. Consider problems that have not been considered worthy of scientific investigation because of the field with which the problem has been traditionally associated.

In seeking out methods to teach problem solving skills, it may be advisable to search for examples and problems from more traditionally female dominated fields such as home economics or nursing. Although these fields have been defined as "nonscience," primarily because they are dominated by women (Ehrenreich & English, 1978; Hynes, 1984), many of the approaches are scientific. Using familiar terminology, equipment, and subjects will allow the student to concentrate on what the problem really asks rather than being put off because she or he does not know what a transformer or trajectory is. Matyas (1985) draws an analogy with males and cooking:

> Envision the thoughts and feelings of an adolescent boy asked to enter the kitchen, recipes and definition list in hand, and to prepare a full meal on which he will consequently be graded. Realize that he is in competition with female peers who, though they also have never done this particular task, have

considerably greater facility with the equipment required. Perhaps by this analogy we can understand the apprehension of the adolescent girl deciding whether or not to take high school physics. (p. 38)

After successful initial problem-solving sessions using familiar terminology and topics, it should be easier for the student to solve similar problems with unfamiliar terminology and topics. Making the transition to unfamiliar territory will insure success in future science courses.

6. Formulate hypotheses focusing on gender as a crucial part of the question asked.

Laboratory exercises in introductory classes may include gender as an assumption or hidden aspect of the question asked. In some cases, a male norm is simply assumed. These assumptions can make female students feel somewhat isolated and distant from the experiment without understanding the reasons for their alienation. Bringing up the issue of gender, correcting laboratory exercises (to include data collection on both males and females, whether they be other animals or humans) where appropriate, and formulating questions to elucidate gender differences or similarities as a variable may bring female students closer to the data. It also constitutes better science because assuming gender does not influence a particular variable is not valid.

An example of a laboratory exercise assuming a male norm and framework is the exercise on the displays of the Siamese Fighting Fish, *Betta spendens* used in introductory biology (Towson State University,, 1984). The exercise implies the only interaction occurring is between males, since only male responses to male, self and female behavior are assessed. The female *Betta* is simply a passive object used to arouse the aggression of the males. Correcting the exercise to include an analysis of the female–female and female–male interaction would convey to the students a more significant role for females, while also constituting better science, as this is the sole laboratory exercise devoted to animal behavior in the course. Just as theories of dominance hierarchies as the only primate organizational behavioral patterns were overturned when female primatologists (Goodall, 1971; Hrdy, 1977; Lancaster, 1975) began to work in the field, some introductory laboratory exercises might demonstrate better science by a focus on issues of gender.

7. Undertake the investigation of problems of more holistic, global scope than the more reduced and limited scale problems traditionally considered.

Modern biology, which emphasizes cell and molecular biology, is reductionistic. The brief time periods allotted for laboratory work coupled with the desire to complete an experiment in one laboratory period result in most laboratory exercises being particularly reductionistic.

Most students lack the extensive background in science, familiarity with the organism studied, and knowledge gained from similar experiments to understand the context and ramifications of the particular experiment completed during the laboratory period. They tend to see the experiment as a singular example of a minute phenomenon occuring in an obscure organism. For example, counting the asci in *Neurospora* appears to them to be a weird activity scientists enjoy for its own sake. They see very little connection between this experiment, genetics in other organisms, and chromosome mapping in humans. All too often the instructor fails to make these important connections explicit.

For female students, it may be especially important for the instructor to spend considerable time describing the global, holistic context of which this experiment is a crucial part. The work of Gilligan (1982) suggests that adolescent girls approach problem solving from the perspective of interdependence and relationship rather than from the hierarchical, reductionistic viewpoint favored by most adolescent boys. Thus females are likely to feel more comfortable in approaching laboratory experiments if they understand the relationship of that experiment to others and the importance of the particular phenomenon being studied for the organism as a whole.

METHODS

1. Use a combination of qualitative and quantitative methods in data gathering.

Some females have suggested their lack of interest in science comes in part from their perception that the quantitative methods of science do not allow them to report their nonquantitative observations, thereby restricting the questions asked to those that they find less interesting. These perceptions are reinforced by textbooks, laboratory exercises, and views of scientific research propagated by the media. In their efforts to teach the objectivity of science and the steps of the scientific method, very few instructors and curricular materials manage to convey the creative and intuitive insights that are a crucial part of most scientific discoveries. For example most of my students are shocked and pleased to learn McClintock could guess exactly how her corn kernels would look before she ever counted them on the ears (Keller, 1983).

Few students have the opportunity to observe the methods by which both qualitative and quantitative data can be combined to explore interesting questions. For example, quantitative physiological data—such as blood pressure, pulse rate, glucose and protein quantities from urinalysis, and weight—may be combined with qualitative assessments given by the patient herself—such as levels of fatigue and nausea—in order to determine the progress of her pregnancy. If so desired, qualitative assessments can be converted to a self-assessed numerical scale to yield a number that can be combined with quantitative data. In the laboratory qualitative observations of animal behavior such as relative activity or passivity can be converted to a numerical scale to be combined with more directly assessed quantitative data.

2. Use methods from a variety of fields or interdisciplinary approaches to problem-solving.

Because of their interest in relationships and interdependence, female students will be more attracted to science and its methods when they perceive its usefulness in other disciplines. Mills College, a small liberal arts college for women, capitalized on this idea in their program for increasing the participation of college women in mathematics-related fields. In addition to other components, their program emphasized interdisciplinary courses stressing the applications of mathematics in courses such as sociology, economics, and chemistry (Blum & Givant, 1982). They also developed a dual degree engineering program, based upon three years at Mills and two years at one of the surrounding engineering schools. At the completion of the five year program, the students receive bachelor's degrees in both liberal arts and engineering (Blum & Givant, 1982).

Many of the students at Mary Baldwin College, another small liberal arts college for women, became biology majors after taking a women's studies course focused on women's health. They sought a better understanding of basic biological processes although their initial attraction to the women's studies course had been to learn more about the psychology of childbirth, social and economic factors affecting teen pregnancy, and mood changes during the menstrual cycle. Frequently, psychology students sought a double major in biology to understand the physiological processes underlying the psychological phenomena they were studying (Sue V. Rosser, 1986).

3. Include females as experimental subjects in experiment designs.

Female students are more likely to perceive the results of the laboratory experiment to be more directly relevant to them if females, whether animal or human, are included as experimental subjects. Considerable criticism has recently (Hamilton, 1985) been leveled at the scientific community for its failure to include females as experimental subjects except when they are overused to test contraceptives or reproductive technologies. The reasons for the exclusion—cleaner data from males due to absence of estrus or menstrual cycles, fear of inducing fetal deformities in pregnant women, and higher incidence of some diseases in males—are practical when viewed from a financial standpoint. However, the exclusion results in drugs that have not been adequately tested in women before marketing and lack of information about the etiology of some diseases in women. In response to this the National Institutes of Health issued guidelines ("NIH Urges Inclusion," 1986) stating that females must be included in the experimental design when the disease occurs in females.

Including females in the experimental design is better science. It introduces the possibility of testing for gender differences caused by the variable under observation. Female students are also likely to feel more included and to see the ramifications of the experiment for their lives.

4. Use more interactive methods, thereby shortening the distance between observer and the object being studied.

Many females find it important to establish a relationship between themselves and the object they are studying. Chodorow's work (1978) in psychological development suggests this desire may be the result of early childrearing experiences in our society which encourage girls to be less autonomous and more dependent than boys. Keller (1985) used Chodorow's work as a basis for her explanation of the distance between subject and object in science to conclude that a masculine approach to the world emphasizes autonomy over relationships and dependence. Because most scientists are men, science has become a masculine province in which the methods, theories, and subjects of interest tend to exclude women and cause us to exclude ourselves from the province. In the teaching of science, most instructors underline the importance of objectivity of the scientist in approaching the subject of study. This is thought to be necessary to establish scientific rigor and school students in the difference between approaches used in the sciences and those of disciplines in the humanities and social sciences. Feminist critics (Haraway, 1978; Keller, 1982) as well as practicing scientists (Bleier, 1984) have pointed out that the portrayal of the scientist as distant from the object of study masks the creative, interactive relationship many scientists have with their experimental subjects.

Because girls and women consider relationships to be an important part of approaching problems, emphasis on a relationship with the object of study will attract females to study science. I have found students to be amazed that scientists can feel very attached and even passionate about their subjects. The biography of Barbara McClintock, *A Feeling for the Organism* (Keller, 1983), and the passion of the scientist Ana about tumors and bacteria expressed by June Goodfield in *An Imagined World* (1981) both surprise students. Jan Harding (1987) summed up the situation very well:

> When school science is presented as objectified and abstracted laws, that enables those whose personalities fit this approach to the world of enabling control and protecting them from emotional demand to feel comfortable. By in large such individuals are males. Changing that presentation of science is likely to attract individuals of different personality types, namely women.

5. Decrease laboratory exercises in introductory courses in which students must kill animals or render treatment that may be perceived as particularly harsh.

Merchant (1979) and Susan Griffin (1978) explored the historical roots of twentieth century mechanistic science which places both women and animals on the nature side of the nature/culture dichotomy. Their works document the extent to which modern mechanistic science becomes a tool men use to dominate both women and animals. Thus many women may particularly empathize with animals being treated harshly or killed for the sake of scientific knowledge.

Federal funding requires an institutional committee to screen experimental designs to insure proper care and use of animals; most scientists also care very much about animals and are unlikely to mistreat or kill an animal unnecessarily in research or teaching. However, killing vertebrate animals in introductory courses may especially discourage female students from pursuing more advanced courses in biology.

A laboratory exercise common in most introductory biology courses involves killing a frog by pithing its brain. I have found many more female students either refuse to pith the frog or register significant discomfort with the act than do male students. One wonders if this laboratory is traditionally included in introductory biology, as Zuleyma Tang Halpin (1989) points out, precisely because it serves as an initiation rite to discourage the students who feel too much empathy with animals from becoming biology majors.

CONCLUSIONS AND THEORIES
DRAWN FROM DATA GATHERED

1. Use precise, gender neutral language in describing data and presenting theories.

Small children given information using generic language such as "mankind" and "he" draw pictures of men and boys when they are asked to visually present the information or story that they have heard (Martyna, 1978). Although adult women have learned that they are supposed to be included in such generic language, some studies (Thorne, 1979) have indicated that women feel excluded when such language is used. Hall and Sandler (1982) have documented the negative effects sexist language has on females in the classroom. Kahle (1985) in her study of secondary school biology classes found that absence of sexism in classroom interactions and curricular materials is important in attracting young women to science.

Because most scientists in our culture are male, science tends to be perceived as a nontraditional area for women. It may become necessary to move beyond the absence of sexism to make particular efforts to correct stereotypes in the student's minds and to emphasize female scientists and their contributions. The necessity for this extra step was brought to my attention by an exercise developed by Virginia Gazzam-Johnson (personal communication, fall, 1985) for her students. She provided students with a bibliography of scientific references. Approximately one third of the names on the list included female forenames and one third were traditional male forenames for our culture. The other third of the authors used only initials for the forenames. When asked to state the gender of the individuals listed, most students assumed all of the people whose names were represented by initials were male. This is particularly ironic because initials were originally used by many female authors to disguise their gender. However, the stereotype of the male scientist is so strong in our culture that, unless clearly identified as female, scientists are assumed to be male.

2. Be open to critiques of conclusions and theories drawn from observations differing from those drawn by the traditional male scientist from the same observations.

Several historical and contemporary (Sayers, 1982) examples exist of the use of biology to justify political and social inequities. If any inequity can be scientifically "proven" to have a biological basis, then the rationale for social pressures to erase that inequity is diminished. In both the nineteenth and twentieth centuries some scientific research has centered on discovering the biological bases for gender differences in abilities to justify women's socially inferior position. Craniometry research and the social Darwinism quickly derived from Darwin's theory of natural selection serve as examples of the flawed science used to "prove" the inferiority of women and non-whites (Sayers, 1982). Feminist critics have stated that some of the work in sociobiology (Bleier, 1984; Hubbard, 1979) and brain lateralization (Bleier, 1988; Star, 1979) constitutes the twentieth century equivalents providing the scientific justification for maintaining the social status quo of women and minorities.

Some women students are consciously or subconsciously aware of these uses of science. They resent this powerful tool being used against them and may react by wishing to avoid science. Instructors can address this problem directly by exposing women to the feminist critiques from the nineteenth and twentieth centuries revealing the flawed experimental designs and conclusions drawn from this gender-differences research. The critiques provide an excellent opportunity to illustrate the problems of faulty experimental design and bias in interpretation. Students may also experience a feeling of empowerment and an increased motivation to study science. Recognizing that well-trained scientists are the individuals most capable of discounting the faulty research which has been used against women should provide a powerful impetus to attract women to science.

3. Encourage uncovering of other biases such as those of race, class, sexual preference, and religious affiliation which may permeate theories and conclusions drawn from experimental observation.

Removing sexism from the classroom and providing an awareness of the feminist critique of science are not sufficient to attract the diversity of individuals needed to correct the bias within science. Science in the United States (and in the Western world) suffers from bias and lack of diversity in other factors besides gender. In addition to being largely a masculine province, it is also primarily a white (with the exception of the recent addition of Asian-Americans) (NSF, 1986) and middle to upper class province. This relatively homogeneous group results in the restricted diversity of scientists compared to the general population. Restricted diversity may lead to excessive similarity in approaches to problem solving and interpretation of data, thereby limiting creativity and introducing bias.

Data collected from programs attempting to recruit and retain minorities in science have been interpreted to show that minorities of both sexes may fail to be attracted to science for some of the same reasons white women are not attracted (Yolanda S. George, 1982). In addition, racism among scientists, both overt and covert, and the use of scientific theories to justify racism are additional powerful deterrents.

Reading *Black Apollo of Science: The Life of Ernest Everett Just* (Manning, 1983) helps to sensitize students to the discrimination and alienation felt by black male scientists. Comparing Manning's work and the black critiques of science with feminist critiques will help to elucidate the separate biases contributed by race and gender (Elizabeth Fee, 1986).

Minority women face double barriers posed by racism and sexism. More research needs to be done to elucidate particular techniques that might help attract and retain minority women, including complex analyses recognizing the intersection of class, race, and gender as factors affecting each individual. Sensitivity of the instructor to these interlocking phenomena in women's lives is a first step toward attracting a diverse population to science.

4. Encourage development of theories and hypotheses that are relational, interdependent, and multicausal rather than hierarchical, reductionistic, and dualistic.

Laboratories in science classes frequently tend to be excessively simplistic and reductionistic. In an attempt to provide clear demonstrations and explanations in a limited span of time, instructors and laboratory manuals avoid experiments focusing on relationships among multiple factors. Well-controlled experiments in a laboratory environment may provide results that have little application to the multivariate problems confronted by scientists outside the classroom and students in their daily lives in the real world. For example, measurement of the increase in blood pressure after running upstairs compared to the rate at rest demonstrates only one of multiple interactive and, often, synergistic factors increasing blood pressure.

Building on the theory of Chodorow (1978) and the research of Gilligan (1982), instructors can capitalize on females' interest in relationships and interaction among factors in introducing and discussing the experiment. Females are likely to be eager to learn how the specific bit of information provided by this particular experiment is likely to influence and be influenced by other related factors. One laboratory instructor expressed the situation in the following way: "The boys won't listen to the instructions; they can't wait to play with the equipment. The girls always want more information about what they're doing and how it relates to other topics we've already studied" (James Robinson, personal communication, September 23, 1987).

Problems with multiple causes from related factors often result in data that are best expressed by gradations along a continuum. Theories of mutual interdependence often best explain such data. These are the types of data and theories traditionally seen as too complex for lower level, introductory courses. These are also the types of theory and data that may be used in approaching problems such as environmental factors affecting fetal development which interest many female students.

PRACTICE OF SCIENCE

1. Use less competitive models to practice science.

Research by Horner (1969) and Phillip Shaver (1976) indicates women learn more easily when cooperative rather than competitive pedagogical methods are used. While male students may thrive on competing to see who can finish the problem first, females prefer and perform better in situations where everyone wins. Emphasizing cooperative methods in the class and laboratory make mathematics and science more attractive to females.

In its program to encourage college women in math-related fields, Mills College takes several steps to change traditional teaching styles: Homework and attendance are required every class period; homework counts one-third toward the final grade; students are encouraged to discuss the assignments and work on them together. In order to reduce the competition and fear of not finishing on time initiated by timed tests, examinations are given in the evening with no time limit, although they must be completed in one sitting (Blum and Givant, 1982).

Because of the current small number of women in science and the lock-step sequencing of the courses, females can be relatively isolated from other women and excluded from informal male networks. Several programs (Daniels & LeBold, 1982; Max, 1982) that have been successful in encouraging women in science and math have emphasized networking and support groups to facilitate cooperative interaction. A necessary element for women's success in engineering programs at MIT was provided by a peer group or team with whom they could cooperate. Male students already had the exam samples from the fraternity files and had "buddies" who could help them (Margaret Dresselhaus, personal communication, 1987).

In addition to cooperative methods, some programs attempt to improve the competitive skills of females. The EQUALS program teaches a variety of problem solving skills for teachers for their classroom use (Kreinberg, 1982).

A study by P. Wheeler and A. Harris (1979) suggests that women benefit from small physics problem solving workshops where they can build confidence. Their study also indicates that women benefit from exercises on test-taking strategies and especially from encouragement in educated risk-taking.

2. Discuss the role of scientist as only one facet which must be smoothly integrated with other aspects of students' lives.

A major issue concerning most females is the possibility and difficulty of combining a scientific career with marriage and/or family. In a longitudinal study of valedictorians from public high schools, Karen Arnold (1987) found that the primary gender difference between male and female valedictorians in choice of major and career was related to issues surrounding marriage and family. Even among the young women choosing to pursue a career in science or engineering later marriage and/or later childbearing were considered as mechanisms permitting them to achieve their career goals. The research of Baker (1983) demonstrated a conflict between "femininity" and science, accounting for the low number of women at the doctoral level in science.

It is clear the issue of the compatibility between a career and family life must be addressed in order for large numbers of young women to be attracted to science. Role models of successful women scientists from a variety of backgrounds who exhibit diverse lifestyles can best address this issue. Many federally funded programs and university-based recruitment efforts emphasize the importance of role models. Remembering the significant role that a mentor or role model played in their own lives, many women scientists are willing to spend large amounts of time speaking to young women. Many of the women's professional organizations have particular outreach role model programs. The Purdue Program in Engineering (Daniels & Lebold, 1982) attributes much of its success to the Society of Women Engineers.

3. Put increased effort into strategies such as teaching and communicating with nonscientists to break down barriers between science and the lay person.

Scientific, mathematical, and medical terminology are frightening and inaccessible to many people in our society. This terminology proliferates as scientific investigation into an area becomes increasingly sophisticated and as its accompanying technology becomes correspondingly more complex. In a survey of girls in British classrooms, Diana Bentley (1985) summarized the attitude of one female in the following way:

> She appears also to have developed a view that as she progresses in her science studies, and indeed as science knowledge in society becomes more detailed, there is an increasing dependence on complex apparatus and this is distancing in its effect. She seems to be saying that her view of science as an accessible activity that ordinary human beings can engage with was a childish

and naive one, and that due to increasing technological knowledge the openness of science to people is decreasing. (p. 163)

The combination of these factors makes many students, particularly females, fear and desire to avoid science and mathematics. Research (Hall & Sandler, 1982) has indicated that females face the additional barrier of having their answers and theories about science devalued because of their speech patterns and other verbal and nonverbal methods of communication. New approaches for communicating scientific information may aid in attracting women to science while opening the door for a new appreciation and valuing of the ideas of females in science.

Lucy Sells (1982) points out that teaching mathematics with the intention to deliver skills and communicate is very different from teaching mathematics with the intention of weeding out all but the top of the class. At the time when many of the instructors were trained, an oversupply of scientists and physicians was expected, therefore teaching techniques were often geared towards selecting the elite. Weeding out teaching styles are less likely to appeal even to very able female students. Tutoring by peers or student majors may be effective techniques for female students.

4. Discuss the practical uses to which scientific discoveries are put to help students see science in its social context.

It will become necessary to restructure the curriculum to include more information on communication skills and ethics. A survey of engineering seniors conducted at Purdue University (Daniels & LeBold, 1982) discovered that female students were more apt than males to give greater importance to educational goals stressing general education, communication skills, and the development of high ethical standards. "However, they were similar to the men in their perception that such goals were not achieved very well" (Daniels & LeBold, 1982, p. 157). The recent cases of scientific fraud (Kohn, 1986) and problems of communication in the scientific community suggest that more information on the topics desired by the women could benefit all. A very persuasive argument to attract women to science is the tremendous usefulness it has for improving people's lives. The positive social benefits of science and technology seem to be overwhelmingly important to females. The research of Jan Harding (1985) shows that girls who choose to study science do so because of the importance of the social implications of the problems science can solve. When asked to solve a particular mechanical problem, boys and girls took a different approach: boys viewed the problem as revolving around the technicalities of producing an apparatus; girls described the problem in its social context or environment, developing a technology to solve a difficulty faced by an elderly person, for example (M. Grant, 1982).

In a study of differential attitudes between boys and girls toward physics, Svein Lie and Eva Bryhni (1983) gave the following summary of their results:

"Taken together we may say that the girls' interests are characterized by a close connection of science to the human being, to society and to ethic and aesthetic aspects. Boys more than girls are particularly interested in the technical aspects of science" (p. 209). This research suggests that programs emphasizing internships or work experience in industrial or government sectors (Daniel & LeBold, 1982) may be particularly important for females because they demonstrate the practical applications of science in aiding people.

Insuring science and technology are considered in their social context with assessment of their benefits for the environment and human beings may be the most important change that can be made in science teaching for all people, both male and female. This change is exemplary of the positive effects that innovative efforts to attract women to science may have. Asking how science might be approached differently to attract females shifts the pressure to change from women to science. Previous efforts to increase the number of women scientists and engineers in the United States have centered primarily on the question of what is wrong with women that they are not attracted to science. This paper asks the question also raised at the 1987 International GASAT Conference: What is wrong with science and science teaching that it fails to attract females? By changing science to consider and encompass feminist perspectives valuing female approaches and concerns, science will begin to include the diversity necessary to help it benefit all human beings.

Chapter 6

Sexism in Textbooks

New Subtleties Replace Overt Stereotypes

A major factor influencing the teaching of science is the choice of textbook. Several research studies (Rebecca Barr, 1988; Michael Cole & Peg Griffin, 1987) have explored the extent to which science teaching is textbook driven, partially due to standardized testing. On the elementary and secondary level, most teachers rely almost exclusively on the textbook for organization of topics, information, method of presentation, and suggestions for activities (Brophy, 1982; Freeman, et al. 1983). At the undergraduate level, instructors are advised to rely heavily, if possible, on the textbook for course organization and content, because students are more comfortable with the continuity and closure which are provided by the congruence of course and text (Wilbert J. McKeachie, 1969). College students are aware that many instructors rely on texts as the major source of information from which tests are constructed, further increasing textbook influence on what students learn in courses (Charles A. Goldsmid & Everett K. Wilson, 1980).

Because the textbook ranges from driving the teaching to serving as a complement to the instruction, it stands as an important element aiding in attracting or deterring people from science. Accuracy in presentation of scientific data, clear and comprehensive coverage of subject matter, and informative, useful pictures, questions, and problems are criteria teachers consider in selecting a textbook. Although these serve as primary criteria for selection, other parameters become relevant when the focus turns to factors deterring women and people of color from science.

Note: This chapter written by Sue V. Rosser and Ellen Potter.

In the early 1970s, several studies explored sexism in the language and illustrations of textbooks (*Avoiding Stereotypes,* 1974; Joan Breiter & Jack Menne, 1974). Other research (Nancy Frazier & Myra Sadker, 1973; Kramarae, 1980) documented possible deleterious effects sexism in textbooks had on girls and women in the classroom. As a result of these studies most textbooks now use gender neutral language and depict women and people of color in illustrations. Blatant sexism and racism in textbooks have been eliminated.

However, women and people of color may still detect more subtle forms of sexism and racism that continue to be conveyed in textbooks. For example, Kahle (1985) and Mariamne Whatley (1988) showed that women and blacks may be highly represented in illustrations while absent from the written content of the text. The roles and contributions of women scientists and ethnic male scientists are frequently omitted or only included on a token basis. Topics of central interest to women (childbirth, menstruation, menopause, lactation) and people of color (sickle cell anemia, lupus) may be overlooked. Harding (1983) and Smail (1983) in separate studies have indicated that certain activities, particularly laboratories and discussions, may be more appealing in interesting girls in science. Many of the techniques particularly attracting girls to science are simply examples of good teaching methods which are equally appealing to boys (Kahle, 1985).

Science educators agree science instruction should include hands-on activities in which students participate in scientific investigations (Cole & Griffin, 1987; Jeffry V. Mallow, 1981). The use of activities contributes both to students' learning and enjoyment of science. Because girls tend to like science less than boys do, affective and motivational concerns are especially important in supporting girls' participation in science (Martin Maehr, 1983; Marjorie Steinkamp, 1984).

Research has established that in science as in other areas of instruction, texts play a decisive role in determining classroom events (Barr, 1988; Cole & Griffin, 1987). One would expect science activities would be especially sensitive to text because teachers would be expected to be particularly apprehensive about assigning investigative activities with procedures not recommended by authorities.

A number of scholars have suggested ways science activities can be useful in encouraging rather than deterring girls' participation in science. Areas frequently mentioned are (a) developing girls' science-related cognitive skills, (b) motivating girls in science by increasing their self-confidence and stimulating their interest, and (c) arranging social participation in order to enhance girls' equal participation and diminish their anxiety.

Many girls have not had the opportunity to develop a number of science related cognitive skills. Joan Skolnick, Carol Langbort, and Lucille Day (1982) describe four skill areas problematic for girls: spatial visualization, including graphing; numerical problem solving and applications; logical reasoning; and scientific investigation. Strengthening girls' skills in these areas should help to erase their lack of confidence and avoidance of subjects requiring these skills.

The reluctance of girls and women to study science is frequently attributed to motivational problems arising from their lack of self-confidence and interest. These are in turn due to the misperception that science involves a collection of obscure facts and mechanical procedures difficult for a female to understand. For this reason, science activities allowing girls to participate in the creation of scientific knowledge, and particularly activities relating to girls' interests and experiences are useful (John Head, 1985; Kahle, 1985). Particularly important to the building of confidence and interest in science in all people is the understanding that there can be more than one correct approach, hypothesis, and solution to a scientific problem and that they can use their ingenuity to participate in scientific investigation. (Phyllis C. Blumenfeld & Judith L. Meece, 1988; John Mergendoller, Virginia Marchman, Alexis Mitman, & Martin Packer, 1988; Rosser, 1986). In addition, females who may be reluctant to approach scientific tools which they consider to be part of the male mechanical domain can benefit from participating in activities in which they can become comfortable with science-related devices (Kahle, 1985; Kahle & Lakes, 1983; Skolnick, et al., 1982).

Finally, it has been suggested that girls' anxiety regarding science can be exacerbated or alleviated by the social context in which they participate (June Shapiro, Sylvia Kramer, & Catherine Hunnerberg, 1981; Elizabeth Stage, Nancy Kreinberg, Jacqueline Eccles, & Joanne Becker, 1985). Opportunities to work at one's own rate, either independently or as an equal member of a cooperative group or pair, and to discuss and raise questions regarding the problems at hand are helpful to girls (Mallow, 1981). Girls frequently require encouragement and a chance to explore without pressure of evaluation or competition (Maehr, 1983).

In an attempt to discover some factors that would deter women and minorities from science, we undertook a project to evaluate sexism in textbooks. Data from the 1976–77 NAEP indicate that a crucial change in girls' attitudes toward science occurs some time between the ages of nine and thirteen. Although nine-year-old girls have significantly less experience with scientific observations and the use of science instruments than nine-year-old boys, the girls *desire* to have such experiences. By the age of thirteen, the girls indicate much less desire for such experiences (Kahle & Lakes, 1983).

Kahle (1985) has indicated that biology may be an important course to observe for student attitudes toward science. Taken by over 80% of high school students nationally (Kahle, 1985), the life sciences also constitute the area in which most of the baccalaureate science degrees obtained by women are earned (NSF, 1986). Therefore, the textbooks and activities used in the life science classes may be critical in attracting girls to science.

Five textbooks adopted by the South Carolina State Department of Education (see Table 6.1 for each of the five textbooks purchased since adoption) were targeted for study because they are used in a life science course during the span between ages nine and thirteen, a critical age for girls' attitudes toward science. (Most South Carolina students do not take biology until grades 9 or 10, which places them at ages 14–16.)

We examined the five textbooks used in the seventh grade life sciences courses in the South Carolina Public Schools to assess the lack of information presented about the achievements, contributions, and roles of women in science; the presence of sexist language and images of women; and the absence of activities in the accompanying activities manuals shown to motivate girls to study science. Underlying this examination was the assumption of the validity and reliability of the research showing that sexist language, limited images of women, lack of information about women's achievements, and selected learning activities fail to attract girls to study science. We did not directly test whether or not those factors motivate girls to study science.

METHODS AND RESULTS

Language

Each textbook was evaluated to determine the number of times and ways sexist language is used. The Association of American Colleges *A Guide to Non-Sexist Language* (1986) was used as the standard against which the words of the texts were evaluated.

Direct sexist language does not occur in any of the five textbooks. Generic pronouns are used unless the antecedent is a named male or female. Occupational stereotypes are not transmitted through the language of the text. For example, it is never assumed a scientist is "he" or a nurse is "she" unless it is appropriate for the specific individual described or depicted.

Table 6.1. South Carolina Seventh Grade Life
Science Textbooks, Listed in
Decreasing Order of Use

Symbol Used in Research	Textbook Publisher
A	D. C. Heath (1984)
B	Charles E. Merrill (1984)
C	Scott, Foresman (1983)
D	Addison-Wesley (1984)
E	Prentice-Hall (1984)

Pictures

The photographs, drawings, and outlines were evaluated to determine the ratio of females compared to males depicted and to assess the nature of the activity illustrated. Specifically, every photograph or drawing was recorded unless it contained a large number of animals or people in it, such as a school of fish, large herd of animals, or a crowd of people. After the picture or drawing was recorded the gender of the animal or person was determined. Sex of animals was considered because many publishers solved the problem of unequal pictorial representation of women and men by substituting pictures of animals for pictures of human beings. If the gender/sex of the animal or person was undeterminable, it was recorded as sex unknown.

Photographs, drawings, and outlines were counted and recorded separately, because it was not obvious that each has an equivalent impact on the student. Photographs are of real people and animals, and might be viewed either as isolated examples or as a representative of the majority of cases. Drawings and outlines represent creations by artists of people, animals, or body silhouettes. Some students might view them as either less real or more normative than photographs. If the gender was not clear from a distinguishing feature of the silhouette, it was recorded as sex unknown.

Animals or people in the process of an activity were recorded as active; animals or people recorded as passive were observing someone or having something done to them. "Scientist" was recorded if a photograph or drawing obviously depicted a scientist or if the caption or surrounding text stated that the picture was of a scientist.

In contrast to the language, the photographs, outlines, and drawings do reflect a sexist bias. The percentages and numbers from the data in Table 6.2 of pictures of animals indicate most animals represented are of unknown or indistinguishable sex. However, when the sex is distinguishable, four of the five textbooks include more pictures of male animals than female animals.

Table 6.2. Photographs of Animals

Textbook	No. of Total Pictures of Animals %	N	No. of Animals Represented	Males %	N	Females %	N	Unknown %	N
A	71	207	289	2.5	7	.3	1	97.2	281
B	52	86	182	7	12	5	9	88	161
C	47	92	189	.5	1	5	9	95	179
D	35	48	135	4	6	2	3	94	126
E	46	55	94	18	17	11	10	71	67

The data in Table 6.3 of photographs of people continue the trend of picturing more males than females; all five texts include more pictures of males. When the pictures are analyzed more carefully for active or passive depictions and representations of scientists, the male bias becomes more pronounced. Four of the five books picture more males in active roles; the fifth text depicts one more active female (29) than male (28). All five of the books picture more male than female scientists; three of the books picture no female scientists. The book that illustrates the most female scientists (6), pictures 15 male scientists.

The data from the drawings of animals (Table 6.4) and people (Table 6.5) are similar to the photograph data from Tables 6.2 and 6.3. Most of the animals are of unknown gender; however, the larger the percentage of animals represented by gender, the larger percentage of males represented. The drawings of people are strongly biased towards males. In all five textbooks two-thirds to three-fours of the drawings represent men or boys. Similarly, many more males than females are shown in active roles. In none of the textbooks was a female scientist drawn although all included at least one male scientist.

The outlines represent humans in a schematic drawing for nongender/sex specific purposes. Outlines are frequently used to show the relative position of structures or organs in the body (i.e., the position of major arteries in the body). Usually, the accuracy of the biological information is not improved by indication of the sex/gender in the outline. When only one sex/gender is

Table 6.3. Photographs of People*

Textbook	No. of Total Pictures of People %	No. of Total Pictures of People N	No. of People Represented	Males %	Males N	Females %	Females N	Unknown %	Unknown N
A	29	84	197	55	108	41	82	4	8
				A 19	37	A 8	15		
				S 8	15	S 3	6		
B	48	80	190	48	91	47	90	5	9
				A 67	61	A 58	52		
				S 18	16	S 0	0		
C	53	103	236	61	143	36	85	3	8
				A 33	77	A 21	50		
				S 1	1	S 0	0		
D	65	90	184	55	102	43	79	2	3
				A 32	58	A 18	34		
				S 3	5	S 1	1		
E	54	64	109	54	59	46	50	0	0
				A 26	28	A 27	29		
				S 39	3	S 0	0		

*A = Active; S = Scientists

Table 6.4. Drawings of Animals

Textbook	No. of Total Drawings Representing Animals %	N	No. of Animals	Males %	N	Females %	N	Unknown Gender %	N
A	77	27	97	0		0		100	97
B	65	32	105	1	1	3	3	96	101
C	50	26	78	0		0		100	78
D	66	33	160	4	7	1	2	94	151
E	84	65	65	20	13	2	1	78	51

used for outlines, the implication is that it represents the norm. The data in Table 6.6 show four of the five books used outlines of the male body only. The fifth book included female outlines for less than 20% of its outlines.

The pictoral data in Summary Table 6.13 demonstrate that male human beings are represented much more frequently than females in all types of pictures. Females constitute less than 50% of photographs in all textbooks. Females are never represented in more than one-third of the drawings and usually are not represented at all in outlines (for four out of the five books).

Table 6.5. Drawings of People*

Textbook	No. of Total Drawings Representing People %	N	No. of People	Males %	N	Females %	N	Unknown Gender %	N
A	23	8	17	71	12	29	5	5	1
				A 75	9	A 20	1		
				S 8	1	S 0	0		
B	35	17	33	76	25	24	8	0	
				A 40	10	A 38	3		
				S 4	1	S 0	0		
C	50	26	39	74	29	26	10	0	
				A 28	11	A 15	6		
				S 4	1	S 0	0		
D	34	17	24	67	16	25	6	4	2
				A 50	12	A 21	5		
				S 13	3	S 0	0		
E	16	12	12	67	8	33	4	0	
				A 25	3	A 8	1		
				S 17	2	S 0	0		

*A = Activity; S = Scientists.

Curricular Content

Integration of information concerning females and women was assessed using two different methods. First, a modification of the Schuster–Van Dyne scheme (1985) (Table 6.7) was used to determine the extent to which the roles and accomplishments of women scientists was included. Integration of information on topics such as menstruation, childbirth, and menopause, particularly relevant to girls and women, into curricular content in the discussion of the reproductive system was included in this scheme.

A second, less direct method involved evaluating descriptions for appeal and order with regard to gender. If a statement was made that only discussed one gender/sex ("Gregor Mendel is considered the father of genetics") it was recorded as an appeal. We defined appeal as positive information attributed to someone of specific gender.

When a career was featured or even mentioned, the gender of the individual described or pictured as holding that career was noted. When both genders were used or shown to discuss a subject, the order of each reference was recorded. For example, if the meiotic process for sperm formation is described before the meiotic process for egg formation in a text, this would be recorded as male listed first.

All five of the books represent a relatively low level of integration of achievements of women scientists and lack information specific to women's health in the curricular content. Two of the books (B and E) are at the lowest level on the Schuster–Van Dyne scheme with the absence of women not noted. They include no descriptions of female scientists and no information such as descriptions of menstruation of particular interest or relevance to female students. The other three books rank at the second lowest level. Two (A and D) describe several female scientists and go into some detail on pregnancy and childbirth, but ignore any active role of the mother. The third (C), while only describing one female scientist, is the only book to describe the menstrual cycle and go into considerable detail about pregnancy.

As the data in Table 6.8 indicate, in all of the books the overwhelming percentage (ranging from 83% to 100%) of appeals were of males. Although

Table 6.6. Body Outlines of People

Textbook	Total No. of Outlines	Males		Females	
		%	N	%	N
A	24	83	20	17	4
B	10	100	10	0	0
C	11	100	11	0	0
D	7	100	7	0	0
E	2	100	2	0	0

Table 6.7. Schuster–Van Dyne Scheme[1]

		Stages of Curriculum Change			
Textbook	Stages	Questions	Incentives	Means	Outcome
B&E	1. Invisible women	Who are the truly great thinkers/actors in history?	Maintaining "standards of excellence"	Back to basics	* Pre-1960s exclusionary core curriculum * Student as "vessel"
A,C,&D	2. Search for missing women	Who are the great women, the female Shakespeares, Napoleons, Darwins?	Affirmative action/compensatory	Add to existing data within conventional paradigms	* "Exceptional" women on male syllabus * Student's needs recognized
	3. Women as disadvantaged, subordinate group	Why are there so few women leaders? Why are women's roles devalued?	Anger/Social justice	Protest existing paradigms but within perspective of dominant group	* "Images of women" courses * "Women in politics" * Women's Studies begins * Links with ethnic, cross-cultural studies * Women-focused courses
	4. Women studied on own terms	What was/is women's experience? What are differences among women? (attention to race, class, cultural difference)	Intellectual	Outside existing paradigms; develop insider's perspective	* Interdisciplinary courses * Student values own experience
	5. Women as challenge to disciplines	How valid are current definitions of historical periods, greatness, norms for behavior? How must our questions change to account for women's experience, diversity, difference?	Epistemology	Testing the paradigms; Gender as category of analysis	* Beginnings of integration * Theory courses * Student collaborates in learning
	6. Transformed, "balanced" curriculum	How can women's and men's experience be understood together? How do class and race intersect with gender?	Inclusive vision of human experience based on difference and diversity, not sameness and generalization	Transform the paradigms	* Reconceptualized, inclusive core * Transformed introductory courses * Empowering of student

[1]Source: Women's Place in the Academy: Transforming the Liberal Arts Curriculumn, copyright 1985 by Rowman & Littlefield Publishers.

81

Table 6.8. Descriptions of Appeal, Scientists, and Careers

Textbook	No. of Total Descriptions That Were of Appeal %	N	No. Appeals Male %	N	No. Appeals Female %	N	No. Male Scientist %	N	No. Female Scientist %	N	No. Male Careers %	N	No. Female Careers %	N
A	40	63	83	52	17	11	52	33	11	7	50	6	50	6
B	33	71	90	64	10	7	60	38	0	0	20	1	80	4
C	32	52	87	45	13	7	42	22	2	1	46	17	54	20
D	51	57	91	52	9	5	70	37	7	4	59	13	41	9
E	32	20	100	20	0	0	80	16	0	0	62	8	38	5

the number of descriptions of male scientists ranged from 16 to 38 in the five books, the maximum number of female scientists described was seven. Two of the books included no descriptions of female scientists.

As the data in Table 6.8 indicate, the number of careers discussed varies considerably among the five books. Two of the books illustrate or describe more careers for women than for men; one book describes an equal number of careers for both sexes. The careers described, however, are often traditional for the gender (i.e., a female nurse).

When both sexes were mentioned in the explanation of a process, the male was almost always listed first (Table 6.9). In one book the female was never listed first. Very frequently even when the female was listed first, the male was still in the more active role ("the egg was fertilized by the sperm").

Table 6.9. Descriptions of Order

Textbook	No. of Total Descriptions That Were of Order %	N	Male Listed First %	N	Female Listed First %	N
A	60	93	82	76	18	17
B	67	147	76	112	25	35
C	68	112	68	76	32	36
D	49	54	78	42	22	12
E	68	42	100	42	0	0

Activities

The sample consisted of 231 activities which were selected from the five texts. Texts varied in the number and kinds of activities included, with Texts A and C having 48 and 45 activities respectively. All activities from these texts were used, and similar numbers of active hands-on science activities (rather than library research activities) were randomly selected so each text was represented by 45 to 48 activities.

Each activity was coded for the presence of skills and motivating elements identified from a review of the research as being important for females (Table 6.10). Activities were also classified as a natural *observation,* a *demonstration* or exercise, or an *experiment.* Reliability, assessed by having two independent individuals code five activities randomly selected from each of the five texts, was .86 using the formula described by Herbert Wright (1967).

A description of the skills and motivating elements examined for their inclusion in science activities is presented in Table 6.10 along with the percentage of activities in which each skill or motivating element was included. Activities most often present opportunities to use the skill of logical reasoning, followed by spatial and numerical skills, with only a few permitting the opportunity for scientific investigative reasoning. The motivating elements most frequently found are the use of science-related manipulatives, of content relevant to females, and of activities that permit more than one answer or that present evidence to be explained rather than a linear explanation. Less frequently seen are the use of the students' own experience, the opportunity to use more than one approach, or the invitation to hypothesize regarding the outcome of the activities. Each text examined provides the opportunity to develop approximately two skills and incorporates approximately two motivating elements. Although texts vary in the number of skills and motivating elements they permit, none falls far below two of each per activity.

It is reasonable to assume that the kinds and numbers of skills and motivational elements in an activity would vary according to the type of activity, with demonstrations perhaps incorporating fewer skills and/or motivating elements than experiments. If this is so, a fair comparison of textbooks would have to take the distribution of types of activities into account because texts differ in the proportion of the three types of activities they include. For example, Text D has a far larger proportion of experiments than do the other texts. Table 6.11 shows activity types are indeed associated with varying numbers of skills and motivating elements, with experiments having considerably higher numbers of both skills and motivating elements than demonstrations and observations. Demonstrations and observations have similar numbers of skills, but observations have more motivating ele-

Table 6.10. Skills and Motivating Elements for Which Activities Were Analyzed

Aspect	Definition	Percentage of Activities in Which Present
Skills		
Logical	Logical reasoning (sorting and classifying, deductive reasoning, combinatorial reasoning, controlling variables, probabilistic reasoning)	80
Spatial	Spatial visualization, drawing, graphing, using charts and tables	64
Numerical	Measuring, understanding numbers, problem-solving with numbers	41
Investigative	Independent scientific investigation (observation, formulating questions and hypotheses; not required to design experiments, collect and analyze data, draw conclusions, and communicate results; requires higher level reasoning beyond logical reasoning skills; requires intellectual effort rather than being algorithmic)	24
Motivating Elements		
Manipulatives	Uses manipulatives related to science and/or teaching (e.g., laboratory equipment not used in usual classes or homemaking)	54
Female-relevant content	Related to interests identified as "feminine" such as bacteriology; food; gardening; nutrition; nuturant nature study such as impacts of environments, reproduction, human body	53
More than one answer	Any part of activity has more than one right answer, due not just to natural variability of measurement; different things may happen or be seen	39
Presentation of evidence	Uses "mystery" approach in which students must provide explanation for evidence, in contrast to linear step-by-step logical exposition or explaining outcome and causes prior to activity	35
Uses own experience	Elicits own prior experience or uses self as the object of investigation	15
More than one approach	Different problem solving behaviors are rewarded, exploration encouraged; chance for individual ingenuity and effort, rather than list of procedures to be followed; distinguishes genuine investigation from highly directed laboratory task	10
Hypothesize fist	Instructions to hypothesize regarding outcome prior to activity	9

Table 6.11. Ranking for Each Text: Skills and Processes by Activity Type[a]

	Textbook					All Texts
	A	B	C	D	E	
ALL ACTIVITIES						
Number of Activities in Category	47	46	48	45	45	231
Skills						
Rank	4	3	2	1	5	
Mean Number	1.85	1.96	2.18	2.66	1.84	2.09
Motivating Elements						
Rank	4	3	2	1	5	
Mean Number	1.85	2.02	2.33	2.68	1.73	2.12
SPECIFIC ACTIVITY TYPES						
Demonstration						
Number of Activities in Category	39	29	38	11	28	145
Skills						
Rank	3	4.5	2	1	4.5	
Mean Number	1.85	1.82	2.02	2.18	1.82	1.91
Motivating Elements						
Rank	4	3	1	2	5	
Mean Number	1.77	1.79	2.07	1.8	1.68	1.84
Experiment						
Number of Activities in Category	6	12	9	26	14	67
Skills						
Rank	4	3	2	1	5	
Mean Number	2.0	2.67	2.78	2.88	1.93	2.55
Motivating Elements						
Rank	4	3	2	1	5	
Mean Number	2.0	2.75	3.40	3.08	1.86	2.72
Observation						
Number of Activities in Category	2	5	1	8	3	19
Skills						
Rank	4	5	1	2	3	
Mean Number	1.5	1.0	3.0	2.6	1.67	1.95
Motivating Elements						
Rank	1	5	3	2	4	
Mean Number	3.0	1.6	2.0	2.6	1.67	2.21

[a] Rank: 1 = most; 5 = fewest.

ments per activity. An examination of the percentage of each of three kinds of activities including each skill and motivating element (Table 6.12) shows this pattern for most of the skills and motivating elements. It is interesting to note, however, that observations are highest in the inclusion of important elements presenting cognitive challenges. These elements include opportunities to use investigative skills, to get more than one answer, to use more than one approach, and to hypothesize about the outcome of an activity before conducting it. Each of the three kinds of activities presents students with a different variety of skills and motivating elements.

Even when the unequal distribution of activities across texts is taken into account, we find that texts differ in their inclusion of elements useful to females with individual texts showing considerable variability in the number of skills and motivating elements they incorporate. As Table 6.11 shows, even when the distribution of activities is controlled, some texts include substantially more skills and motivating elements facilitating females' participation in science than do others. This comparison is clarified by the rankings included on Table 6.11, where each text's rank for numbers of skills and motivating elements is displayed separately for each kind of activity as well as for all activities. Text D, which ranks best for overall activities, is ranked first or second for each cell; Text E, which is worst, is almost always

Table 6.12. Percentage of Activities for Each Activity Type Containing Each Skill and Motivating Element

	Demonstration	Experiment	Observation
	n = 145	n = 67	n = 19
Skills			
Logical	.74	.95	.73
Spatial	.67	.65	.42
Numerical	.36	.58	.26
Investigative	.14	.36	.53
Motivating Elements			
Manipulatives	.47	.76	.26
Female-relevant content	.48	.52	.53
More than one answer	.33	.43	.68
Presentation of evidence	.19	.75	.26
Uses own experience	.20	.09	.05
More than one approach	.10	.04	.37
Hypothesize first	.08	.05	.12

ranked fourth or fifth for its inclusion of skills and motivating elements in all three kinds of activities.

DISCUSSION

This project represents the only research on the evaluation of science texts and activities manuals for the factors examined in this study. Other research on science textbooks has focused only on the sexism of the language and images of women (Kahle, 1985) or the photographs (Whatley, 1988). Steinkamp (1984) and Susan L. Melnick, Christopher Wheeler, and Barbara B. Gunnings (1983) have examined varieties of activities and approaches which may interest girls in science. Research evaluating the integration of women's roles and achievements into textbooks has been restricted largely to the humanities and social sciences (Tetreault, 1985). This project demonstrates the first examination of science textbooks for this integration; it also represents the first attempt to examine textbooks and activities manuals for all factors.

Careful analysis of the five textbooks used for teaching seventh grade life science in the South Carolina public schools reveals that overt forms of sexism, such as use of the masculine pronouns as generic and exclusion of females from illustrations, does not occur. Careers for both men and women are described when material on careers is included in the text.

However, more subtle forms of sexism pervade all of the texts. They all picture more males than females (Summary Table 6.13) and picture males more frequently in active roles. Most scientists pictured or described are men in all of the textbooks. Two of the books include no description of a female scientist while three books include no picture of a female scientist (Summary Table 6.14). Picturing and describing male scientists primarily provide few role models for girls aspiring to be scientists.

Using the male body as the generic schematic outline and describing more men or describing the male role first also occurred in all of the text-

Summary Table 6.13. Pictoral Depictions of Human Males and Females

Textbook	Photographs		% Drawings		% Outlines	
	Male	Female	Male	Female	Male	Female
A	55	41	71	29	83	17
B	48	47	76	24	100	0
C	61	36	74	26	100	0
D	55	43	67	25	100	0
E	54	46	67	33	100	0

Summary Table 6.14. Descriptions of Appeals, Scientists, and Careers

Textbook	% Appeals		% Scientist		No. of Careers		Sex Listed First	
	Male	Female	Male	Female	Male	Female	Male	Female
A	83	17	52	11	6	6	82	18
B	90	10	60	0	1	4	76	24
C	87	13	42	2	17	20	68	32
D	91	9	70	7	13	9	78	22
E	100	0	80	0	8	5	100	0

books. Emphasizing the male, coupled with the small amount of information about the accomplishments of women in science and topics of interest to girls, constitute other subtle forms of sexism occurring in all of the texts.

Although probably not as detrimental as the more overt forms of sexism, subtle sexism may still deter young women from careers in science. The work of Kahle (1985) suggests that pictures of women in lab coats are inadequate to attract women to science. Meaningful contributions of women in science need to be discussed in the text and the illustrations need to include women in nontraditional occupations and active roles (Ann Haley-Oliphant, 1985). The work of Whatley (1988) documents the powerful impact illustrations can have in transmitting information that may even be contrary to what is presented in the text.

Using only male outlines to show the location of organ systems in the human body or to show where humans fit in a schematic drawing reinforces the message to students that males are the norm, the standard. Picturing and discussing male scientists and mostly including activities in which students are asked to do further research into the work of a male scientist buttresses the stereotype that only male scientists are worthy of research and only their ideas are worthy of recognition.

This investigation found substantial differences between texts in their inclusion of elements encouraging to girls in scientific activities. It suggests that females whose teachers selected activities from Text D would have the opportunity to learn more of the skills they need and have more motivating experiences in science than those whose teachers used activities from Text E, and so would be more likely to develop and pursue a successful interest in science. Implicit in this conclusion is the assumption that girls will be better served if activities include more rather than fewer skills girls have been shown to need and if they incorporate more rather than fewer elements the research suggests will be motivating to them. An examination of the list of skills and motivating elements (Table 6.10) provides support for this assumption, because all of these features represent what we would agree is good science pedagogy. Increasing the quantity of these features in activities would not create a muddle of confusing or overextended experiences; rather they would more accurately represent the skills and operations used by scientists and so provide girls and boys the opportunity to experience them.

Many of the skills needed by females could be readily incorporated into activities. For example, teachers could require students to use logical reasoning and to plan investigations rather then providing them with ready-made solutions and procedures. They could incorporate spatial and visual skills by having students create drawings, graphs, tables, and charts to describe their findings.

Likewise, many motivating elements readily lend themselves to a variety of activities. For example, teachers could routinely ask students to hypothesize about the expected outcomes of their activities, instead of telling them what they are likely to find in advance. This would be congruent with the "mystery" approach in which students must explain the evidence uncovered, rather than simply providing the examples for the teacher's explanations and descriptions of causes and processes. Too few activities draw on the students' own experiences, focus on the students themselves, or have more than one possible outcome or answer, and far too few permit or encourage individual ingenuity or creativity in conducting investigations. The result is girls (and boys) frequently misperceive science as a body of established knowledge accessible to only a few extraordinary individuals. The low proportion of activities requiring these higher level investigative skills is especially disturbing, because higher level thinking both motivates student interest and is a prerequisite for effective functioning as a scientist (Steinkamp, 1984; Susan S. Stodolsky, 1988).

As an example of differing approaches to the same subject matter, we find that activities designed to familiarize students with joints and their movements are included in some form in all of the texts. One text merely asks students to observe a diagram or model of a skeleton and to fill in a chart using information gathered from the model and provided in the text. Other texts ask students to construct joints from animal bones and to experiment with differing kinds of attachments and examine their movements. Still other activities ask students to analyze joint movement by experimenting with various movements of their own bodies, and ask students how changing their joints would affect their ability to move. Some texts limit their questions to requests for bone names and similar information, while others require careful observation and encourage speculation regarding functions and adaptive values of joints. Thus some texts require students to practice many skills, motivating them with the challenge to think creatively, while others provide ready-made answers. Teachers could readily incorporate many facilitative elements themselves.

The planned analysis of activities for social aspects was deleted because so few activities mentioned social arrangements. Teachers could themselves encourage a cooperative, accepting, and challenging classroom environment for shared inquiry, whether or not it is suggested by the text. They can make sure all members of a team or paired work group have equivalent roles and responsibilities, and that questioning, intellectual self-confidence, and effort are encouraged in a task-focused noncompetitive environment.

None of the five textbooks is ideal; they all suffer from several forms of sexist bias. However differences exist among the books in the kinds and extent of sexism (see Summary Tables 6.13 and 6.14). For example one text (A) which showed less sexism than the others in pictures and content, was not strong in motivating elements for females. It is better than any of the other texts on the whole in picturing females, in describing female scientists, and in including nontraditional careers for women. Another book (B) was probably the worst in reinforcing stereotypical opinions of females and males. Males were pictured as lumberers, policemen, scientists, and in other typically male occupations. Females were usually pictured in a shopping setting or as mothers. The descriptions reinforced the idea of women as mothers/mates. The chapters mentioning females most often were those on reproduction. However, in contrast, this same book pictured a higher percentage of females and careers for women than the other books and was intermediate in terms of motivating activities.

A third book (E) that always described the male first, described no female scientists, had fewest activities to motivate girls, and also had 100% of its appeals towards males, described more careers for females than any other book. The text (D) best in motivating elements showed intermediate degrees of sexism for other factors.

To attract talented young women to study and actively pursue careers in science we must become aware of the many factors currently deterring them. The data from this study provide information about one of the basic deterrents: the material presented in the textbooks and activities manuals.

Selection of a textbook solely on the basis of its female-friendly characteristics is difficult. A book picturing larger numbers of females and discussing more careers for women than another book may, in contrast, have fewer appeals in which a positive characteristic is attributed to women or fewer activities to motivate female students. Although one or two books may be decidedly more sexist, it is difficult to find a book that is uniformly female-friendly. When the myriad of other factors—such as clarity and completeness in coverage of subjects, accuracy in scientific information, and useful questions, problems, and illustrations, which are also of major importance in textbook selection—is added to the consideration of sexism, choosing a textbook becomes a complex issue. Evaluating sexist language and images of women, level of integration of information concerning women into curricular content, and activities better preparing and motivating females must become a significant factor in that choice, however, if we hope to attract larger numbers of women to science.

Chapter 7

Warming up the Classroom Climate for Women

Faculty, students, and administrators are showing renewed interest in eliminating sexism in its various forms from their institutions and from their science classrooms in an attempt to attract more women to science. A beginning step taken in many classes and development workshops for faculty and administrators toward elimination is providing information about the diverse ways women experience sexism daily on the campus. The series of "Chilly Climate" papers produced by the Project on the Status and Education of Women of the AAC (Hall & Sandler 1982, 1984; Bernice R. Sandler & Roberta M. Hall, 1986) serve as the resource guide for extensive material about sexism in language, nonverbal behavior, and teaching approaches that create a chilly climate in the classroom particularly detrimental to female students. The series also documents the more subtly sexist problem of the absence of women's roles, experiences, and achievements from curricular content and the overt problem of sexual harassment: factors preventing women students from enjoying full equality of educational opportunity. They point out that these problems tend to be most severe in science and engineering because these are nontraditional areas for women. Because of these factors the climate in science classrooms tends to be especially chilly, or female-unfriendly.

Lectures and discussions based on the information from the "Chilly Climate" series provide excellent avenues for educating administrators, students, and faculty. Active participation in exercises will reinforce the ideas presented in lectures and discussion. The purpose of the following group of five exercises is to provide active participation for a group of individuals learning about sexism. Each exercise has been developed to focus on a particular aspect of sexism developed in the "Chilly Climate" series. All five exercises might be used together in a workshop introducing the diverse forms of sexism. Each exercise may also be used separately to reinforce information presented in depth in a workshop on a particular topic such as gender and language or curricular reform in the science classroom.

DEFINING SEXISM AND ITS RELATIONSHIP TO CHILLY CLIMATE ISSUES

Purpose

This exercise allows participants to express definitions of sexism and suggest interpretations of how sexism may contribute to a chilly climate in the classroom for women.

Who

Students, faculty, and administrative staff can all benefit from defining and hearing the definitions and interpretations of the others in the group.

When

"Defining Sexism and Its Relationship to Chilly Climate Issues" serves as an ideal exercise to open a workshop or discussion on the chilly climate topic. Although the exercise is particularly effective to crystallize the thoughts of participants who have read the chilly climate papers in preparation for the session, the exercise may be modified slightly for participants who have not read the papers in advance.

Why

The exercise provides the group with a common basis, to which everyone has had an opportunity to contribute, with which to begin a discussion of chilly climate issues. After hearing the definitions of others, participants are likely to recognize that members of the group hold diverse viewpoints.

Where

No particular setting is necessary for the exercise. It is desirable that participants have a table or other flat surface on which to write their definitions on index cards.

How

"Defining Sexism and Its Relationship to Chilly Climate Issues " may provide participants with an activity as they arrive waiting for the session to begin. Each participant should be given a 3 × 5 index card upon entering the room.

The following directions facilitate the exercise:

1. Ask each participant to write a definition of sexism and a statement of how sexism is related to creating a chilly climate in the classroom for women on an index card. (If participants have not read the chilly climate papers before the session, ask them how they think that sexism might create a chilly climate in the classroom for women.)
2. Collect the cards from all individuals.
3. Read all of the cards aloud to the group without comment. If the group is particularly large or if time is short, every second or third card might be read. However, it is important that the group realize that the cards read were not pre-selected.
4. Ask the group for their comments about the definition of sexism and its relationship to chilly climate issues.

Outcome

For most groups, this exercise becomes an avenue for breaking the ice, uniting the group, and providing a common ground for beginning the session.

PRONOUNS AS POWER

Purpose

This exercise emphasizes the point that gendered pronouns, even when used generically, evoke a mental image of an individual whose sex corresponds with the gender of the pronoun, thereby excluding individuals of the opposite sex.

Who

Students, faculty, and administrators can all benefit from this exercise.

When

"Pronouns As Power" might be used to initiate a discussion or lecture on the importance of language, including a chilly classroom climate for women, in conveying sexism. Alternatively it might be used as a closing statement after such a discussion or in response to the question "Why do women feel excluded by terms like mankind and he which are used generically to include all individuals?"

Where

No special equipment or settings are necessary for the exercise.

Why

Many individuals, particularly men, fail to understand the exclusion that women feel when so-called generic language (man) and pronouns (he, his) are used (Martyna, 1978). If the generic pronouns are truly inclusive, then the same message and feeling should be conveyed by a passage when such generic pronouns are switched to female pronouns. After reading a familiar passage in which female pronouns have been substituted for generic pronouns, most people begin to comprehend that generic language is not really inclusive.

How

The following information may be helpful in completing the exercise:

1. Select a passage that is familiar and that conveys a message of power or impact. People may not care if they are included in passages conveying little of significance or import. A passage from the Bible, the Constitution or other famous document carries the necessary significance and familiarity for most people.
2. Ask the group to listen to the passage as you read it aloud.
3. Read the passage aloud to the group, changing the original language from masculine nouns and pronouns to feminine nouns and pronouns. Change supposed generic terms such as mankind to truly generic words such as humanity that convey the same meaning.

A sample passage:

> Then God said, "Let us make woman in our image, after our likeness; and let them have dominion over the fish of the sea, and over the birds of the air, and over the cattle, and over all the earth, and over every creeping thing that creeps upon the earth." So God created woman in her own image, in the image of God she created her; female and male she created them. (Gen. 1:26–27.)

> Then the Lord God said, "It is not good that the woman should be alone; I will make her a helper fit for her." So out of the ground the Lord God formed every beast of the field and every bird of the air, and brought them to the

woman to see what she would call them; and whatever the woman called every living creature, that was its name. The woman gave names to all cattle, and to the birds of the air, and to every beast of the field; but for the woman there was not found a helper fit for her. So the Lord God caused a deep sleep to fall upon the woman, and while she slept took one of her ribs and closed up its place with flesh; and the rib which the Lord God had taken from the woman she made into a man and brought him to the woman. Then the woman said,
"This at last is bone of my bones and flesh of my flesh; he shall be called Man, because he was taken out of Woman."
Therefore a woman leaves her mother and her father and cleaves to her husband, and they become one flesh. And the woman and her husband were both naked, and were not ashamed. (Gen. 2:18–25.)

4. After the participants have listened to the passage, ask them to describe their reaction to hearing the passage with the reversed nouns and pronouns.

Outcome

Most individuals state that the familiar passage contains a slightly different meaning for them when the pronouns have been reversed. The women often express feelings of empowerment, inclusion, and authority after hearing the passage. Men usually express feelings of distance and exclusion.

GENDER DIFFERENCES IN EXPERIENCES WITH CHILLY CLIMATE ISSUES AND SEXISM

Purpose

The purpose of this exercise is to provide participants with a physical representation of how chilly climate issues and sexism may have affected their education or career.

Who

This exercise is useful to raise the awareness of students, faculty, or administrators to sexism and chilly climate issues that may differentially affect women and men. Although it may be most effective when used with a faculty department, class of students, or unit, it may be modified slightly (see below) to be used with groups consisting of faculty, staff, and students from throughout the institution. The exercise can only be used in a group containing both males and females.

Why

Individuals who hear the information about chilly climate issues and sexism may not clearly understand these incidents occur much more frequently in women's lives than in men's lives. This exercise causes each person to see that sexism more frequently affects women than men.

When

This exercise is most effective when used after a presentation about chilly climate issues and sexism; it is a particularly effective response to the question: "Do sexism and chilly climate issues really affect women more than men?"

Where

A rectangular room or hallway free of chairs or other obstructions is the ideal space in which to permit the free movement of the number of people in the group.

How

The following instructions will help to orient the group to the exercise:

1. Ask the group to imagine that a line runs from one end of the room to the other. They should imagine that one end of the room or line corresponds with agree strongly, always, or ten; the other end of the room or line corresponds with disagree strongly, never, or zero. In between the two ends are the points one through nine which correspond to the gradations between always and never (i.e., the midpoint between the two ends of the room corresponds to "sometimes" or "neither agree nor disagree").
2. Ask the individuals in the group to stand and to place themselves arbitrarily along the imaginary line.
3. Tell the group that you will read a series of 12 statements. After each statement each individual should move to the position on the imaginary line that corresponds with her or his experience in light of that statement.
4. Each person is asked to notice not only his or her position after each statement but also to be aware of the gender distribution along the imaginary line after each statement.

Statements

The following statements should be read for a group of faculty. Remind the individuals to be aware of the position of males compared to females, as well as their own position after each statement.

1. I find that I have trouble picturing or including myself when I hear terms like mankind.
2. I think that males are superior to females in mathematical or visuo-spatial ability.
3. I often find myself being interrupted or ignored by my colleagues.
4. I have been sexually harassed by an employer or professor.
5. A professor or colleague has questioned whether or not I am serious about my chosen career.
6. I worry a considerable amount about how well my career plans will fit in with my plans for a relationship and/or family.
7. I have been questioned by my department chair or dean about my plans for marriage or family.
8. All of my classes include information about contributions made by famous people of my sex.
9. Several times when I was in college, a professor made comments to me about my clothes or physical appearance.
10. I find that I learn the names of the individuals of the opposite sex in my classes better than the names of the people of my own sex.
11. A factor in the choice of my major was that it is an appropriate or traditional field for a person of my sex.
12. At least half of the faculty members in my department are of the same sex that I am.

Modifications

The statements may be modified in varying ways to more appropriately fit the backgrounds of individuals in the group. For example, statement seven might be changed to the following for a group consisting solely of students: "I have been questioned by my advisor or a professor about my plans for marriage or family." Statement 12 might be modified to the following for a group consisting entirely of staff: "At least half of the employees in my department or division are of the same sex as I am."

Outcome

After all of the statements have been read, the group can be asked about the differences in gender distributions they observed after each statement. This exercise provides most groups with a physical demonstration that although some individuals of both genders may have similar experiences corresponding to particular statements, gender differences in experiences are usually revealed by these statements. Specifically, sexism and chilly climate issues occur more frequently in the lives of women than men.

Exceptions

In certain fields such as nursing, which are more traditionally dominated by females, statements 8 and 12 in particular may show the reverse of the usual chilly climate pattern (i.e., women will strongly agree with these statements and men will strongly disagree with them). If participants in the group come from diverse fields which include equal numbers of individuals from disciplines with extremely strong patterns of male or female dominance, gender differences on some statements may be obscured even though sexism exists in that discipline. For example, if 50% of the group were composed of engineers (a strongly male dominated field) and the other 50% of the group were composed of nurses (a strongly female dominated field), equal numbers of men and women would be likely to agree with statements 8, 10, 11, and 12. These exceptions and others resulting from the particularities of the group such as wide variation in age or deviation of this individual department from the national norm in terms of gender distribution, should be discussed when assessing the outcome of the exercise.

INCORPORATING SCHOLARSHIP ON WOMEN INTO A TRADITIONAL DISCIPLINARY COURSE

Purpose

This exercise facilitates discussion of course revision to include new scholarship on women in traditional disciplinary (i.e., non-women's studies) course offerings.

Who

Faculty who hold some familiarity with recent feminist research and who are open to revising their traditional introductory or advanced course to include the new scholarship are the most likely group to profit from this exercise by changing their course syllabi. The exercise permits students to review courses they have taken and recognize how those courses might be improved and changed. This realization may lead students to demand such information in future courses.

When

Faculty in institutions that have adopted curricular reforms requiring inclusion of information on women's studies and ethnic studies in general education courses will have compelling interest in the exercise. Faculty who have recently been exposed through faculty development seminars, presentations at professional meetings, or reading the literature to recent feminist research may also be eager to consider syllabus revision. However, the exercise can be successfully used to introduce the new scholarship to faculty and students.

Why

Feminist research represents the cutting edge of scholarship in many disciplines. In addition to women's studies courses, this research must be integrated into traditional departmental courses. Even faculty who are knowledgeable about the new scholarship and eager to integrate it into their courses may not know how to begin transformation. This exercise provides an avenue to initiate that process.

Where

No particular setting is necessary for the exercise. A chalkboard or flip chart for the facilitator and a table or flat surface on which the participants may write are useful.

How

In anticipation of this exercise, each participant is asked to bring a course syllabus. The facilitator presents the McIntosh (1984), Schuster–Van Dyne (1985), or Tetreault (1985) scheme as a model representing phases of curricular development. Each participant then evaluates her or his course syllabus against the phase model to determine the extent to which the course transformation has occurred. Then participants consider what might be done to further transform this course to the next stage.

Model

I prefer to use the McIntosh model developed for phases of curricular integration in history to illustrate transformation. This model is less complex and is therefore more easily comprehended after an oral presentation:

Phase I

Womanless History. This is the very traditional approach to the discipline, which is exclusive in that only great events and men in history are deemed worthy of consideration.

Phase II

Women in History. Heroines, exceptional women, or an elite few who are seen to have been of benefit to culture, as defined by the traditional standards of the disciplines, are included in the study.

Phase III

Women as a Problem, Anomaly, or Absence in History. Women are studied as victims, as deprived or defective variants of men, or as protesters, with "issues." Women are at least viewed in a systematic context because class, race, and gender are seen as interlocking political phenomena. Categories of historical analysis still are derived from those who had the most power.

Phase IV

Women as History. The categories for analysis shift and become racially inclusive, multifaceted, and filled with variety; they demonstrate and validate plural versions of reality. This phase takes account of the fact that because women have had half of the world's lived experience, we need to ask what that experience has been and to consider it as half of the history. This causes faculty to use evidence and source materials that they are not in the habit of using.

Phase V

History Redefined and Reconstructed to Include Us All. Although this history will be a long time in the making, it will help students to sense that women are both part of and alien to the dominant culture and the dominant version of history. It will create more usable and inclusive constructs that validate a wider sample of life.

Examples from art, literature, psychology, and biology may be used to illustrate the use of the model in diverse disciplines (Sue V. Rosser, 1987).

Outcome

Few participants will leave the room with a revised course syllabus. However, the exercise provides most with ideas for beginning course transformation in their science disciplines. With the exception of biology, it is unlikely most science professors will be able to envision course revision beyond stage two. In biology, a professor who is also well-educated in women's studies scholarship should be able to revise the course to stage three or four (Rosser, 1986).

STEREOTYPES AFFECT DISCUSSIONS
OF SEXUAL HARASSMENT POLICY

Purpose

This exercise demonstrates that stereotypes surrounding factors such as gender, position, or rank, and known previous sexual history may influence discussion of sexual harassment policy. Specifically, the stereotypic labels worn by individuals affect their contributions to the discussion, the perceptions of their remarks by other group members, and the extent to which the group permits them to influence the discussion.

Who

Groups containing individuals of both genders holding different positions in the institution are appropriate for this exercise. Probably more learning occurs when individuals representing both genders and wide diversity of positions (students, faculty, administrative staff) comprise the group. However, the exercise may be used with single sex groups containing participants of similar institutional status.

When

Modifications in the question given to the group for discussion make the exercise appropriate for use at different points in a sexual harassment discussion. It may provide an effective mechanism for an institution that is developing its official policy on sexual harassment to begin discussion with various groups throughout the institution about the policy; the exercise provides a means for educating various constituencies in the college or university about the policy and some of the difficulties that may arise in its implementation. The exercise may also be used during a general discussion of sexism and its connection with sexual harassment without reference to a specific policy of sexual harassment.

Where

The ideal setting for this exercise is a room in which a small circle of six to eight chairs can be surrounded by a circle of chairs large enough to accommodate the other participants in the group. The inner circle should be easily visible to everyone in the outer circle. Although no particular limit need to be placed on the size of the group, the exercise is likely to be more effective for groups containing between 20 and 30 people.

Why

Stereotypic labels resulting from gender status within the organization, and knowledge of personal information, including sexual history may affect the influence that an individual has in discussions of most topics. However, controversial subjects such as sexual harassment may particularly evoke stereotypic responses because of lack of information about the topic and embarrassment about discussing sexual issues. This exercise provides an avenue to raise the awareness of group participants of the role stereotypic labeling may be playing in the dynamics of group discussion.

How

The group role play may be carried out in the following way:

1. Select six or eight people from the larger group to participate in the role play. Choose an approximately equal number of individuals of each sex. If the positions of individuals within the institution are known, try to choose small group participants who represent a variety of ranks.
2. Ask the six or eight small group participants to sit in a circle with the remainder of the larger group sitting in a surrounding circle.
3. Select a previously prepared label to place on the forehead of each small group participant. The label should be as different as possible from the true gender, rank, and known sexual history of the individual on whom the label is being placed. (For example, a male department chair might receive the label "female untenured professor. Ignore me.") Each small group participant is *not* permitted to see her or his own label. However, each participant must show the label to all participants in both the smaller and larger groups.

Labels

Labels may be mailing labels or any other suitable material which may be temporarily affixed to the forehead. The following sorts of descriptors may be written in magic marker on the labels.

1. Male Department Head. Tell me I'm right.
2. Female Sorority member. Tell me I'm cute.
3. Male professor who harasses students sexually.
4. Female student who has been sexually harassed.
5. Male student accused of acquaintance rape.
6. Female untenured professor. Ignore me.
7. Male football coach. Tell me I'm a good ol' boy.
8. Female director of Women's Studies. Tell me I'm radical.

Instructions

Give the following instructions to the participants in the smaller group:

1. The topic for discussion is "What should be the sexual harassment policy for our institution?" (If a sexual harassment policy has already been developed for the institution then the question might be "What is our sexual harassment policy and how does it affect the different campus constituencies?")
2. Everyone in the group must participate in the discussion.
3. Because this is a role play, you must react and respond to other participants according to their label, not by what you know about their true gender, rank, or sexual history.
4. You must try to guess what your own label says by observing the reaction of other participants to you. At the end of the discussion you will be asked what you think your label is.
5. You will have 15 minutes for the role play/discussion. Give the participants in the surrounding larger group the following instructions:

- Observe the group dynamics in the smaller group during the discussion.
- After the discussion you will be asked to comment upon what the exercise revealed regarding the way that stereotypic labels affect discussions of sexual harassment policy.

Outcome

If everyone in the small group does participate according to the instructions, most individuals are able to guess fairly accurately what their label might be. Some men who hold powerful positions are surprised by how differently their responses are treated when they are wearing a label such as "Female untenured professor. Ignore me." Students and women are similarly amazed at the positive reinforcement they receive when wearing a label such as "Male department head. Tell me I'm right." Larger group observers normally have insightful comments about the impact of these stereotypic labels upon the discussion of the topic.

CONCLUSION

The presence of sexism in language and classroom behaviors combined with the absence of information about the achievements, roles, and experiences of women from most curricular content leaves many female students feeling somewhat distant, different, and alienated from what they are learning. Sexism may be particularly severe in cases where women are attempting to enter fields in science and engineering which are not perceived as traditional arenas for women. Small inequities occurring in the classroom may have a cumulative negative effect upon a female student's self-esteem, choice of major, and career plans. If these inequities are aggravated by an overt form of sexism such as sexual harassment, the effects on the women are likely to be more severe; dropping the course, changing majors, or dropping out of post-secondary school entirely represent frequent reactions to sexual harassment.

These exercises stimulate faculty and staff to provide a comfortable learning environment for female students. Overcoming sexism as a barrier to learning and including more information about women in curricular content are ways to begin to warm up the science classroom climate for women, making it more female-friendly.

Chapter 8

Conclusion

*What I Learned From the Bag Lady Scientist and
the Nobel Laureate James Watson*

Several months ago I was at a midwestern university where I was serving as the Visiting Scholar in women's studies for the week. After a public lecture that had been well attended and well received the night before, I was looking forward to giving the smaller, brown bag lunch seminar on "Good Science: Can It Ever Be Gender Free?" This university was unique among American universities because it not only had a well established women's studies program and science departments that included an unusually large number of women, but it also boasted three feminist scientists who taught in women's studies. I had been brought to the institution precisely because these three women faculty had created a core of science faculty and students, particularly in biology, who were interested in issues in feminism and science. This was quite different from the motivating force behind my visits to most campuses; usually the women's studies faculty invite me, hoping to stir up some interest on the part of their scientific colleagues who are oblivious, if not downright hostile, to feminism.

The first person to enter the room was an elderly woman. Although she badly needed some dental work and a shampoo, her demeanor was of the type that I had come to associate with certain crusty, older women in academia. She approached me quite directly, informed me that she was eighty years old, and stated that at least we had something in common because we were both scientists. I wasn't quite certain what her remark implied we did not hold in common—presumably an interest in feminism rather than some more tangible characteristic such as age.

As other people entered the room, they appeared to frown or seem vaguely displeased when they noticed the presence of the elderly woman and avoided sitting near her or becoming engaged in conversation with her. I mentally noted that she must not be popular with her colleagues. Soon several of the people I had met the previous evening engaged me in conversation and I forgot about the presence of the elderly woman until my lecture began.

During my lecture, I encountered a frown and narrowed eyes whenever I made eye contact with the woman. It was difficult to ascertain whether this came from determined concentration or hostility towards my remarks.

As soon as the lecture ended, her hand shot up. She told me that she did not agree with what I had said. In her view science was objective and neutral and was certainly not biased by gender in the questions explored, experimental subjects used, data gathered, nor interpretations and theories drawn. She did not think that the small number of women in science had anything to do with discrimination; in her view, women were not attracted to science because they were unwilling to work as hard as she had. She then launched into a lengthy monologue explaining how she had developed the Talent Search Program for Westinghouse and initiated science fairs for secondary school students both nationally and internationally. She stated that girls could succeed in science just as easily as boys as long as they were willing to work as hard.

Almost as soon as the elderly scientist opened her mouth, the other people in the room began to fidget and try to get her to be quiet. Finally, the person next to her told her in a sharp tone that she must be quiet and let someone else speak. I was not surprised by her remarks. I had entertained similar comments before from both male and female scientists of her generation and younger. Many scientists assume that the scientific method insures perfect objectivity and freedom from any bias.

I assumed that her colleagues were embarrassed by the fact that she had not grasped the subtle aspects of my argument about how science might represent a masculine province not only in numbers of males in science but also in terms of questions studied, approaches taken, and conclusions drawn. Undoubtedly, she had made similar remarks before at other presentations and her colleagues were frustrated by her unwillingness to conform to social cues regarding group interest in a question and appropriate length for comments.

After responding to questions from other individuals, I again called on the elderly scientist, who had continued to raise her hand during the entire discussion. She proceeded to state that she thought my ideas were rather silly and asked how many women scientists were in the room. Of the ten women who raised their hands, she asked how many agreed with my ideas and found them to be an adequate depiction of the situation for women in science. When they agreed, she shook her head and began to vehemently express her opinion that science was not subject to bias and that all women had to do to succeed in science was to work hard.

Another individual cut her off in a rude manner and after a few more questions and a round of applause, the group dispersed. Because I was late for an appointment with a faculty member, I did not have an immediate opportunity to talk with anyone who had attended the seminar.

Later that afternoon, the elderly scientist was the topic of conversation among the women's studies faculty. Much to my surprise I learned that she was not a professor emeritus who had lost the respect of her colleagues; she was a bag lady. It was true that she was a scientist; she had developed the Westinghouse Talent Search and initiated science fairs all over the United States and the world. Somehow she had never held a "regular job" with benefits. Never having become a part of the system, she had no retirement or pension in her old age. She slept in the lounge on the fifth floor of the science building and attended seminars, eating at the receptions to supplement her meager food allowance from Social Security.

I was shocked. Part of the shock came from the system that had turned this well-educated scientist into a bag lady; more of the shock came from the recognition of *who* insisted that success comes to women if they work hard enough in science. It was the bag lady, who would be deemed by most as not successful, who insisted that individual women were responsible for their own success. It was the women scientists in the room, including me, mostly tenured professors, successes by most counts, who saw bias and flaws within the system.

A further shock came from the realization that the remarks made by the bag lady scientist were similar to comments I had heard over the last decade from a substantial fraction of women scientists. Recognition that a scientist turned bag lady had raised the same concerns pushed me to assess the status in the scientific profession of the other individuals who had held similar views. Although sometimes such comments had been expressed during discussions in a public forum in which the status of the individual remained unknown to me, more frequently I had heard the views in more informal settings in which I knew or could inquire about the status of the person who expressed them.

Perhaps selective memory was operating. However, all of the individuals I could recall who had insisted most vehemently that women could succeed in science if they worked just as hard as men fell into one of two categories. First, they did not hold "regular" positions in the scientific establishment in academia, government, or industry. For example, if they were in universities, they were not in tenure-track positions. Instead they were lecturers or continuing post-doctoral researchers who worked in someone else's lab. Second, they did hold "regular" jobs but their rank and/or position was substantially less than other scientists, both male and female, with comparable training and experience. The people in both of these groups did not hold influential or decision making positions in the scientific establishment. They tended to be on the margins of the system of influential committees (grant peer review, promotion and tenure, executive committees of professional associations), both in institutions and nationally, which form the scientific establishment.

In contrast, in my memory, the most vocal critiques of the system, reports of active discrimination, and discomfort with perceived gender bias in scientific theories came from women well-established within the scientific hierarchy. It was often the female department chair or woman who served on the review panel of the most prestigious national foundation who most severely criticized the system. It seemed that those most successful and securely entrenched in the system could best see and understand its biases. Did the bag lady scientist versus the tenured professor scientist disagreement on this issue represent a microcosm of a more widespread phenomenon of women in science?

Numerous ideas leap to mind that complicate this overly simplified dichotomy. First, this idea is based on retrospective perceptions of vocalized opinions rather than data from a systematic survey made of either a random or representative sample of women scientists. Second, the group of women scientists who elect to attend talks on feminism and science or become involved in discussions on the topic is self-selective. It seems quite likely that many successful women scientists may overtly reject feminism or may consciously decide not to become involved with feminist issues, particularly those they perceive as affecting their professional lives, for fear it will be detrimental to their careers. This stance has been documented for women who are successful in other traditionally male career paths (Clara H. Greed, 1988) and has been suggested for women in science (Evelyn Fox Keller, 1987). Furthermore, many of the women in marginal positions in science who are feminists and/or have experienced discrimination may be unable to attend seminars because of their low status positions. If they are present at the talks they may not feel the need to make comments if they are in agreement with the speaker or they may be unwilling to talk due to perceived vulnerability resulting from their low status position.

Recognizing the problems with the categorization of which women scientists accept the potential positive impact of feminism on science, I was still intrigued by what this might mean in a practical sense. If the goal is to change the status quo of science to include more women in order to expand the questions asked, experimental subjects used, types of data gathered, and theories drawn, then discovering the group likely to provide the impetus for this goal is important. The bag lady versus tenured professor dichotomy suggests that the drive for change is likely to come from well-established women scientists in theoretical and decision making positions, rather than from women scientists who hold more marginal positions or who are outside the system.

This would imply that attracting more women to science and working to secure and advance women already in the scientific hierarchy are indeed important keys for bringing about a feminist transformation of science. Although increasing the numbers of women in an area has traditionally been seen as a first step toward feminism, some recent work (Greed, 1988) on women in traditionally male career fields has documented that increasing the number of women does not necessarily lead to increased feminism. Demographic trends and predicted shortages of scientists in the 1990s have caused NSF, AAAS, and other national scientific organizations to seek methods to attract women to science and to retain and advance them within the hierarchy (Widnall, 1988). It is to be hoped that increasing the numbers of women in science will result in an increase in the impact of feminism on science.

An incident involving the Nobel laureate James Watson which occurred several weeks later increased support for that hope. I had been invited to a major southern university by the departments of Genetics and Zoology and the Women's Studies Program to speak on "Feminist Perspectives on Science: Is Reconceptualization Possible?" In the evening and day following my talk, several people commented to me that during the last week, the university had sponsored two talks in which diametrically opposed views on women scientists had been presented. Earlier in the week many individuals had been shocked by Nobel laureate James Watson's statement that American science is losing its cutting edge because there are too many women in biology and too many Asians in physics.

I was not particularly surprised to learn about Watson's remark; he had previously made racist and sexist statements to the public and press in spoken and written form (Watson, 1985). What did amaze me was the recognition that although superficially he and I appeared to be making statements that were directly opposite, on another level we were saying very much the same thing. Both of us were asserting our belief that large numbers of women (or minorities) in a field could affect not only the practice of science but also the conceptions of questions asked, methods of data gathering, and formulation of theories. Where Watson and I differ centers on the point of the desirability of such a change. He favors maintaining the status quo of science as a province of the white, middle class Western male with all the biases, both positive and negative, that are implied by their relatively homogeneous, restrictive approach to the physical, natural world. I favor opening science to women and minorities and aiding them in reaching theoretical and decision making positions in the scientific hierarchy. As indicated by the bag lady versus established woman scientist difference, this may provide the most effective avenue for changing science to be more accessible, varied, and humane. As more women and people from differing races, classes, and ethnic backgrounds become scientists, the science they evolve is likely to reflect their rich diversity of perspective.

References

Alexander, Richard D. (1987). *The biology of moral systems*. New York: Aldine de Gruyter.

Arditti, Rita. (1980). Feminism and science. In R. Arditti, P. Brennan, & S. Cavrak (Eds.), *Science and liberation* Boston: South End Press.

Arnold, Karen. (1987, July). *Retaining high achieving women in science and engineering*. Paper presented at Women in Science and Engineering: Changing Vision to Reality conference, University of Michigan, Ann Arbor. Sponsored by the American Association for the Advancement of Science.

Association of American Colleges. (1984). The new scholarship on women. *The Forum for Liberal Education*, 6(5), 2.

Association of American Colleges. (1985). *Integrity in the college curriculum: A report to the academic community*. Washington, DC: Author.

Association of American Colleges. (1986). *A guide to non-sexist language*. Washington, DC: Author.

Astin, Alexander. (1977). *Four critical years: Effects of college on beliefs, attitudes and knowledge*. San Francisco, CA: Jossey-Bass.

Avoiding stereotypes: Principles and applications. (1974). Boston, MA: Houghton Mifflin.

Baker, Dale. (1983, November). Can the difference between male and female science majors account for the low number of women at the doctoral level in science? *Journal of College Science Teaching*, 102–107.

Barash, David. (1977). *Sociobiology and behavior*. New York: Elsevier.

Barr, Rebecca. (1988). Conditions influencing content taught in nine fourth-grade mathematics classrooms. *The Elementary School Journal*, 88(4), 387–411.

Bartlett, Katherine T. (1988). Feminism unmodified: Discourses on life and law and real rape. *Signs: Journal of Women in Culture and Society*, 13(4), 879–885.

Baxter, James Phinney. (1946). *Scientists against time*. Cambridge, MA: The MIT Press.

Belenky, Mary Field, Clinchy, Blythe McVicker, Goldberger, Nancy Rule, & Tarule, Jill Mattuck. (1986). *Women's ways of knowing*. New York: Basic Books.

Bennett, William J. (1984). *To reclaim a legacy: A report on the humanities in higher education*. Washington, DC: National Endowment for the Humanities.

Bentley, Diana. (1985). Men may understand the words, but do they know the music? Some cries de coeur in Science education. In *Supplementary Contributions to the Third Girls and Science and Technology Conference* (pp. 160–168). London: Chelsea College, University of London.

Birke, Lynda. (1986). *Women, feminism, and biology: The feminist challenge.* New York: Methuen.

Bleier, Ruth. (1976). Myths of the biological inferiority of women: An exploration of the sociology of biological research. *University of Michigan Papers in Women's Studies, 2,* 39–63.

Bleier, Ruth. (1979). Social and political bias in science: An examination of animal studies and their generalizations to human behavior and evolution. In R. Hubbard & M. Lowe (Eds.), *Genes and gender II: Pitfalls in research on sex and gender* (pp. 49–70). New York: Gordian Press.

Bleier, Ruth. (1984). *Science and gender: A critique of biology and its theories on women.* Elmsford, NY: Pergamon Press.

Bleier, Ruth. (1986). Sex differences research: Science or belief? In R. Bleier (Ed.), *Feminist approaches to science* (pp.147–164). Elmsford, NY: Pergamon Press.

Bleier, Ruth. (1988). Science and the construction of meanings in the neurosciences. In S.V. Rosser (Ed.), *Feminism within the science and health care professions: Overcoming resistance.* Elmsford, NY: Pergamon Press.

Bloom, Allan. (1987). *The closing of the American mind.* New York: Simon & Schuster.

Blum, Lenore, & Givant, Steven. (1982). Increasing the participation of college women in mathematics-related fields. In S. Humphreys (Ed.), *Women and minorities in science.* American Association for the Advancement of Science Selected Symposia Series. Boulder, CO: Westview Press.

Blumenfeld, Phyllis C., & Meece, Judith L. (1988). Task factors, teacher behavior, and students' involvement and use of learning strategies in science. *The Elementary School Journal, 88*(3), 235–250.

Boyer, Ernest L. (1987). *College: The undergraduate experience in America.* New York: The Carnegie Foundation for the Advancement of Teaching.

Breiter, Joan, & Menne, Jack. (1974). *A procedure for textbook evaluation illustrated by an analysis of fifth grade social studies texts.* Bethesda, MD. (ERIC Document Reproduction Service, No. ED 132 130)

Brophy, Jere E. (1982). How teachers influence what is taught and learned in classrooms. *The Elementary School Journal, 83*(1).

Campbell, Patricia. (1986, March). What's a nice girl like you doing in a math class? *Phi Delta Kappan,* 516–520.

Carson, Rachel. (1962). *Silent spring.* New York: Fawcett Press.

Chodorow, Nancy. (1978). *The reproduction of mothering: Psychoanalysis and the sociology of gender.* Berkeley and Los Angeles: The University of California Press.

Cole, Michael, & Griffin, Peg. (1987). *Contextual factors in education: Improving science and mathematics education for minorities and women.* Madison, WI: Wisconsin Center for Education Research.

College Placement Council. (1979, March). College Placement Council salary survey.

Corea, Gena, Klein, Renate Duelli, Hamner, Jalna, Holmes, Helen B., Hoskins, Betty, Kishwar, Madhu, Raymond, Janice, Rowland, Roberta, Steinbacher, R. (1980). *Man-made women: How new reproductive technologies affect women.* Bloomington, IN: Indiana University Press.

Cronkite, Ruth, & Perl, Teri. (1982). A short-term intervention program: Math science conferences. In S. Humphreys (Ed.), *Women and minorities in science.* American Assocation for the Advancement of Science Selected Sympsosia Series. Boulder, CO: Westview Press.

Daniels, Jane, & LeBold, William. (1982). Women in engineering: A dynamic approach. In S. Humphreys (Ed.), *Women and minorities in science.* American Association for the Advancement of Science Selected Symposia Series. Boulder, CO: Westview Press.

Dawkins, Richard. (1976). *The selfish gene.* New York: Oxford University Press.

Dearman, N. B., & Plisko, V. W. (1981). *The condition of education.* Washington, DC: National Center for Education Statistics.

Dill, Bonnie T. (1983). Race, class, and gender: Prospects for an all-inclusive sisterhood. *Feminist Studies, 9*(1), 131–150.

Dowie, Mark, & Johnston, Tracy. (1977). A case of corporate malpractice and the Dalkon Shield. In C. Dreifus (Ed.), *Seizing our bodies.* New York: Vintage Books.

Ehrenreich, Barbara, & English, Deirdre. (1978). *For her own good: 150 years of the experts advice to women.* Garden City, NY: Anchor Books.

Erikson, Erik H. (1963). *Childhood and society* (2nd ed.). New York: W. W. Norton.

Fausto-Sterling, Anne. (1985). *Myths of gender.* New York: Basic Books.

Fee, Elizabeth. (1981). Is feminism a threat to scientific objectivity? *International Journal of Women's Studies, 4*(4), 213–233.

Fee, Elizabeth. (1982). A feminist critique of scientific objectivity. *Science for the people, 14*(4), 8.

Fee, Elizabeth. (1983). Women's nature and scientific objectivity. In M. Lowe & R. Hubbard (Eds.), *Women's nature: Rationalizations of inequality.* Elmsford, NY: Pergamon Press.

Fee, Elizabeth. (1986). Critiques of modern science: The relationship of feminism to other radical epistemologies. In R. Bleier (Ed.), *Feminist approaches to science.* Elmsford, NY: Pergamon Press.

Feminist Women's Health Centre, Frankfurt, Federal Republic of Germany. (1987). Chernobyl and after. In P. Spallone & D. L. Steinberg (Eds.), *Made to order: The myth of reproductive and genetic progress.* Elmsford, NY: Pergamon Press.

Fennema, Elizabeth, & Sherman, Julie. (1977). Sex related differences in mathematics achievement, spatial visualization and affective factors. *American Educational Research Journal, 14*, 51–71.

Fossey, Dian. (1983). *Gorillas in the mist.* Boston: Houghton Mifflin.

Frazier, Nancy, & Sadker, Myra. (1973). *Sexism in school and society.* New York: Harper & Row.

Freeman, Donald J., Kuhs, Therese M., Porter, Andrew C., Floden, Robert E., Schmidt, William H., & Schwille, John R. (1983). Do textbooks and tests define a national curriculum in elementary school mathematics? *The Elementary School Journal, 83*(5).

Gallup, George H. (1983). *The Gallup Poll: Public opinion 1982.* Wilmington, DE: Scholarly Resources.

George, Yolanda S. (1982). Affirmative action programs that work. In S. Humphreys (Ed.), *Women and minorities in science.* American Association for the Advancement of Science Selected Symposia Series. Boulder, CO: Westview Press.

Gilligan, Carol. (1982). *In a difference voice: Psychological theory and women's development.* Cambridge, MA: Harvard University Press.

Goldsmid, Charles A., & Wilson, Everett K. (1980). *Passing on sociology: The teaching of a discipline.* Belmont, CA: Wadsworth.

Goodall, Jane. (1971). *In the shadow of man.* Boston: Houghton Mifflin.

Goodfield, June. (1981). *An imagined world.* New York: Penguin Books.

Gornick, Vivian. (1983). *Women in science: Portraits from a world in transition.* New York: Simon & Schuster.

Gould, Stephen Jay. (1981). *The mismeasure of man.* New York: W. W. Norton.

Grant, M. (1982). Prized projects. *Studies in Design Education, Craft and Technology, 15*(1).

Greed, Clara H. (1988). Is more better? With reference to the position of women chartered surveyors in Britain. *Women's Studies International Forum, 11*(3), 187–197.

Griffin, Susan. (1978). *Women and nature: The roaring inside her.* New York: Harper & Row.

Haber, Louis. (1979). *Women pioneers of science.* New York: Harcourt Brace Jovanovich.

Haley-Oliphant, Ann. (1985). International perspectives on the status and role of women in science. In J. B. Kahle (Ed.), *Women in science.* Philadelphia: Falmer Press.

Hall, Roberta M., & Sandler, Bernice R. (1982). *The classroom climate: A chilly one for women?* Washington, DC: Association of American Colleges.

Hall, Roberta M., & Sandler, Bernice R. (1984). *Out of the classroom: A chilly campus climate for women?* Washington, DC: Association of American Colleges.

Halpin, Zuleyma Tang. (1989). Scientific objectivity and the concept of "The Other." *Women's Studies International Forum, 12*(3), 285–294.

Hamilton, Jean. (1985). Avoiding methodological biases in gender-related health research. In *Women's health report of the Public Health Service Task Force on women's health issues.* Washington, DC: U.S. Department of Health and Human Services Public Health Service.

Haraway, Donna. (1978). Animal sociology and a natural economy of the body politic, Part I: A political physiology of dominance; Animal sociology and a natural economy of the body politic, Part II: The past is the contested zone: Human nature and theories of production and reproduction in primate behavior studies. *Signs: Journal of Women in Culture and Society, 4*(1), 21–60.

Haraway, Donna. (1989). Monkeys, aliens, and women: Love, science, and politics at the intersection of feminist theory and colonial discourse. *Women's Studies International Forum, 12*(3), 295–312.

Hardin, J., & Dede, C. J. (1978). Discrimination against women in science education. *The Science Teacher, 40,* 18–21.

Harding, Jan. (1983). *Switched off: The science education of girls.* Schools Council Programme 3, York, England: Longman Resources Unit.

Harding, Jan. (1985). Values, cognitive style and the curriculum. In *Contributions to the Third Girls and Science and Technology Conference,* Chelsea College, London: University of London.

Harding, Jan. (1987, July). *International panel debate: Gender and science issues.* Paper presented at Women in Science and Engineering: Changing Vision to Reality conference, University of Michigan, Ann Arbor. Sponsored by the American Association for the Advancement of Science.

Harding, Sandra. (1986). *The science question in feminism.* Ithaca, NY: Cornell University Press.

Head, John. (1985). *The personal response to science.* Cambridge, London: Cambridge University Press.

Hein, Hilde. (1981). Women and science: Fitting men to think about nature. *International Journal of Women's Studies, 4,* 369–377.

Hirsch, E.D., Jr. (1987). *Cultural literacy: What every American needs to know.* Boston: Houghton Mifflin.

Hoffman, Joan C. (1982). Biorhythms in human reproduction: The not-so-steady states. *Signs: Journal of Women in Culture and Society, 7*(4), 829–844.

Hoffman, Lois Wladis. (1972). Early childhood experiences and women's achievement motives. *Journal of Social Issues, 28*(2), 129–55.

Hoffman, Lois Wladis. (1974). Fear of success in males and females: 1965 and 1971. *Journal of Consulting and Clinical Psychology, 42,* 353–58.

Hoffman, Nancy. (1987). Women's studies and the higher education reports. *Perspectives, 17*(2), 42–52.

Holliday, Laurel. (1978). *The violent sex: Male psychobiology and the evolution of consciousness.* Guerneville, CA: Bluestocking Books.

Holy Bible. (1953). (revised standard version) (pp.1–3). New York: Thomas Nelson & Sons.

Horner, Matina S. (1969). Fail: Bright women. *Psychology Today, 3,* pp. 36–38.

Hrdy, Sarah B. (1977). *The langurs of Abu: Female and male strategies of reproduction.* Cambridge, MA: Harvard University Press.

Hrdy, Sarah B. (1979). Infanticide among animals: A review, classification and examination of the implications for the reproductive strategies of females. *Ethology and Sociobiology, 1,* 3–40.

Hrdy, Sarah B. (1981). *The woman that never evolved.* Cambridge, MA: Harvard University Press.

Hrdy, Sarah B. (1984). Introduction: Female reproductive strategies. In M. Small (Ed.), *Female primates: Studies by women primatologists.* New York: Alan Liss.

Hrdy, Sarah. (1986). Empathy, polyandry, and the myth of the coy female. In R. Bleier (Ed.), *Feminist approaches to science.* Elmsford, NY: Pergamon Press.

Hubbard, Ruth. (1979). Have only men evolved? In R. Hubbard, M. S. Henifin, & B. Fried (Eds.), *Women look at biology looking at women.* Cambridge, MA: Schenkman.

Hubbard, Ruth. (1983). Social effects of some contemporary myths about women. In M. Lowe & R. Hubbard (Eds.), *Woman's nature: Rationalizations of inequality.* Elmsford, NY: Pergamon Press.

Hubbard, Ruth. (1985). Putting genes in their place. *The Women's Review of Books, 2*(4), 7–8.

Hubbard, Ruth, & Lowe, Marian. (1979). Introduction. In R. Hubbard & M. Lowe (Eds.), *Genes and gender II: Pitfalls in research on sex and gender.* New York: Gordian Press.

Humphreys, Sheila. (1982). Effectiveness of science career conferences. In S. Humphreys (Ed.), *Women and minorities in science.* American Association for the Advancement of Science Selected Symposia Series. Boulder, CO: Westview Press.

Hynes, H. Patricia. (1984, November/December). Women working: A field report. *Technology Review, 37ff*

Hynes, H. Patricia. (1989). *The recurring silent spring.* Elmsford, NY: Pergamon Press.

Jaggar, Alison M. (1983). *Feminist politics and human nature.* Totowa, NJ: Rowman & Allanheld.

Jenkins, Mercilee M. (1983). Removing bias: Guidelines for student—faculty communication. A part of the series of booklets *Sex and gender in the social sciences: Reassessing the introductory course.* Annandale, VA: Speech Communication Association.

Kahle, Jane. (1983). *The disadvantaged majority: Science education for women.* Burlington, NC: Carolina Biological Supply Company. AETS Outstanding Paper for 1983.

Kahle, Jane B. (1985). *Women in science.* Philadelphia: Falmer Press.

Kahle, Jane B., & Lakes, Marsha K. (1983). The myth of equality in science classrooms. *Journal of Research in Science Teaching, 20,* 131–140.

Keller, Evelyn Fox. (1982). Feminism and science. *Signs: Journal of Women in Culture and Society, 7*(3), 589–602.

Keller, Evelyn Fox. (1983). *A feeling for the organism: The life and work of Barbara McClintock.* New York: W. H. Freeman.

Keller, Evelyn Fox. (1984, November/December). Women and basic research: Respecting the unexpected. *Technology Review,* 44–47.

Keller, Evelyn Fox. (1985). *Reflections on gender and science.* New Haven, CT: Yale University Press.

Keller, Evelyn Fox. (1987). Women scientists and feminist critics of science. *Daedalus,* 77–91.

Keller, Evelyn Fox. (1989). Holding the center of feminist theory. *Women's Studies International Forum, 1*(3), 313–318.

Kelly, Alison. (1981). *The missing half.* Manchester, England: Manchester University Press.

Kirschstein, Ruth L. (Ed.) (1985). *Women's health: Report of the Public Health Service Task Force on Women's Health Issues 2.* Washington, DC: U.S. Department of Health and Human Services Public Health Service.

Klein, Ethel. (1984). *Gender politics: From consciousness to mass politics.* Cambridge, MA: Harvard University Press.

Kohn, Alexander. (1986). *Fraud prophets.* New York: Basil Blackwell.

Kramarae, Cheris (Ed.). (1980). *The voices and words of women and men.* London: Pergamon Press.

Kramarae, Cheris, & Treichler, Paula. (1986). *A feminist dictionary*. London: Pandora Press.

Kreinberg, Nancy. (1982). EQUALS: Working with educators. In S. Humphreys (Ed.), *Women and minorities in science*. American Association for the Advancement of Science Selected Symposia. Boulder, CO: Westview Press.

Kuhn, Thomas S. (1970). *The structure of scientific revolution* (2nd ed.). Chicago: The University of Chicago Press.

Lakoff, Robin. (1975). *Language and woman's place*. New York: Harper & Row.

Lancaster, Jane. (1975). *Primate behavior and the emergence of human culture*. New York: Holt, Rinehart & Winston.

Leavitt, Ruth R. (1975). *Peaceable primates and gentle people: Anthropological approaches to women's studies*. New York: Harper & Row.

Leibowitz, Lila. (1975). Perspectives in the evolution of sex differences. In R. R. Reiter (Ed.), *Toward an anthropology of women*. New York: Monthly Review Press.

Levinson, Daniel J., Darrow, Charlotte M., Klein, Edward B. Levinson, Maria H., & McKee, Braxton. (1974). The psychosocial development of men in early adulthood and the mid-life transition. In D.F. Ricks, A. Thomas, & M. Ross (Eds.), *Life history research in psychotherapy*, 3. Minneapolis: University of Minnesota Press.

Lewontin, Richard C., Rose, Steven, & Kamin, Leon J. (1984). *Not in our genes: Biology, ideology, and human nature*. New York: Pantheon.

Lie, Svein, & Bryhni, Eva. (1983). Girls and physics: Attitudes, experiences and underachievement. *Contributions to the Second Girls and Science and Technology Conference* (pp. 202–211). Oslo, Norway: University of Oslo, Institute of Physics.

Lowe, Marian. (1978). Sociobiology and sex differences. *Signs: Journal of Women in Culture and Society, 4*(1), 118–125.

Lowe, Marian. (1983). The dialectic of biology and culture. In M. Lowe & R. Hubbard (Eds.), *Woman's nature: Rationalizations of inequality*. Elmsford, NY: Pergamon Press.

MacKinnon, Catharine A. (1987). *Feminism unmodified: Discourses on life and law*. Cambridge, MA and London: Harvard University Press.

Maehr, Martin. (1983). On doing well in science: Why Johnny no longer excells; Why Sarah never did. In S. Paris, G. Olson, & H. Stevenson (Eds.), *Learning and motivation in the classroom*. Hillsdale, NJ: Lawrence Erlbaum Associates.

Malcolm, Shirley M. (1983, July 31). An assessment of programs that facilitate increased access and achievement of females and minorities in K-12 mathematics and science education. Washington, DC: American Association for the Advancement of Science, Office of Opportunities in Science.

Mallow, Jeffry V. (1981). *Science anxiety: Fear of science and how to overcome it*. New York: Van Nostrand Reinhold.

Manning, Kenneth R. (1983). *Black Apollo of science: The life of Ernest Everett Just*. New York: Oxford University Press.

Martyna, Wendy. (1978). What does "he" mean? Use of the generic masculine. *Journal of Communication, 28*, 131–138.

Marwick, C. (1983). Holdup of toxic shock data ends during trial in Texas. *Journal of the American Medical Association, 250*(24), 3267–3269.

Matyas, Marsha L. (1985). Obstacles and constraints on women in science. In J. B. Kahle (Ed.), *Women in science*. Philadelphia: Falmer Press.

Max, Claire E. (1982). Career paths for women in physics. In S. Humphreys (Ed.), *Women and minorities in science*. American Association for the Advancement of Science Selected Symposia. Boulder, CO: Westview Press.

McIntosh, Peggy. (1984). The study of women: Processes of personal and curricular revision. *The Forum for Liberal Education, 6*(5), 2–4.

McKeachie, Wilbert J. (1969). *Teaching tips: A guidebook for the beginning college teacher*. Lexington, MA: D. C. Heath.

McLeod, S. (1987). In N. Reingold & M. Rothenberg (Eds.), *Scientific colonialism: A cross-cultural comparison*. Washington, DC: Smithsonian Institution Press.

McMillen, Liz. (1987). More colleges and more disciplines incorporating scholarship on women into the classroom. *Chronicle of Higher Education*, A15–A17.

McNamee, Harriet, & Fix, Dorothy. (1986). Art workshop in S. Coulter, K. Edgington, & E. Hedges (Eds.), *Resources for curriculum change*. Towson, MD: Towson State University.

Means, Russell. (1980, December). The future of the earth. *Mother Jones*. As cited in S. Harding (1986), *The science question in feminism*. Ithaca, NY: Cornell University Press.

Melnick, Susan L., Wheeler, Christopher W., & Gunnings, Barbara B. (1983). *Can science teachers promote gender equity in their classrooms? How two teachers do it*. Paper presented at the meeting of the Educational Research Association, Montreal, Canada. (ERIC Document Reproduction Service No. ED 255 355)

Menand, Louis. (1987, May 25). Mr. Bloom's planet. *New Republic*, pp. 38–41.

Merchant, Carolyn. (1979). *The death of nature: Women, ecology and the scientific revolution*. New York: Harper & Row.

Mergendoller, John R., Marchman, Virginia A., Mitman, Alexis L., & Packer, Martin J. (1988). Task demands and accountability in middle grade science classes. *The Elementary School Journal, 88*(3), 251–265.

Messing, Karen. (1983). The scientific mystique: Can a white lab coat guarantee purity in the search for knowledge about the nature of women? In M. Lowe & R. Hubbard (Eds.), *Woman's nature: Rationalizations of inequality*. Elmsford, NY: Pergamon Press.

Money, John, & Ehrhardt, Anke A. (1972). *Man and woman, boy and girl*. Baltimore, MD: The Johns Hopkins University Press.

Mozans, H. J. (1974). *Woman in science—1913*. Cambridge, MA: The MIT Press.

National Assessment of Educational Progress. (1978, December). *Science Achievement in the Schools* (Science Report No.08-S-01). Denver, CO: Education Commission of the States.

National Institute for Education. (1984). *Involvement in learning*. (Final Report of the Study Group on the Conditions of Excellence in American Higher Education). Washington, DC: U.S. Government Printing Office.

National Research Council. (1986). *Summary report, 1985 doctorate recipients from United States universities*. Washington, DC: U.S. Government Printing Office.

National Science Foundation. (1982). *Science and engineering education: Data and information*. (NSF 82-30). Washington, DC: Author.

National Science Foundation. (1986). *Report on women and minorities in science and engineering*. Washington, DC: Author.

National Science Foundation. (1987). *Human talent for competitiveness*. (NSF 87-24). Washington, DC: Author.

National Science Foundation. (1988). *Women and minorities in science and engineering*. (NSF 88-301). Washington, DC: Author.

National Women's Studies Association. (1988). *Membership directory*. College Park, MD: University of Maryland.

Needham, Joseph. (1976). History and human values: A Chinese perspective for world science and technology. In H. Rose & S. Rose (Eds.), *Ideology of/in the natural sciences*. Cambridge, MA: Schenkman. As cited in S. Harding (1986), *The science question in feminism*. Ithaca, NY: Cornell University Press.

NIH urges inclusion of women in clinical study populations (1986, 16[2]). *National News and Development*, p. 3.

Noonan, John F. (1980). *White faculty and black students: Examining assumptions and practices*. (Paper available from the Center for Improving Teaching Effectiveness, Virginia Commonwealth University, Richmond).

Nulty, Peter. (1989). The hot demand for new scientists. *Fortune, 120*(3), 155–163.

Nussbaum, Martha. (1987). Undemocratic vistas. *The New York Times Book Review*, pp. 20–26.

Odum, H. T. (1957). *Ecological monographs, 27*, 55–112. Ecological Society of America.

Office of Technology Assessment. (1985). *Demographic trends and the scientific and engineering workforce*. Washington, DC: Author.

Office of Technology Assessment, Commission on Professionals in Science and Technology. (1986). *Manpower Comments, 23*(l), 5.

Office of Technology Assessment (1987). *New developments in biotechnology background paper: Public perceptions of biotechnology* (OTA-BP-BA-45). Washington, DC: Author.

Ogilvie, Marilyn B. (1986). *Women in science: Antiquity through the nineteenth century*. Cambridge, MA: The MIT Press.

Pion, Georgine M., & Lipsey, Mark W. (1981). Public attitudes toward science and technology: What have the surveys told us? *Public Opinion Quarterly 45*.

Remick, Helen, & Miller, Kathy. (1978, May). Participation rates in high school mathematics and science courses. *The Physics Teacher*, 280–282.

Rich, Frank. (1988, September 9). In "plow" and "butterfly:" New leads and new light. *The New York Times*, pp.15–17.

Rose, Hilary, & Rose, Steven. (1980). The myth of the neutrality of science. In R. Arditti, P. Brennan, & S. Cavrak (Eds.), *Science and liberation*. Boston: South End Press.

Rose, R. M., Holaday, J. W., & Bernstein, I. S. (1971). Plasma testosterone, dominance rank, and aggressive behavior in male rhesus monkeys. *Nature, 231*, 366–368.

Rosser, Sue V. (1982). Androgyny and sociobiology. *International Journal of Women's Studies, 5*(5), 435–444.

Rosser, Sue V. (1986). *Teaching science and health from a feminist perspective: A practical guide*. Elmsford, NY: Pergamon Press.

Rosser, Sue V. (1987). Gender balancing the curriculum. *Carolina View, 3*, 17–20.

Rosser, Sue V. (1988). Women in science and health care: A gender at risk. In S. V. Rosser (Ed.), *Feminism within the science and health care professions: Overcoming resistance*. Elmsford, NY: Pergamon Press.

Rosser, Sue V. (1989a). Teaching techniques to attract women to science. *Women's Studies International Forum, 12*(3), 363–378.

Rosser, Sue V. (1989b). Warming up the classroom climate for women. *Feminist Teacher, 4*(1), 8–12.

Rossiter, Margaret W. (1982). *Women scientists in America: Struggles and strategies to 1940*. Baltimore, MD: The Johns Hopkins University Press.

Rowell, Thelma. (1974). The concept of social dominance. *Behavioral Biology, 11*, 131–154.

Rubin, Vera. (1986, July/August). Women's work: For women in science, a fair shake is still elusive. *Science, 86*, pp. 58–65.

Sadker, Myra, & Sadker, David. (1979). *Between teacher and student: Overcoming sex bias in the classroom*. Unpublished report by the Non-Sexist Teacher Education Project of the Women's Educational Equity Act Program, U.S. Department of Health, Education, and Welfare, Office of Education.

Sandler, Bernice R., & Hall, Roberta M. (1986). *The campus climate revisited: Chilly for women faculty, administrators, and graduate students*. Washington, DC: Association of American Colleges.

Sayers, Janet. (1982). *Biological politics: Feminist and anti-feminist perspectives*. London and New York: Tavistock Publications.

Schuster, Marilyn, & Van Dyne, Susan. (1985). *Women's place in the academy: Transforming the liberal arts curriculum*. Totowa, NJ: Rowman & Allanheld.

Sells, Lucy. (1975). *Sex and discipline differences in doctoral attrition*. Unpublished Ph.D. thesis. University of California at Berkeley.

Sells, Lucy. (1982). Leverage for equal opportunity through mastery of mathematics. In S. Humphreys (Ed.), *Women and minorities in science.* Boulder, CO: Westview Press.

Shapiro, June, Kramer, Sylvia, & Hunerberg, Catherine. (1981). *Equal their chances: Children's activities for non-sexist learning.* Englewood Cliffs, NJ: Prentice-Hall.

Shaver, Phillip. (1976). Questions concerning fear of success and its conceptual relatives. *Sex roles, 2*, 205–220.

Skolnick, Joan, Langbort, Carol, & Day, Lucille. (1982). *How to encourage girls in math and science: Strategies for parents and educators.* Englewood Cliffs, NJ: Prentice-Hall.

Smail, Barbara. (1983). *Getting science right for girls. Contributions to the Second Girls and Science and Technology Conference* (pp. 30–40). Oslo, Norway: University of Oslo, Institute of Physics.

Stage, Elizabeth K., Kreinberg, Nancy, Eccles, Jacqueline, & Becker, Joanne R. (1985). Increasing the participation and achievement of girls and women in mathematics, science, and engineering. In S. Klein (Ed.), *Handbook for achieving sex equity through education.* Baltimore, MD: The Johns Hopkins University Press.

Stallings, Jane. (1980). *Comparisons of men's and women's behaviors in high school math classes.* Washington, DC: National Institute of Education.

Star, Susan Leigh. (1979). Sex differences and the dichotomization of the brain: Methods, limits and problems in research on consciousness. In R. Hubbard & M. Lowe (Eds.) *Genes and gender II: Pitfalls in research on sex and gender.* New York: Gordian Press.

Steinkamp, Marjorie. (1984). Motivational style as a mediator of adult achievement in science. *Advances in Motivation and Achievement, 2*, 281–316.

Stodolsky, Susan S. (1988). *The subject matter: Classroom activity in math and social studies.* University of Chicago Press: Chicago.

Tetreault, Mary K. (1985). Stages of thinking about women: An experience-derived evaluation model. *Journal of Higher Education, 5*(4), 368–384.

Thorne, Barrie. (1979, September 13–15). *Claiming verbal space: Women, speech and language in college classrooms.* Paper presented at the Research Conference on Educational Environments and the Undergraduate Women, Wellesley College, Wellesley, Mass.

Thorne, Barrie, & Henley, Nancy (Eds.). (1975). *Language and sex: Difference and dominance.* Pittsburgh, PA: Know.

Towson State University. (1984). *Contemporary general biology lab book* (3rd Ed.) Towson, MD: Towson State University.

Trivers, Robert L. (1972). Parental investment and sexual selection. In B. Campbell (Ed.), *Sexual selection and the descent of man.* Chicago, IL: Aldine.

U.S. Department of Health, Education, and Welfare, Office of Education. (1978). *Taking sexism out of education.* (The National Project on Women in Education, HEW Publication No. OE 77-01017). Washington, DC: U.S. Government Printing Office.

Watson, James. (1985, April). Quoted in *Science, 12*, p. l60.

Whatley, Mariamne. (1988). Photographic images of blacks in sexuality texts. *Curriculum Inquiry, 18*(2), 137–155.

Wheeler, P., & Harris, A. (1979). *Performance differences between males and females on the ATP physics test.* Berkeley, CA: Educational Testing Service.

Widnall, Sheila E. (1988). Amercian Association for the Advancement of Science Presidential lecture: Voices from the pipeline. *Science, 241*, 1740–1745.

Wilson, Edward O. (1975). *Sociobiology: The new synthesis.* Cambridge, MA: Harvard University Press.

Wilson, Edward O. (1978). *On human nature.* Cambridge, MA: Harvard University Press.

Winick, M. (1975). Nutritional disorders during brain development. In D. B. Tower (Ed.), *The clinical neurosciences.* New York: Raven Press. As cited in R. Bleier (1984), *Science and gender: A critique of biology and its theories on women.* Elmsford, NY: Pergamon Press.

Wright, Herbert. (1967). *Recording and analyzing child behavior.* New York: Harper & Row.

Yerkes, R. M. (1943). *Chimpanzees.* New Haven: Yale University Press.

Zimmerman, Bill, et al. (1980). People's science. In R. Arditti, P. Brennan, & S. Cavrak, (Eds.), *Science and liberation* (pp.299–319). Boston: South End Press.

Zimmerman, Don H., & West, Candace. (1975). Sex roles, interruptions and silences in conversation. In B. Thorne & N. Henley (Eds.), *Language and sex: Difference and dominance.* Rowley, MA: Newbury House.

Supplemental Bibliography

FEMINISM AND SCIENCE

Abel, Elizabeth, & Abel, Emily K. (Eds.). (1983). *The Signs reader: Women, gender, and scholarship.* Chicago: University of Chicago Press.

Addelson, Kathryn Pyne. (1985). Doing science. *Proceedings: Philosophy of Science Association, 2,* 543–548. East Lansing, MI: Philosophy of Science Association.

Allen, David & Wolfgram, Beverly. (1988, April–June). Nursing, therapy, and social control: Feminist science and systems-based family therapy. *Health Care for Women International,* 9(2), 107–124.

Alper, J. S. (1985). Sex differences in brain asymmetry: A critical analysis. *Feminist Studies, 11,* 7–37.

Arditti, Rita, & Minden, Shelley (1983, Winter). Comment on Haraway's "In the beginning was the word." *Signs, 9,* 330–335.

Arditti, Rita, Brennan, Pat, & Cavrak, Steve (Eds.). (1980). *Science and liberation.* Montreal: Black Rose Books.

Asquith, Peter, & Kitcher, Philip (Eds.). (1985). Sex and gender in the construction of science. *Proceedings: Philosophy of Science Association, 2,* 12. East Lansing, MI: Philosophy of Science Association.

Asquith, Peter, & Giere, Ronald N. (Eds.). (1980). *Proceedings: Philosophy of Science Association.* East Lansing, MI: Philosophy of Science Association.

Bagehot, Walter. (1978, December). Biology and women's rights. *Popular Science Monthly, 14,* 201–213.

Baker, Susan W. (1980). Biological influences on human sex and gender. *Signs, 6,* 80–96.

Barnet, Rosalind, & Baruch, Grace. (1978). Women in the middle years: A critique of research and theory. *Psychology of Women Quarterly, 3,* 187–197.

Beldecos, Athena, Bailey, Sarah, Gilbert, Scott, Hicks, Karen, Kenschaft, Lori, Niemczyk, Nancy, Rosenberg, Rebecca, Schaertel, Stephanie, & Wedel, Andrew. (Biology and Gender Study Group). (1988, Spring). The importance of feminist critique for cell biology. *Hypatia, 3,* 61–76.

Note: Faye Chadwell was primarily responsible for the extensive bibliography.

Benston, Margaret. (1986, November). Questioning authority: Feminism and scientific experts. *Resources for Feminist Research, 15,* 71–73.

Bentley, Diana, & Watts, D. Michal. (1986). Courting the positive virtues—A case for feminist science. *European Journal of Science Education, 8*(2), 121–134.

Benton, David, Brian, Paul, & Haug, Marc. (Eds.). (1985). *The aggressive female.* Montreal: Eden Press.

Bernstein, Irwin. (1981). Dominance: The baby and the bathwater. *Behavioural and Brain Sciences, 4,* 419–457.

Birke, Lynda (Ed.). (Brighton Women and Science Group). (1980). *Alice through the microscope: The power of science over women's lives.* London: Virago Press.

Birke, Lynda. (1984). Outgrowing selfish genes. *New Socialist, 16,* 40–42.

Birke, Lynda. (1986). *Women, feminism and biology: The feminist challenge.* Great Britain: Wheatsheaf.

Birke, Lynda, Rose, Hilary, & Rose, Steven. *The new right and the nature of human nature.* Unpublished manuscript.

Birke, Lynda, & Vines, Gail. (1987). Beyond nature versus nurture: Process and biology in the development of gender. *Women's Studies International Forum, 10*(6), 555–570.

Bleier, Ruth. (1976). Myths of the biological inferiority of women: An exploration of the sociobiology of biological research. *University of Michigan Papers in Women's Studies, 2,* 39–63.

Bleier, Ruth. (1978, Autumn). Bias in biological and human sciences: Some comments. *Signs, 4*(1), 159–162.

Bleier, Ruth. (1979, Spring). Difficulties of detecting sexist biases in the biological sciences. *Creative Woman Quarterly, 2*(4).

Bleier, Ruth. (1982). Comments on Haraway's "In the beginning was the word: The genesis of biological theory." *Signs, 7*(3), 725–727.

Bleier, Ruth. (1984). *Science and gender: A critique of biology and its theories on women.* Elmsford, NY: Pergamon Press.

Bleier, Ruth (Ed.). (1986). *Feminist approaches to science.* Elmsford, NY: Pergamon Press.

Bonner, Jill. (1980, April 11). The cult of objectivity in the physical sciences. *Choices for science: Proceedings of a symposium sponsored by the Mary Ingram Bunting Institute of Radcliffe College* (pp. 52–57). Cambridge, MA: Mary I. Bunting Institute.

Borque, Susan C., & Warren, Kay B. (1987, Fall). Technology, gender, and development. *Daedalus, 116,* 173–197.

Breines, Wini, Cerullo, Margaret, & Stacey, J. (1978). Social biology, family studies, and anti-feminist backlash. *Feminist Studies, 4*(1), 43–67.

Brown Parlee, Mary. (1978, November). The sexes under scrutiny: From old biases to new theories. *Psychology Today,* 64–68.

Burfoot, Annette. (1987, December). Impediments to feminist acts in science. *Resources for Feminist Research, 16,* 25–26.

Cambridge Women's Studies Group (Eds.). (1981). *Women in society: Interdisciplinary essays.* London: Virago Press.

Chasin, Barbara. (1977, May-June). Sociobiology: A sexist synthesis. *Science for the People, 9*(3) 27–31.

Cheney, J. (1987, Summer). Eco-feminism and deep ecology. *Environmental Ethics, 9,* 115–145.

Cliquet, R. L. (1984). The relevance of sociobiological theory for emancipatory feminism. *Journal of Human Evolution, 13*(1), 117–127.

Condry, John, & Condry, Sandra. (1976). Sex differences: A study in the eye of the beholder. *Child Development, 47,* 812–819.

Dagg, Anne Innis. (1983). *Harem and other horrors: Sexual bias in behavioral biology.* Waterloo, Ontario: Otter Press.

Dagg, Anne Innis. (1984, November). Sexist language and science. *Resources for Feminist Research, 13,* 32–33.

Davies, Katherine. (1988, June–July). What is ecofeminism? *Women and Environments, 10,* 4–6.

De Konnick, Maria. (1986, November). Que serait une approach feministe de la science? *Resources for Feminist Research, 15,* 62–64.

de Lauretis, Teresa (Ed.). (1986). *Feminist studies, critical studies.* Bloomington, IN: Indiana University Press.

Donchin, Anne. (1986, Fall). The future of mothering: Reproductive technology and feminist theory. *Hypatia, 1,* 121–138.

Dugdale, Ann. (1988, April–June). A feminist critique of the masculinity of scientific knowledge. *Philosophy and Social Action, 14,* 53–64.

Dunlop, Margaret J. (1986, November). Is a science of caring possible? *Journal of Advanced Nursing, 11*(6), 661–670.

Easlea, Brian. (1980). Witch-hunting, magic and the new philosophy: An introduction to the debates of the scientific revolution, 1450–1750. Brighton, Sussex: Harvester Press.

Easlea, Brian. (1983). *Fathering the unthinkable: Masculinity, scientists, and the nuclear arms race.* London: Pluto Press.

Easlea, Brian. (1981). *Science and sexual oppression: Patriarchy's confrontation with woman and nature.* London: Weidenfeld and Nicholson.

Emery, Merrelyn. (1988, April–June). A feminized science: From theory to practice. *Philosphy and Social Action, 14,* 23–35.

Fausto-Sterling, Anne. (1980, Winter). Women's studies and science. *Women's Studies Newsletter, 8*(1), 4–7.

Fausto-Sterling, Anne. (1981). The myth of neutrality: Race, sex and class in science. *Radical Teacher, 19,* 21–25.

Fausto-Sterling, Anne. (1981). Women and science. *Women's Studies International Quarterly, 4*(1), 41–50.

Fausto-Sterling, Anne. (1985). *Myths of gender: Biological theories about women and men.* New York: Basic Books.

Fausto-Sterling, Anne. (1985, Summer). The new research on women: How does it affect the natural sciences? *Women's Studies Quarterly, 13,* 30–32.

Fausto-Sterling, Anne. (1987, Fall). Society writes biology/Biology constructs gender. *Daedalus, 116*(4), 61–76.

Fausto-Sterling, Anne. (in press). *Women: A biological fantasy.* New York: Basic Books.

Fausto-Sterling, Anne, & English, Lydia L. (1986). Women and minorities in science. *Radical Teacher, 30,* 16–20.

Fee, Elizabeth. (1979). Nineteenth-century craniology: The study of the female skull. *Bulletin of the History of Medicine, 53,* 415–433.

Fee, Elizabeth. (1981, September-October). Is feminism a threat to scientific objectivity? *International Journal of Women's Studies, 4*(4), 378–392.

Fee, Elizabeth (Ed.). (1983). *Women and health: The politics of sex in medicine.* Farmingdale, NY: Baywood.

Fee, Elizabeth. (1982, July-August). A feminist critique of scientific objectivity. *Science for the People, 14*(4), 5–8 & 30–33.

Feldman, Jacqueline. (1975). The savant and the midwife. *Impact of Science on Society, 25*(2), 125–136.

Feldman, Jacqueline. (1988, April-June). Feminist critiques of science. *Philosophy and Social Action, 14,* 37–52.

Franklin, Sarah, & McNeil, Maureen. (1988, Fall). Reproductive futures—Recent literature and current feminist debates on reproductive technologies. *Feminist Studies, 14*(3), 545.

Ginzberg, Ruth. (1987, Fall). Uncovering gynocentric science. *Hypatia,* 89–105.

Goddard, Nancy, & Henifin, Mary Sue. (1984, Winter). A feminist approach to the biology of women. *Women's Studies Quarterly, 12,* 11–18.

Goodman, Madeleine J., & Goodman, Lenn Evan. (1981, September-October). Is there a feminist biology? *International Journal of Women's Studies, 4*(4), 393–414.

Gould, Carol (Ed.). (1984). *Beyond domination: New perspectives on women and philosophy.* Totowa, NJ: Rowman & Allanheld.

Gould, Carol C., & Watofsky, Mary W. (Eds.). (1976). *Women and philosophy: Toward a theory of liberation.* New York: G. P. Putnam.

Grady, Kathleen E. (1981). Sex bias in research design.*Psychology of Women Quarterly, 5*(4), 628–636.

Griffin, Susan. (1978). *Women and nature: The roaring inside her.* New York: Harper and Row.

Gulbrandsen, Evelyn. (1988). Feminism, science, and social change. *Communication and Cognition, 21*(2), 149–155.

Haas, Violet B., & Perrucci, Carolyn C. (Eds.). (1984). *Women in scientific and engineering professions.* Ann Arbor, MI: University of Michigan Press. Papers presented at the National Conference on Women in the Professions: Sciences, Social Sciences, and Engineering, Purdue University, March 20-21, 1981.

Hall, Diana Long. (1974). Biology, sex hormones and sexism in the 1920s. *Philosophical Forum, 5,* 81–96.

Hall, Diana Long, & Long, D. (1977). *The scholar and the feminist IV.* New York: Barnard College Women's Center.

Hanen, Marsha, & Neilsen, Kai (Eds.). (1987). *Science, morality, and feminist theory: Canadian Journal of Philosophy* (supplementary volume). Calgary, Alberta: University of Calgary Press.

Haraway, Donna. (1976). *Crystals, fabrics, and fields: Metaphors of organicism in Twentieth-century developmental biology.* New Haven and London: Yale University Press.

Haraway, Donna. (1978). Animal sociology and a natural economy of the body politic (Parts 1 and 2). *Signs, 4*(1), 21–60.

Haraway, Donna. (1978). Reinterpretation or rehabilitation: An exercise in contemporary marxist history of science. *Studies in the History of Biology, 2,* 193–209.

Haraway, Donna. (1979, Spring-Summer). The biological enterprise: Sex, mind and profit: From human engineering to sociobiology. *Radical History Review, 20,* 206–234.

Haraway, Donna. (1981, Spring). In the beginning was the word: The genesis of biological theory. *Signs, 6*(3), 469–481.

Haraway, Donna. (1981–1982, Winter-Spring). The high cost of information in post World War II evolutionary biology: Ergonomics, semiotics, and the sociobiology of communications systems. *Philosophical Forum, 12* (2–3), 244–278.

Haraway, Donna. (1982, March). Class, race, sex, scientific objects of knowledge—A marxist-feminist perspective on the social construction of productive nature and some political consequences. *Argument, 24,* 200–213.

Haraway, Donna. (1983, March-April). A manifesto for cyborgs: Science, technology, and socialist feminism in the 1980s. *Socialist Review, 80,* 65–107.

Haraway, Donna. (1983). Signs of dominance: From a physiology to a cybernetics of primate society. *Studies in the History of Biology, 6,* 129–219.

Haraway, Donna. (1984–1985, Winter). Teddy bear patriarchy: Taxidermy in the Garden of Eden, New York City, 1908–1936. *Social Text II,* 20–64.

Haraway, Donna. (1988, Fall). Situated knowledges—The science question in feminism and the privilege of partial perspective. *Feminist Studies, 14*(3), 575–599.

Haraway, Donna. (1989). *Primate visions: Gender, race, and nature in the world of modern science.* New York: Routledge.

Haraway, Donna. (n.d.) The struggles for a feminist science. *Women: A journal of Liberation, 6*(2), 20–25.

Harding, Jan (Ed.). (1986). *Perspectives on gender and science.* London, New York, and Philadelphia: Falmer Press.

Harding, Sandra. (1977). Does objectivity in social science require value neutrality? *Soundings, 60*(4), 351–366.

Harding, Sandra. (1978). Four contributions values can make to the objectivity of social science. *PSA, 1,* 199–209.

Harding, Sandra. (1979) January 6). *Is science objective?* Paper presented at the annual meeting of the Association for the Advancement of Science, Houston, Texas.

Harding, Sandra (1986). *The science question in feminism.* Ithaca, NY: Cornell University Press.

Harding, Sandra (Ed.). (1987). *Feminism and methodology.* Bloomington, IN: Indiana University Press.

Harding, Sandra. (1987, Fall). The method question. *Hypatia, 2* 19–35.

Harding, Sandra. (1988). Feminism, epistemology and science—Introduction. *Communication and Cognition, 21*(2), 125–128.

Harding, Sandra, & Hintikka, Merrill B. (Eds.). (1983). *Discovering reality: Feminist perspectives on epistemology, metaphysics, methodology, and philosophy of science.* Dordrecht, Holland: D. Reidel.

Harding, Sandra, & O'Barr, Jean F. (Eds.). (1987). *Sex and scientific inquiry.* Chicago: University of Chicago Press.

Hartnett, Oonagh, Boden, Gill, & Fuller, Mary. (Eds.). (1978). *Sex-role stereotyping.* London: Tavistock.

Hein, Hilde. (1981, September-October). Women and science: Fitting men to think about nature. *International Journal of Women's Studies, 4*(4), 369–377.

Heldke, Lisa. (1987, Fall). John Dewey and Evelyn Fox Keller: A shared epistemological tradition. *Hypatia, 2* 120–140.

Herschberger, Ruth. (1970). *Adam's rib.* New York: Harper & Row.

Hoagland, Sarah Lucia. (1979). *Naming, describing, explaining: Deception and science.* Paper presented at the Annual Meeting of the American Association for the Advancement of Science.

Hrdy, Sarah Blaffer. (1981). *The woman that never evolved.* Cambridge, MA: Harvard University Press.

Hubbard, Ruth. (1984, Winter). Reflections of a feminist biologist on human sexuality and reproduction. *Women's Studies Quarterly, 12,* 2–5

Hubbard, Ruth. (1988). Science, facts and feminism. *Hypatia, 3*(1), 5–18.

Hubbard, Ruth. (1985, August). *History, science, and gender.* Soundrecording of discussion with Bonnie Smith and Elizabeth Fee. Research Triangle Park, NC, National Humanities Center.

Hubbard, Ruth. (in press). *The politics of women's biology.* New Brunswick, NJ: Rutgers University Press.

Hubbard, Ruth, Henifin, Mary Sue, & Fried, Barbara (Eds.). (1979). *Women look at biology looking at women.* Cambridge, MA: Schenkman.

Hubbard, Ruth, Henifin, Mary Sue, & Fried, Barbara (Eds.). (1982). *Biological woman: The convenient myth.* Cambridge, MA: Schenkman.

Hubbard, Ruth, & Lowe, Marian (Eds.). (1979). *Genes and gender II: Pitfalls in research on sex and gender.* New York: Gordian Press.

Hyde, Janet S. (1981). How large are cognitive gender differences: A meta-analysis using ω^2 and d. *American Psychologist, 36,* 892–901.

Imber, Barbara, & Tuana, Nancy. (1988, Spring). Feminist perspectives on science. *Hypatia, 3,* 139–144.

Irigaray, Luce, & Bove, Carol Mastrangelo (translator). (1987, Fall). Is the subject of science sexed? *Hypatia, 2* 65–87.

Jacklin, Carol N. (1981). Methodological issues in the study of sex-related differences. *Developmental Review, 1*, 266–273.

Jacobus, Mary, Shuttleworth, Sally, & Keller, Evelyn Fox (Eds.). (1989). *Body/politics: Women, literature and the discourse of science*. New York: Routledge.

Jaeger, M. E. (1987). What is the subject of feminist science—Comment. *International Journal of Science Education, 9*(2), 153–158.

James, William. (1982). *Essays in religion and morality*. Cambridge, MA: Harvard University Press.

Kahle, Jane Butler. (1985). *Women in science: A report from the field*. London, New York, and Philadelphia: Falmer Press.

Kammer, Anne E., Granose, Cherlyn S., & Sloan, Jan B. (compilers). (1979). *Science, sex, and society*. Washington, DC: Women's Educational Equity Act Program, Department of Health, Education, and Welfare.

Kann, Mark E. (Ed.). (1983). *The future of American democracy*. Philadelphia: Temple University Press.

Keller, Evelyn Fox. (1978). Gender and science. *Psychoanalysis and Contemporary Thought, 1*, 409–433.

Keller, Evelyn Fox. (1979). Cognitive repression in physics. *American Journal of Physics, 47*, 718–721.

Keller, Evelyn Fox. (1979, September). Nature as "her." Paper presented at Second Sex Conference, New York Institute for the Humanities.

Keller, Evelyn Fox. (1980). Baconian science: A hermaphroditic birth. *Philosophical Forum 9*, 229–308.

Keller, Evelyn Fox. (1980). Feminist critique of science: A forward or backward move? *Fundamenta Scientiae, 1*, 341–349.

Keller, Evelyn Fox. (1981, September-October). Women and science: Two cultures or one? Commentary on Hein, Lowe, Fee, and Goodman and Goodman. *International Journal of Women's Studies, 4*(4), 414–419.

Keller, Evelyn Fox. (1982, Spring). Feminism and science. *Signs, 7*(3), 589–602.

Keller, Evelyn Fox. (1983, September-October). Feminism as an analytic tool for the study of science. *Academe, 69*(5), 15–21.

Keller, Evelyn Fox. (1984, September). Feminism and natural science. *Argument, 26*, 719–724.

Keller, Evelyn Fox (1984 November-December). Women and basic research: Respecting the unexpected. *Technology Review 87*, 44–47.

Keller, Evelyn Fox (1985 March). *Does gender have an effect on science?* Videorecording of a speech made at the University of Virginia, Women's Studies Program.

Keller, Evelyn Fox (1985). *Reflections on gender and science*. New Haven, CT: Yale University Press.

Keller, Evelyn Fox (1987 Fall). The gender/science system: Or is sex to gender as nature is to science? *Hypatia*, 37–49.

Keller, Evelyn Fox (1987). On the need to count past two in our thinking about gender and science. *New Ideas in Psychology, 5*(2), 275–287.

Keller, Evelyn Fox. (1987). Women scientists and feminist critics of science. *Daedalus, 116*(4), 77–91.

Keller, Evelyn Fox (1988 Summer/Fall). Feminist perspectives on science studies. *Science, Technology, and Human Values, 13*(3–4), 235–249.

Kelly, Alison. (1978). Feminism and research. *Women's Studies International Quarterly, 1*(3), 225–232.

Kelly, Alison. (1981). *The missing half*. Manchester: Manchester University Press.

Keohane, Nannerl O., Rosaldo, Michele Z., & Gelpi, Barbara C. (Eds.). (1982). *Feminist theory, a critique of ideology*. Chicago: University of Chicago Press.

Kimball, Meredith M. (1981). Women and science: A critique of biological theories. *International Journal of Women's Studies, 4,* 318–338.

Kinsbourne, Marcel. (1980). If sex differences in brain lateralization exist, they have yet to be discovered. *Behavioural and Brain Sciences, 3,* 241–242.

Kleiman, Devra G. (1977). [Review of *Sociobiology: The new synthesis*]. *Signs, 3* 293–295.

Lambert, Helen H. (1978). Biology and equality: A perspective on sex differences. *Signs, 4*(1), 97–117.

Leavitt, Judith W., Gordan, Linda, & Bleier, Ruth. (1988, Fall). A decade of feminist critiques in the natural sciences—An address. *Signs, 14*(1) 182–195.

Levin, Margarita. (1988). Caring new world, feminism and science. *American Scholar, 57*(1) 100–106.

Lloyd, Barbara, & Archer, John (Eds.). (1976). *Exploring sex differences.* London: Academic Press.

Longino, Helen. (1981, Fall). Scientific objectivity and feminist theorizing. *Liberal Education, 67,* 181–195.

Longino, Helen. (1983). Beyond "bad science." *Science, Technology, and Human Values, 8*(1), 7–17.

Longino, Helen. (1983). Scientific objectivity and the logics of science. *Inquiry, 25*(1), 85–106.

Longino, Helen. (1987, Fall). Can there be a feminist science? *Hypatia,* 51–64.

Longino, Helen. (1988, Fall). Science, objectivity, and feminist values. *Feminist Studies, 14*(3), 561.

Longino, Helen, & Doell, Ruth. (1983, Winter). Body, bias, and behavior: A comparative analysis of reasoning in two areas of biological science. *Signs, 9*(2), 206–277.

Lootens, Tricia. (1984, October). Feminist science: A meaningful concept? *Off our Backs, 14,* 13.

Lowe, Marian. (1978). Sociobiology and sex differences. *Signs, 4*(1), 118–125.

Lowe, Marian. (1980, Spring). Reply to Ralls. *Signs, 5,* 546–547.

Lowe, Marian. (1981, September–October). Cooperation and competition in science. *International Journal of Women's Studies, 4*(4), 362–369.

Lowe, Marian, & Hubbard, Ruth (Eds.). (1983). *Woman's nature: Rationalizations of inequality.* Elmsford, NY: Pergamon Press.

Maccoby, Eleanor. (1970). Feminine intellect and the demands of science. *Impact of Science on Society, 20*(1), 13–28.

MacCormack, Carol P. (1977). Biological events and cultural control. *Signs, 3*(2), 93–100.

MacCormack, Carol P, & Strathern, Marilyn (Eds.). (1980). *Nature, culture, and gender.* New York: Cambridge University Press.

Magner, Lois. (1978). Women and the scientific idiom. *Signs, 4*(1), 61–80.

Manthorpe, Catherine. (1985, March). Feminists look at science. *New Scientist, 105*(1446), 29–31.

Martin, Jane Roland. (1988, April). Science in a different style. *American Philosophical Quarterly, 25*(2), 129–140.

Martin, Jane Roland. (1989). Ideological critiques and the philosophy of science. *Philosophy of Science, 56*(1), 1–22.

Mathieu, Nicole-Claude. (1978) Man-culture and woman-nature? *Women's Studies International Quarterly, 1*(1), 55–66.

McGlone, Jeannette. (1982). Faulty logic fuels controversy. *Behavioural and Brain Sciences, 5,* 312–314.

McGlone, Jeannette. (1980). Sex differences in human brain asymmetry: A critical survey. *Behavioural and Brain Sciences, 3,* 215–263.

Menzies, Heather. (1987, May-June). In his image: Science and technology as ideology. *This Magazine, 21,* 31–34.

Merchant, Carolyn. (1980). *The death of nature: Women, ecology, and the scientific revolution.* San Francisco: Harper & Row.

Merchant, Carolyn. (1981). Earthcare. *Environment, 23*(5), 6–12.

Merchant, Carolyn. (1982, September). Isis consciousness raised. *ISIS, 73,* 398–409.

Messing, Karen. (1986, November). What would a feminist approach to science be? *Resources for Feminist Research, 15,* 65–66.

Miles, Angela R., & Finn, Geraldine. (1982). *Feminism in Canada.* Montreal: Black Rose Books.

Montagu, Ashley. (1953). *The natural superiority of women.* New York: Macmillan.

Morais, Nina. (1982). A reply to Hardaker on: The woman question. *Popular Science Monthly, 221,* 74–75.

Morgan, Elaine. (1972). *The descent of woman.* New York: Stein & Day.

Mosedale, Susan Sleeth. (1978, Spring). Science corrupted: Victorian biologists consider "the woman question." *Journal of the History of Biology, 11,* 1–55.

Nemiroff, Greta Hofmann. (1987). *Women and men: Interdisciplinary readings on gender.* Montréal: Fitzhenry and Whiteside.

Nelson, Lynn Hankinson. (1987). Some remarks on the issues feminist critiques of science raise for empiricism. Ph.D. dissertation, Temple University. *Dissertation Abstract International, 48*(02), SECA: 413.

Nowotny, Helga, & Rose, Hilary (Eds.). (1979). *Countermovements in the sciences: Sociology of science yearbook.* Dordrecht, Holland: D. Reidel.

Oakley, Ann. (1979). A case of maternity: Paradigms of women as maternity cases. *Signs, 4*(4), 607–631.

Oldroyd, David, & Langham, Ian (Eds.). (1983). *The wider domain of evolutionary thought.* Dordrecht, Holland: D. Reidel.

Olser, Margaret J. (1980). Sex, science, and values: A critique of sociobiological accounts of sex differences. *Proceedings of the Third Annual Meeting of the Canadian Research Institute for the Advancement of Women,* 119–124.

Pakszys, Elzbieta. (1988). Feminism, sciences, epistemology—Three issues. *Communication and Cognition, 21*(2), 141–143.

Peterson, Anne C., & Wittig, Michele A. (Eds.). (1979). *Sex-related differences in cognitive functioning developmental issues.* New York: Academic Press.

Pffaflin, Sheila M. (1984, October). Women, science, and technology. *American Psychologist, 39,* 1183–1186.

Plumwood, Val. (1986, June). Ecofeminism: An overview and discussion of positions and arguments. *Australian Journal of Philosophy,* supp. 64, 120–138.

Plumwood, Val. (1988, Spring). Women, humanity, and nature. *Radical Philosophy, 48,* 16–24.

Potter, Elizabeth. (1988, Spring). Modeling the gender politics in science. *Hypatia, 3*(1), 19–33.

Prentice, Susan. (1988, June-July). Taking sides: What's wrong with ecofeminism? *Women and Environments, 10,* 9–10.

Purdy, Laura. (1986, Spring) Nature and nurture: A false dichotomy. *Hypatia, 1,* 167–174.

Ralls, Katherine. (1980, Spring). Comment on Lowe's "Sociobiology and sex differences." *Signs, 5,* 544–546.

Ranck, Shirley Ann. (1979). Points of theological convergence between feminism and postmodern science. *International Journal of Women's Studies, 2*(4), 386–397.

Raymond, Janice G. (1982, May). Medicine as patriarchal religion. *Journal of Medicine and Philosophy, 7,* 197–216.

Reed, Evelyn. (1978). *Sexism and science.* New York: Pathfinder Press.

Reskin, Barbara F. (1978). Sex differentiation and the social organization of science. *Sociological Inquiry, 48* (3–4), 6–37.

Richards, Barry (Ed.). *Capitalism and infancy.* London: Free Association Books.

Reissman, Catherine K. (1983, Summer). Women and medicalization: A new perspective. *Social Policy, 14*(1), 3–18.

Roberts, Joan L. (Ed.). (1976). *Beyond intellectual sexism: A new woman, a new reality.* New York: David McKay.

Rogers, Leslie J. (1983, November). Hormonal theories for sex differences: Politics disguised as science. *Sex Roles, 9,* 1109–1114.

Rose, Hilary. (1983). Hand, brain and heart: A feminist epistemology for the natural sciences. *Signs, 9*(1), 73–90.

Rose, Hilary. (1984, April). Is a feminist science possible? Paper presented at Massachusetts Institute of Technology, Women's Studies Program.

Rose, Hilary. (1988). Comment on Schiebinger's "The history and philosophy of women in science: A review essay." *Signs, 13*(2), 377–380.

Rose, Hilary. (1988). Dreaming the future. *Hypatia, 3*(1), 119–138.

Rose, Hilary, & Rose, Steven (Eds.). (1976). *The radicalization of science: Ideology of/in the natural sciences.* London Macmillan.

Rose, Steven (Ed.). (Dialectics of Biology Group). (1982). *Against biological determinism.* London: Allison and Busby.

Rosser, Sue V. (1982). Genetic androgyny and sociobiology. *International Journal of Women's Studies, 5*(5), 435–444.

Rosser, Sue V. (1984, January-February). A call for feminist science. *International Journal of Women's Studies, 7*(1), 3–10.

Rosser, Sue V. (1987, Fall). Feminist scholarship in the sciences: Where are we now and when can we expect a theoretical breakthrough? *Hypatia, 1,* 5–17.

Rosser, Sue V. (1988). *Feminism within the science and health care professions: Overcoming resistance.* Elmsford, NY: Pergamon Press.

Rosser, Sue V. (1988). Good science: Can it ever be gender free? *Women's Studies International Forum, 11*(1), 13–19.

Rossi, Alice S. (Ed.). (1974). *The feminist papers.* New York: Bantam Press.

Rothschild, Joan A. (1981). A feminist perspective on technology and the future. *Women's Studies International Quarterly, 4*(1), 65–74.

Rothschild, Joan A. (Ed.). (1983). *Machina ex dea: Feminist perspectives on technology.* Elmsford, NY: Pergamon Press.

Ruse, Michael (1981). *Is science sexist: And other problems in biomedical science* (pp. 219–244). Dordrecht, Holland: D. Reidel.

Ruse, Michael (1985). Biological science and feminist values. *Proceedings: Philosophy of Science Association 1984, 2,* (pp. 525–542). East Lansing: MI: Philosophy of Science Association.

Russett, Cynthia E. (1989). *Sexual science: Victorian constructions of womanhood.* Cambridge, MA: Harvard University Press.

Salleh, A.K. (1984, Winter). Deeper than deep ecology: The eco-feminist connection. *Environmental Ethics, 6,* 339–346.

Sapiro, Virginia. (Ed.). (1985). *Women, biology and public policy.* Beverly Hills, CA: Sage Publications.

Sayers, Janet. (1979). Anatomy is destiny: Variations on a theme. *Women's Studies International Quarterly, 2*(1). 19–32.

Sayers, Janet. (1980). Biological determinism, psychology, and the division of labour by sex *International Journal of Women's Studies, 3*(3), 241–260.

Sayers, Janet. (1982). *Biological politics: Feminist and antifeminist perspectives.* London: Tavistock.

Sayers, Janet. (1987). *Analyzing gender: A handbook of social science research.* Newbury Park, CA: Sage Publications.

Sayers, Janet. (1987). Feminism and science—Reason and passion. *Women's Studies International Forum, 10*(2), 171—179.

Scheinin, Rose. (1981). The rearing of women for science, engineering and technology. *International Journal of Women's Studies, 4*(4), 339–347.

Schiebinger, Londa. (1987). The history and philosophy of women in science: A review essay. *Signs, 12*(2), 305–332.

Schiebinger, Londa. (1988). Reply to Rose. *Signs, 13*(2), 380–384.

Segerberg, Marsha. (1979, March). Re/de/e/volving: Feminist theories of science. *Off Our Backs, 9*, 12–13.

Sherman, Julia. (1978). *Sex-related cognitive differences: An essay on theory and evidence.* Springfield, IL: Charles C. Thomas.

Shields, Stephanie. (1975). Functionalism, Darwinism and the psychology of women: A study in social myth. *American Psychologist, 30*, 739–754.

Shields, Stephanie. (1978, December 7). Sex and the biased scientist. *New Scientist, 80*, 752–754.

Shields, Stephanie. (1982). The variability hypothesis: The history of a biological model of sex differences in intelligence. *Signs, 7*(4), 769–797.

Shteir, Ann B. (1986, November). A connecting link: Women, popularization, and the history of science. *Resources for Feminist Research, 15*, 38–39.

Simon, Thomas. (1988, April-June). Feminist science and participatory democracy. *Philosophy and Social Action, 14*, 13–22.

Sloane, Ethel. (1985). *Biology of women (2nd ed.).* New York: John Wiley & Sons.

Smith, Dorothy E. (1974). The social construction of documentary reality. *Sociological Inquiry, 44*, 258–267.

Smith, Dorothy E. (1978). A peculiar eclipsing: Women's exclusion from man's culture. *Women's Studies International Quarterly, 1*(4), 281–296.

Smith, Joan. (1982). Sociobiology and feminism: The very strange courtship of competing paradigms. *Philosophical Forum, 13*, 281–308.

Smith-Rosenberg, Caroll. (1972). The hysterical woman: Sex roles and role conflict in 19th century America. *Social Research, 39*, 652–678.

Smith-Rosenberg, Carroll, & Rosenberg, Charles. (1973). The female animal: Medical and biological views of woman and her role in 19th century America. *Journal of American History, 59*, 332–356.

Smith-Rosenberg, Carroll, & Rosenberg, Charles. (1976). *No other gods: On science and American thought.* Baltimore, MD: The Johns Hopkins University Press.

Soble, Allan. (1983). Feminist epistemology and women scientists. *Metaphilosophy, 14*, 291–307.

Spanier, Bonnie B. (1986). Women's studies and the natural sciences: A decade of change, *Frontiers, 8*(3), 66–72.

Spender, Dale (Ed.). (1981). *Men's studies modified: The impact of feminism on the academic disciplines.* Elmsford, NY: Pergamon Press.

Standish, Leanna J. (1982, September-October). Women, work, and the scientific enterprise. *Science for the People, 14*, 12–18.

Stark, Evan, Flitcraft, Anne, & Frazier, William. (1979). Medicine and patriarchal violence: The social construction of a private event. *International Journal of Health Services, 9*, 461–493.

Stark-Adamec, Cannie. (1981, September-October). Women and science. *International Journal of Women's Studies 4*(4), 311–318.

Stoll, Clarice Stasz. (1973). *Sexism: Scientific debates.* Palo Alto, CA: Addison-Wesley.

Tanner, Nancy. (1981). *On becoming human.* New York: Cambridge University Press.

Tanner, Nancy, & Zihlman, Adrienne. (1976). Woman in evolution: Part I: Innovation and selection in human origins. *Signs, 1*, 585–608.

Tedesco, Marie. (1978). Science and feminism: Conceptions of female intelligence and their effect on American feminism 1859–1920. Ph.D. dissertation, Georgia State University. *Dissertation Abstracts International, 39* (02), SECA: 1028.

Teitelbaum, Michael S. (Ed.). (1976). *Sex differences: Social and biological perspectives.* New York: Doubleday.

Tiles, Mary. (1986). Mathesis and the masculine birth of time. *International Studies in the Philosphy of Science, I*(1), 16–35.

Tobach, Ethel, Gianutsos, John, Toppoff, Howard, & Gross, Charles G. (Eds.). (1974). *The four horsemen: Racism, sexism, militarism, and social Darwinism.* New York: Behavioral Publications.

Tobach, Ethel, & Rosoff, Betty. (1978). *Genes and gender I.* New York: Gordian Press.

Tomm, Winnie. (Ed.). (1989). *Effects of feminist approaches on research methodology.* Waterloo, Ontario: Wilfrid Laurier University Press for the Calgary Institute for the Humanities. Papers presented at a conference held at the University of Calgary, January 1987.

Tosi, Lucia. (1975). Women's scientific creativity. *Impact of Science on Society. 25*(2), 105–114.

Traweek, Sharon. (1984, November-December). High-energy physics: A male preserve. *Technology Review,* 42–43.

Traweek, Sharon. (1988, Summer/Fall). Feminist perspectives on science studies—commentary. *Science, Technology and Human Values, 13*(3–4), 250–253.

Trecker, Janice Law. (1974). Sex, science, and education. *American Quarterly, 26*(4), 352–366.

Triplette, Marianne. (Ed.). (1983). *Women's studies and the curriculum.* Winston-Salem, NC: Salem College.

Tuana, Nancy. (1983). Re-fusing nature/nurture. *Women's Studies International Forum, 6*(6), 621–632.

Tuana, Nancy. (1986, Spring). A response to Purdy's nature and nurture: A false dichotomy. *Hypatia, 1,* 175–178.

Tuana, Nancy. (1986). Re-presenting the world: Feminism and the natural science. *Frontiers, 8*(3), 73–78.

Tuana, Nancy (Ed.). (1987). Feminism and society I [special issue]. *Hypatia, 2*(3).

Tuana, Nancy (Ed.). (1988). Feminism and society II [special issue]. *Hypatia, 3*(1).

Tuana, Nancy. (1988, Spring). The weaker seed: The sexist bias of reproductive theory. *Hypatia, 3,* 35–59.

Vetterling-Braggin, Mary (Ed.). (1982). *"Masculinity", "femininity" and "androgyny": A modern philosophical discussion.* Totowa, NJ: Littlefield, Adams, & Company.

Vicinus, Martha (Ed.). (1973). *Suffer and be still: Women in the Victorian age.* Bloomington, IN: Indiana University Press.

Vines, Gail. (1985, September). Science is big enough for the both of us. *New Scientist, 107,* 55–56.

Warren, K. J. (1987, Spring). Feminism and ecology: Making connections. *Environmental Ethics, 9,* 3–20.

Watts, Meredith W. (1984). *Biopolitics and gender.* New York: Haworth Press.

Whitbeck, Caroline. (1982, May). Women and medicine: An introduction. *Journal of Medicine and Philosophy, 7,* 119–133.

Whitelegg, Elizabeth. (Ed.). (1982). *Changing experience of women.* Oxford: Martin Robertson.

Wittig, Michele A. (1976). Sex differences in intellectual functioning: How much of a difference do genes make? *Sex Roles, 2,* 63–74.

Wittig, Michele A. & Peterson, Anne C. (Eds.). (1979). *Sex-related differences in cognitive functioning: Developmental issues.* New York: Academic Press.

Wylie, Alison & Okruhlik, Kathleen. (1987, September). Philosophical feminism: Challenges to science. *Resources for Feminist Research, 16,* 12–15.

Zihlman, Adrienne. (1979). Women in evolution, Part II: Subsistence and social organization among early hominids. *Signs, 4,* 4–20.

Zimmerman, E. (1987, Spring). Feminism, deep ecology, and environmental ethics. *Environmental Ethics, 9,* 21–44.

Zita, Jacquelyn N. (1988, Spring). The feminist question of the science question in feminism. *Hypatia, 3,* 157–168.

Zita, Jacquelyn N. (1988, Spring). The premenstrual syndrome: Dis-easing the female cycle. *Hypatia, 3,* 77–99.

FEMINIST PEDAGOGY

Ackerhalt, Esther Judith. (1986). Toward the feminist transformation of the nursing curriculum: Development of a women's studies course for nurses in an academic setting. Ph.D dissertation, Columbia University Teacher's College, New York.

Allen, Carolyn. (1981). Feminist teachers: The power of the personal. *Feminist pedagogy: Positions and points of view.* Women's Studies Research Center, Working Paper Series 3. Madison, WI: University of Wisconsin.

Allen, Katherine R. (1988, January). Integrating a feminist perspective into family studies courses. *Family Relations, 37,* 29–35.

Andrist, Linda. (1988, February). A feminist framework for graduate education in women's health. *Journal of Nursing Education, 27,* 66–70.

Apple, Michael W. (1988). *Teachers and texts: A political economy of class and gender relations in education.* New York: Routledge.

Arnold, Lois. (1975). Marie Curie was great, but. . . . *School Science and Mathematics, 75*(7), 577–584.

Astin, Helen, & Hirsch, Werner Z. (Eds.). (1978). *Higher education of women.* New York: Praeger.

Barkey, Jeanne, & Davis, Karen. (1982, June 16–20). *Feminism through education.* Papers presented at the National Women's Studies Association Conference. Humboldt, California.

Beck, Evelyn Torton. (1981). Self-disclosure and the commitment to social change. *Feminist pedagogy: Positions and points of view.* Women's Studies Research Center, Working Paper Series, 3. Madison, WI: University of Wisconsin.

Belenky, Mary F., Clinchy, Blythe M., Goldberger, Nancy, & Tarule, Jill M. (1986). *Women's ways of knowing: The development of self, body, and mind.* New York: Basic Books.

Bell, Lee. (1987, Fall/Winter). Hearing all our voices: Applications of feminist pedagogy to conferences, speeches, and panel presentations. *Women's Studies Quarterly, 15,* 74–80.

Benson, Ruth C. (1972). Women's studies: Theory and practice. *American Association of University Professors Bulletin, 58*(3), 283–286.

Bergmann, Barbara R. (1987, Fall). Women's roles in the economy: Teaching the issues. *Journal of Economic Education, 18,* 393–407.

Berlak, Ann, & Berlak, Harold (1981). *Dilemmas of schooling: Teaching and social change.* New York: Methuen.

Bleier, Ruth. (1982). *Women's studies: Its impact on society, technology, and the arts.* Sound-recordings, Office of Women's Studies, University of Wisconsin-Milwaukee.

Bleier, Ruth (Ed.). (1986). *Feminist approaches to science.* Elmsford, NY: Pergamon Press.

Blumhagen, Kathleen, & Johnson, Walter (Eds.). (1978). *Women's studies.* Westport, CT: Greenwood Press.

Bouchard, Pierette. (1986–1987, December/January). Pratique feministe en education: Transformer radicalement la pédagogie. [Feminism applied to education: Radically transforming pedagogy]. *Resources for Feminist Research, 15,* 15–17.

Bowles, Gloria, & Klein, Renate Duelli. (1983). *Theories of women's studies*. Boston: Routledge & Kegan Paul.

Boxer, Marilyn J. (1982). For and about women: The theory and practice of women's studies in the United States. *Signs, 7*(3), 661–695.

Bridges, Amy, & Hartmann, Heidi. (1975, Winter). Pedagogy by the oppressed. *Review of Radical Political Economics, 6*(4) 75–79.

Briscoe, Anne M., & Pffaflin, Sheila (Eds.). (1979). *Expanding the role of women in science*. New York: New York Academy of Sciences.

Bunch, Charlotte. (1979). Not by degrees. *Quest, 5*(1), 7–18.

Bunch, Charlotte, & Pollack, Sandra. (1983). *Learning our way: Essays in feminist education*. Trumansburg, NY: Crossing Press.

Cayleff, Susan E. (1988, Spring/Summer). Teaching women's history in a medical school: Challenges and possibilities. *Women's Studies Quarterly, 16*, 97–109.

Caywood, Cynthia L., & Overing, Gillain R. (Eds.). (1987). *Teaching writing: Pedagogy, gender, and equity*. Albany, NY: State University of New York Press.

Clinchy, Blythe, & Belenky, Mary. (1984). Connected education for women. *Journal of Education, 167*,(3) 28–45.

Collins, Georgia C. (1981, April). Feminist approaches to art education. *Journal of Aesthetic Education, 15*, 83–94.

Collins, Patricia Hill. (1986). The emerging theory and pedagogy of black women's studies. *Feminist Issues, 6*(1), 3–17.

Conway, Jill K. (1987, Fall). Politics, pedagogy, and gender. *Daedalus, 116*, 137–152.

Culley, Margo, & Portuges, Catherine (Eds.). (1985). *Gendered subjects: The dynamics of feminist teaching*. Boston: Routledge & Kegan Paul.

Davaney, Sheila G. (Ed.). (1981). *Feminism and process thought*. New York: Mellen Press.

Davis, Barbara Hillyer (Ed.). (1985). Feminist education [special issue]. *Journal of Thought, 20*(3).

Deegan, Mary Jo. (1988, April). Transcending a patriarchal past: Teaching the history of women in sociology. *Teaching Sociology, 16*(2), 141–150.

Dervin, Brenda. (1987, Fall). The potential contribution of feminist scholarship to the field of communication. *Journal of Communication, 37*(4), 107–120.

Dittman, Linda. (1985). Inclusionary practices: The politics of syllabus design. *Journal of Thought, 20*(3), 37–47.

Dumont, Jeanne. (1983, Fall). Feminist pedagogy at National Women's Studies Association: Making information accessible. *National Women's Studies Association Newsletter, 1*(4).

Eisenstein, Zillah R. (Ed.). (1979). *Capitalist patriarchy and the case for socialist feminism*. New York: Monthly Review Press.

Evans, Mary. (1982, Spring). In praise of theory: The case for women's studies. *Feminist Review, 10*, 61–74.

Farley, Margaret A. (1984). Feminist ethics in the Christian ethics curriculum. *Horizons, 11*(2), 361–372.

Farnham, Christine (Ed.). (1987). *The impact of feminist research in the academy*. Bloomington, IN: Indiana University Press.

Farrant, Patricia A. (Ed.). (1986). *Strategies and attitudes: Women in educational administration: A book of readings*. Washington D.C: National Association for Women Deans, Administrators, and Counselors. (ERIC Document Reproduction. Service No. ED 285 439)

Fausto-Sterling, Anne. (1982). Course closeup: The biology of gender. *Women's Studies Quarterly, 10*, 17–19.

Fausto-Sterling, Anne, & English, Lydia L. (1985). *Women and minorities in science: An interdisciplinary course*. Wellesley, MA: Wellesley College Center for Research on Women.

Ferguson, Ann. (1982). Feminist teaching: A practice developed in undergraduate courses. *Radical Teacher, 18*, 26–69.

Fisher, Berenice. (1982). Professing feminism: Feminist academics and the women's movement. *Psychology of Women Quarterly, 7*(1), 55–69.

Fisher, Berenice. (1982). What is feminist pedagogy? *Radical Teacher, 19,* 26–29.

Fitzgerald, Ann. (1978, March). Teaching interdisciplinary women's studies. *Great Lakes College Association Faculty Newsletter,* 2–3.

Flax, Jane. (1978). Critical theory as a vocation. *Politics and Society, 8*(2), 202–223.

Flax, Jane. (1987, Summer). Postmodernism and gender relations in feminist theory. *Signs, 12*(4), 621–643.

Folsom, Jack. (1983, Spring). Teaching about sexism and language in a traditional setting: Surmounting the obstacles. *Women's Studies Quarterly, 11,* 12–15.

Fortune, Janet Cummings. (1987). Toward a feminist pedagogy: Relationships, experience, and liberation. Ed. D. dissertation, University of North Carolina at Greensboro. *Dissertation Abstract International, 49* (07), SECA: 1995.

Fox-Genovese, Elizabeth. (1979, Fall). The personal is not political enough. *Marxist Perspectives, 1,* 94–113.

Freeman, Jo. (1973). The feminist scholar. *Quest, 5*(1), 26–36.

Freire, Paulo. (1973). *Pedagogy of the oppressed.* New York: Seabury Press.

Freire, Paulo. (1985). *The politics of education: Culture, power, and liberation.* South Hadley, MA: Bergin & Garvey.

Friedman, Susan Stanford. (1985). Authority in the feminist classroom: A contradiction in terms? *Feminist pedagogy: Positions and points of view.* Women's Studies Research Center, Working Paper Series, 3. Madison, WI: University of Wisconsin Press.

Froschl, Merle, Odarenko, Dora J., & Weinbaum, Sandy. (1977). Women's lives, women's works—Feminist approaches to high school curriculum. *Journal of Research and Development in Education, 10*(4), 12–19.

Garside Allen, Christine. (1975). Conceptual history as a methodology for women's studies. *McGill Journal of Education, 10*(1), 49–58.

Geiger, Susan, & Zita, Jacqueline N. (1985). White traders: The caveat emptor of women's studies. *Journal of Thought, 20*(3), 106–121.

Giroux, Henry. (1981). *Ideology, culture, and the process of schooling.* Philadelphia, PA: Temple University Press.

Giroux, Henry. (1986). Radical pedagogy and the politics of student voice. *Interchange, 17*(1), 48–69.

Gonzales, Sylvia. (1980, Summer). Toward a feminist pedagogy for Chicana self-actualization. *Frontiers, 5*(2), 48.

Gordon, Linda. (1975). A socialist view of women's studies. *Signs, 1*(2), 539–566.

Grant, Julia. (1982). The dynamics of the women's studies classroom. *Radical Teacher, 22,* 24.

Gross, Michael. (1984, Winter). The science of "strange females": A course on hormones and homosexuality. *Women's Studies Quarterly, 7*(4), 6–10.

Grossman Kahn, Diana. (1978). Interdisciplinary studies and women's studies: Questioning answers and creating questions. *The structures of knowledge, Proceedings of the 4th Annual Great Lakes College Association Women's Studies Conference,* 20–24.

Grumet, Madeleine. (1981). Conception, contradiction, and curriculum. *Journal of Curriculum Theorizing, 3*(1), 287–298.

Grumet, Madeleine. (1981). Pedagogy for patriarchy: The feminization of teaching. *Interchange, 12*(2–3), 165–184.

Gundersen, Joan R. (1986, November). Re-visioning the past: Toward a more inclusive telling of history. *History Teacher, 20*(1). 51–62.

Guttentag, Marcia. (1978). Evaluating women's studies: A decision theoretic approach. *Signs, 3*(4), 884–890.

Haecker, Dorothy A. (1984, Spring). Thoughts on feminist teaching. *National Women's Studies Association Newsletter, 2,* 4–5.

Hall, Roberta M. (1982). *The classroom climate: A chilly one for women?* Washington, D.C.: Project on the Status and Education of Women.

Halpern, Carol, & Samuelson, Marlene. (1985). Our progress and struggles as feminists teaching biology. *Feminist Teacher, 1*(4), 10–14.

Hearn, Pamela. (1987). Things you were never told about teaching women's studies. *Women's Studies, 13*(4), 373–379.

Howe, Florence. (1978). Breaking the disciplines. *The structures of knowledge, Proceedings of the 4th Annual Great Lakes College Association Women's Studies Conference, 34–37.*

Howe, Florence. (1982, April). Feminist scholarship: The extent of the revolution. *Change, 14,* 12–20.

Howe, Florence. (1984). *Myths of coeducation: Selected essays, 1964–1983.* Bloomington, IN: Indiana University Press.

Hubbard, Ruth. (1978, March). *Feminism in academia: Its problematics and problems.* Paper presented at Expanding the Role of Women in the Sciences Conference, sponsored by the New York Academy of Sciences and the Association for Women in Science Educational Foundation.

Johnson, Marilyn. (Ed.). (1982, Fall). Special Issue: Teaching psychology of women. *Psychology of Women Quarterly, 7,* 3–104.

Kahle, Jane Butler, & Hickman, Faith M. (1981). *New directions in biology teaching.* Reston, VA: National Association of Biology Teachers.

Keohane, Nannerl O., Rossaldo, Michele K., & Gelpi, Barbara C. (Eds.). (1982). *Feminist theory: A critique of ideology.* Chicago: University of Chicago Press.

Ketchum, Sara Ann. (1980, Summer). Female culture, woman culture, and conceptual change: Toward a philosophy of women's studies. *Social Theory and Practice, 6,* 151–162.

King, Ynestra. (1981). Feminist pedagogy and technology—Reflections on the Goddard Feminism and Ecology Summer Program. *Women's Studies International Quarterly, 4*(3), 370–372.

Kipp, Rita. (1981). The feminist critique: Plans and perspectives. *The structure of knowledge, Proceedings of the 4th Annual Great Lakes College Association Women's Studies Conference, 49–53.*

Klein, Renate D. (1978). The dynamics of the women's studies classroom: A review essay of the teaching practice of women's studies in higher education. *Women's Studies International Forum, 10*(2), 187–206.

Kolodny, Annette. (1980, Spring). Dancing through the minefield; Some observations on the theory, practice, and politics of a feminist literary criticism. *Feminist Studies, 6,* 1–25.

Kritek, Phyllis, & Glass, Laurie. (1978, March). Nursing: A feminist perspective. *Nursing Outlook, 26,* 182–190.

Lafontaine, Phyllis Watts. (1981). Non-sexist education: Toward the emergence of an alternative curriculum paradigm for women's studies programs. Ph.D. dissertation, Ohio State University. *Dissertation Abstracts International, 42*(02), SECA: 526.

Laird, Susan. (1988). Reforming women's true profession—A case of feminist pedagogy in teacher education. *Harvard Educational Review, 58*(4), 449–463.

Lambie, William. (1988, March). Feminism and schools. *Education Digest, 53,* 19–21.

Langland, Elizabeth, & Gove, Walter (Eds.). (1983). *A feminist perspective in the academy: The difference it makes.* Chicago: University of Chicago Press.

Lather, Patti. (1984, March). Critical theory, curricular transformation and feminist mainstreaming. *Journal of Education, 166,* 49–62.

Lather, Patricia Ann. (1983). Feminism, teacher education, and curricular change: Women's studies as counter-hegemonic work. Ph.D. dissertation, Indiana University. *Dissertation Abstract International, 44*(10), SECA: 3182.

Leiss, William.(1974). Critical theory and its future. *Political Theory, 2*(3), 330–349.

Lenihan, Genie O., & Rawlins, Melanie E. (1987, Spring). The impact of a women's studies program: Challenging and nourishing the true believers. *Journal of the National Association of Women Deans, Administrators, and Counselors, 50*(3), 3–10.

Lerner, Gerda. (1972). On the teaching and organization of feminist studies. *Female Studies, 5*, 34–37.

Levin, Tobe, & Miller-Goeder, Janet. (1984, Summer). Feminist teaching in a military setting: Co-operation or subversion. *Women's Studies Quarterly, 12*, 13–15.

Loewenstein, Sophie F. (1976). Integrating content on feminism and racism into social work curriculum. *Journal of Education for Social Work, 12*(1), 91–96.

Longenecker, Marlene, & Hyers, Suzanne. (1983, Summer). NWSA '83: Feminist education: Quality and equality convention update. *National Women's Studies Association Newsletter, 1*, 2–4.

Lord, Sharon. (1982). Toward the psychology of women: Examination of a teaching-learning model. *Psychology of Women Quarterly, 7*(1), 70–80.

Loring, Katherine (Ed.). (1984). *Feminist pedagogy and the learning climate, Proceedings of the 9th Annual Great Lakes College Association Women's Studies Conference, November 4–6, 1983.* Ann Arbor, MI: Great Lakes College Association Women's Studies Program.

Maher, Frances. (1985). Pedagogies for the gender-balanced classroom. *Journal of Thought, 20*(3), 48–64.

Maher, Frances. (1987, March). Inquiry teaching and feminist pedagogy. *Social Education, 51*, 186–188.

Maher, Frances. (1987). Toward a richer theory of feminist pedagogy: A comparison of liberation and gender models for teaching and learning. *Journal of Education, 169*(3), 91–100.

Mahony, Pat. (1988). Oppressive pedagogy: The importance of process in women's studies. *Women's Studies International Forum, 11*(2), 103–108.

Martin, Jane Roland. (1985). *Reclaiming a conversation: The ideal of the educated woman.* New Haven: Yale University Press.

Mazza, Karen A. (1983, April 16–20). *Feminist perspectives and the reconceptualization of the disciplines.* Paper presented at the American Educational Research Association, Montréal, Canada.

McCandless, Amy T. (1987). Patriarchy and pedagogy—The effect of patriarchal ideology on the higher education of southern women. Paper presented at the First Southern Conference on Women's History, Converse College, Spartanburg, SC.

McIntosh, Peggy. (1983). *Interactive phases of curricular re-vision: A feminist perspective.* Wellesley, MA: Wellesley College Center for Research on Women.

McRobbie, Angela. (1982). The politics of feminist research: Between talking, text, and action. *Feminist Review, 126*, 46–57.

Miller, Francesca. (1988, Spring/Summer). Precedent and pedagogy: Teaching the history of women in Latin America. *Women's Studies Quarterly, 16*, 110–117.

Miller, Janet L. (1983). The resistance of women academics: An autobiographical account. *Journal of Educational Equity and Leadership, 3*(2), 101–109.

Miller, Janet L. (1982, Winter). The sound of silence breaking: Feminist pedagogy and curriculum theory. *Journal of Curriculum Theorizing, 4*(1), 5–11.

Miller, Nancy K. (1981). Mastery, identity, and the politics of work, a feminist teacher in the graduate classroom. *Feminist pedagogy: Positions and points of view.* Women's Studies Research Center, Working Paper Series 3. Madison, WI: University of Wisconsin.

Minnich, Elizabeth. (1982, April). A devastating conceptual error: How can we not be feminist scholars? *Change, 14*, 7–9.

Mitrano, Barbara. (1979). Feminism and curriculum theory: Implications for teacher education. Ed. D. dissertation, University of Rochester. *Dissertation Abstract International, 40*(03), SECA: 1417.

Mitrano, Barbara. (1979). Feminist theology and curriculum theory. *Journal of Curriculum Studies, 11*(3), 211–220.

Mitrano, Barbara. (1981, Summer). Feminism and curriculum theory: Implications for teacher education. *Journal of Curriculum Theorizing, 5–85.*

Morgan, Kathryn P. (1987, September). The perils and paradoxes of feminist pedagogy. *Resources for Feminist Research, 16,* 49–52.

Mumford, Laura Stempel. (1985). "Why do we have to read all this old stuff?" Conflict in the feminist theory classroom. *Journal of Thought, 20*(3), 88–96.

Omolade, Barbara. (1987, Fall/Winter). A black feminist pedagogy. *Women's Studies Quarterly, 15,* 32–39.

Partington, Geoffrey. (1985). The same or different—Curricular implications for feminism and multiculturalism. *Journal of Curriculum Studies, 17*(3), 275–292.

Peters, Helene. (1983, June 26–30). *Feminist theory and feminist pedagogy: The existential woman.* Paper presented at the National Women's Studies Association Conference, Columbus, Ohio.

Pierson, Ruth, & Prentice, Alison (1982, Spring). Feminism and the writing and teaching of history. *Atlantis, 7,* 37–46.

Ramalho, Tania. (1985). Towards a feminist pedagogy of empowerment: The male and female voices in critical theory. Ph.D. dissertation, Ohio State University. *Dissertation Abstract International, 46*(06), SECA: 1757.

Ray, Gloria Jean. (1980). An investigation of students', faculty's, and parents' attitudes towards a modified home economics curriculum from a feminist perspective. Ed.D. dissertation, University of Massachusetts. *Dissertation Abstract International, 42*(02), SECA: 533.

Reason, Peter, & Rowan, John. (Eds.). (1981). *Human inquiry.* London: John Wiley & Sons.

Reinharz, Shulamit, Bumbyk, Marti, & Wright, Janet. (1982). Methodological issues in feminist research: A bibliography of literature in women's studies, sociology and psychology. *Women's Studies International Forum, 6*(4).

Reuben, Elaine. (1978). In defiance of the evidence: Notes on feminist scholarship. *Women's Studies International Quarterly, 1*(3), 215–218.

Rich, Adrienne. (1979). *On lies, secrets, and silence: Selected prose, 1966–1978.* New York: W. W. Norton.

Richardson, Laurel, Fonow, Mary Margaret, & Cook, Judith. (1985, April). From gender seminar to gender community. *Teaching Sociology, 12*(3), 313–324.

Richardson, Nancy D. (1985). Feminist theology, feminist pedagogy—An experimental program of the Women's Theological Center. *Journal of Feminist Studies in Religion, 1*(2), 115–120.

Roberts, Helen (Ed.). (1981). *Doing feminist research.* London: Routledge & Kegan Paul.

Rosser, Sue V. (1986). *Teaching science and health from a feminist perspective: A practical guide.* Elmsford, NY: Pergamon Press.

Rosser, Sue V. (1987). Science and health-related women's studies courses: A report after 10 years in the academy. *Feminist Teacher, 2*(2), 30–34.

Rothenberg, Paula. (1985). Teaching about racism and sexism: A case history. *Journal of Thought, 20*(3), 122–136.

Roy, Paula A., & Schen, Molly. (1987, Fall/Winter). Feminist pedagogy: Transforming the high school classroom. *Women's Studies Quarterly, 15,* 110–115.

Rutherford, Millicent Alexander. (1977). Feminism and the secondary school curriculum, 1890–1920. Ph.D. dissertation, Stanford University. *Dissertation Abstract International, 38*(03), SECA: 1205.

Salzman-Webb, Marilyn. (1972). Feminist studies: Frill or necessity? *Female Studies, 5,* 64–67.

Schniedewind, Nancy. (1983). *Open minds to equality: A sourcebook of learning activites to promote race, sex, class, and age equality.* Englewood Cliffs, NJ: Prentice Hall.

Schniedewind, Nancy. (1985). Cooperatively structured learning: Implications for feminist pedagogy. *Journal of Thought, 20*(3), 74–87.

Schniedewind, Nancy, & Maher, Frances. (1987). *Women's Studies Quarterly* [special issue on feminist pedagogy]. *15*(3 & 4).

Schuster, Marilyn R., & Van Dyne, Susan R. (Eds.). (1985). *Women's place in the academy: Transforming the liberal arts curriculum.* Totowa, NJ: Rowman & Allanheld.

Shakeshaft, Charol. (1986, March). A gender at risk. *Phi Delta Kappan,* 499–503.

Sherwin, Susan. (1972). Women's studies as a scholarly discipline: Some questions for discussion. *Female Studies, 5,* 114–116.

Shor, Ira. (1980). *Critical teaching and everyday life.* Boston: South End Press.

Showalter, Elaine, & Ohmann, Carol (Eds.). (1971). *Teaching about women.* Pittsburgh, PA: Know.

Shrewsbury, Carolyn M. (1983, Fall). Conference sessions on feminist pedagogy. *National Women's Studies Association Newsletter, 1*(4).

Shrewsbury, Carolyn M. (1987, Fall/Winter). Feminist pedagogy: A bibliography. *Women's Studies Quarterly, 15,* 116–124.

Shrewsbury, Carolyn M. (1987, Fall/Winter). What is feminist pedagogy? *Women's Studies Quarterly, 15,* 6–14.

Siporin, Rae Lee (Ed.). (1972). *Women and education: A feminist perspective.* Pittsburgh, PA: Know.

Smolen, Bonnie. (1979). Psychoanalysis and feminist scholarship: Toward a women's studies curriculum in counseling and psychology. Ed.D. dissertation, University of Massachusetts. *Dissertation Abstracts International, 40* (08), SECB: 3971.

Spanier, Bonnie, Bloom, Alexander, & Boroviak, Darlene (Eds.). (1984). *Toward a balanced curriculum: A sourcebook for initiating gender integration projects.* Cambridge, MA: Schenkman.

Special section: Women's studies. (1982, April). *Change, 14*(3), 12–46.

Spender, Dale (Ed.). (1981). *Men's studies modified: The impact of feminism on the academic disciplines.* Elmsford NY: Pergamon Press.

Spender, Dale. (1983). *Invisible women: The schooling scandal.* London: Readers' and Writers' Press.

Spillers, Hortense J. (1981). Unloosening the double bind: A pedagogy for liberation. *Feminist pedagogy: Positions and points of view.* Women's Studies Research Center, Working Papers Series Madison, WI: University of Wisconsin.

Stanley, Liz, & Wise, Sue. (1983). *Breaking out: Feminist consciousness and feminist research.* Boston: Routledge & Kegan Paul.

Stimpson, Catherine. (1973, September). The new feminism and women's studies. *Change,* 43–48.

Stimpson, Catherine. (1973). What matter mind: A theory about the practice of women's studies. *Women's Studies, 1*(3), 293–314.

Stimpson, Catherine. R. (1987, September/October). Women's studies: The idea and the ideas. *Liberal Education, 73*(4), 34–38.

Strauss, Mary Jo, (1983, Fall). Feminist education in science, mathematics, and technology. *Women's Studies Quarterly, 11,* 23–25.

Tabakin, Geoffrey Allan. (1983). Feminist theory and the development of curriculum for use in schools. Ph.D. dissertation, University of Wisconsin-Madison. *Dissertation Abstract International, 44* (05), SECA: 1326.

Tetreault, Mary K., Arch, Elizabeth, & Kershner, S. (1982, June 16–20). *The inclusion of women and the conception of a discipline.* Paper presented at the National Women's Studies Association Conference, Humboldt, CA.

Thoen, Gail. (1983). Women alone, alive, and thriving—An innovative curriculum for the nontraditional student. *Journal of College Student Personnel, 24*(2), 162–163.

Tobias, Sheila. (1978). Women's studies: Its origins, organization and prospects. *Women's Studies International Quarterly, 1*(1), 85–97.

Torrey, Jane. (1987, October). Phases of feminist re-vision in the psychology of personality. *Teaching of Psychology, 14*(3), 155–160.

Trebilcot, Joyce. (Ed.). (1983). *Mothering: Essays in feminist theory.* Totowa, NJ: Rowman & Allanheld.

Walker, Stephen, & Burton, Len. (Eds.). (1983). *Gender, class, and education.* Sussex, England: Fulmer Press.

Wallston, Barbara Strudler. (1981, Summer). What are the questions in psychology of women? A feminist approach to research. *Psychology of Women Quarterly, 5,* 597–617.

Whyte, Karen. (1988, June). "Can we learn this? We're just girls."—Visions and strategy. *Resources for Feminist Research, 17,* 6–9.

Winkler, Barbara Scott. (1983, June 26–30). *On comparing feminist and Marxist pedagogy.* Paper presented at the National Women's Studies Association Annual Conference, Columbus, Ohio.

Woodhull, Amy, Lowry, Nancy, & Henifin, Mary Sue. (1985). Teaching for change: Feminism and the sciences. *Journal of Thought, 20*(3), 162–173.

FEMINIST THEORY

Abel, Elizabeth, & Abel, Emily K. (Eds.). (1983). *The Signs reader: Women, gender, and scholarship.* Chicago: University of Chicago Press.

Anderson, Margaret L. (1983). *Thinking about women: Sociological and feminist perspectives.* New York: Macmillan.

Asquith, Peter, & Giere, Ronald (Eds.). (1981). Proceedings: Philosophy of Science Association, 2. East Lansing, MI: Philosophy of Science Association.

Bordo, Susan. (1987). *The flight to objectivity: Essays on Cartesianism and culture.* Albany, NY: State University of New York Press.

Bowles, Gloria, & Klein, Renate Duelli (Eds.). (1983). *Theories of women's studies.* Boston, MA: Routledge & Kegan Paul.

Bunch, Charlotte. (Ed.). (1981). *Building feminist theory: Essays from Quest.* New York: Longman Press.

Code, Lorraine B. (1981, July-October). Is the sex of the knower epistemologically significant? *Metaphilosophy, 12,* 267–276.

Davaney, Sheila (Ed.). (1981). *Feminism and process thought.* New York: E. Mellen Press.

Dinnerstein, Dorothy. (1988, June-July). What does feminism mean? *Women and Environments, 10,* 7–8.

Eisenstein, Hester. (1983). *Contemporary feminist thought.* Boston, MA: G.K. Hall.

Flax, Jane. (1978). Critical theory as a vocation. *Politics and Society, 8*(2), 202–223.

Flax, Jane. (1987, Summer). Postmodernism and gender relations in feminist theory. *Signs, 12*(4), 621–643.

Flax, Jane. (1988, Fall). Postmodernism and gender relations in feminist theory—Reply. *Signs, 14*(1), 201–203.

Frye, Marilyn. (1983). *The politics of reality: Essays in feminist theory.* Trumansburg, NY: Crossing Press.

Genova, Judith. (1988, Spring). Women and the mismeasure of thought. *Hypatia, 3,* 101–117.

Glennon, Lynda. (1979). *Women and dualism: A sociology of knowledge analysis.* New York: Longman.

Gould, Carol (Ed.). (1984). *Beyond domination: New perspectives on women and philosophy.* Totowa, NJ: Rowman & Allanheld.

Grant, Judith. (1987, Fall). I feel therefore I am: A critique of female experience as the basis for a feminist epistemology. *Women and Politics, 7*(3), 99–114.

Grosz, Elizabeth A. (1987). Feminist theory and the challenge to knowledges. *Women's Studies International Forum, 10*(5), 475–480.

Haber, Barbara (Ed.). (1983). *The women's annual.* Boston, MA: G.K. Hall.

Hanen, Marsha & Nielsen, Kai (Eds.). (1987). *Science, morality, and feminist theory.* Calgary, Alberta: University of Calgary Press.

Harding, Sandra. (1979). The social function of the empiricist conception of mind. *Metaphilosophy, 10,* 38–47.

Harding, Sandra. (1982). Is gender a variable in conceptions of rationality? A survey of issues. *Dialectica, 36,* 225–242.

Harding, Sandra. (1983). Common causes: Toward a reflexive feminist theory. *Women and Politics, 3*(4).

Harding, Sandra & Hintikka, Merrill B. (Eds.). (1983). *Discovering reality.* Dordrecht, Holland: D. Reidel.

Harding, Sandra, & O'Barr, Jean (Eds.). (1987). *Sex and scientific inquiry.* Chicago: University of Chicago Press.

Harstock, Nancy. (1983). *Money, sex, and power: Toward a feminist historical materialism.* New York: Longman.

Hawkesworth, Mary E. (1988, August). Feminist rhetoric—Discourses on the male monopoly of thought. *Political Theory, 16*(3), 444–467.

Held, Virginia. (1985, Summer). Feminism and epistemology: Recent work on the connection between gender and knowledge. *Philosophy and Public Affairs, 14,* 296–307.

Hull, Gloria T., Scott, Patricia B., & Smith, Barbara (Eds.). (1982). *All the women are white, all the blacks are men, but some of us are brave: Black women's studies.* New York: Feminist Press.

Jagger, Alison M. (1983). *Feminist politics and human nature.* Totowa, NJ: Rowman & Allanheld.

Jassen-Jurreit, Marielouise, & Moberg, Verne (Translator). (1982). *Sexism: The male monopoly on history and thought.* New York: Farrar, Straus & Giroux, (German edition published in 1976)

Kelly, Joan. (1979). The doubled vision of feminist theory: A postscript to the "Women and Power Conference." *Feminist Studies, 5,* 216–227.

Keohane, Nannerl O., Rosaldo, Michelle Z., & Gelpi, Barbara. (1982). *Feminist theory, a critique of ideology.* Chicago: University of Chicago Press.

King, Deborah K. (1988, Fall). Multiple jeopardy, multiple consciousness—The context of a black feminist ideology. *Signs, 14*(1), 42–72.

Lloyd, Genevieve. (1984). *The man of reason: "Male" and "female" in western philosophy.* Minneapolis, MN: University of Minnesota Press.

MacKinnon, Catharine A. (1982, Spring). Feminism, marxism, method and the state: An agenda for theory. *Signs, 7*(3), 515–544.

MacKinnon, Catharine A. (1983), Feminism, marxism, method, and the state: Toward a feminist jurisprudence. *Signs, 8*(4), 635–658.

McMillan, Carol. (1982), *Women, reason, and nature: Some philosophical problems with feminism.* Princeton, NJ: Princeton University Press.

Midgley, Mary, & Hughes, Judith. (1983). *Women's choices: Philosophical problems facing feminism.* New York: St. Martin's Press.

Nicholson, Linda J. (Ed.). (1989). *Feminism/postmodernism.* New York: Routledge.

Nye, Andrea. (1989). *Feminist theory and the philosophies of man.* London and New York: Croom Helm.

Sabrosky, Judith A. (1979). *From rationality to liberation: The evolution of feminist ideology.* Westport, CT: Greenwood Press.

Smith, Dorothy. (1983). *Knowledge reconsidered: A feminist overview.* Ottawa, Ontario: Canadian Research Institute for the Advancement of Women.

Spender, Dale (Ed.). (1985). *For the record: The making and meaning of feminist knowledge.* London: The Women's Press.

Stanley, Liz & Wise, Sue. (1983). *Breaking out: Feminist consciousness and feminist research.* Boston: Routledge & Kegan Paul.

Swerdlow, Amy, & Lessinger, Hanna. (Eds.). (1983). *Class, race, and sex: The dynamics of control.* Boston, MA: G.K. Hall.

Trebilcot, Joyce (Ed.). (1983). *Mothering: Essays in feminist theory.* Totowa, NJ: Rowman & Allanheld.

Tress, Daryl McGowan. (1988, Fall). Postmodernism and gender relations in feminist theory—Comment. *Signs, 14*(1), 196–200.

Vetterling-Braggin, Mary (Ed.). (1982). *"Femininity", "masculinity", and "androgyny": A modern philosophical discussion.* Totowa, NJ: Littlefield, Adams.

Weed, Elizabeth (Ed.). (1989). *Coming to terms: Feminism/theory/politics.* New York: Routledge.

WOMEN AND SCIENCE

Part One: Women Scientists

Abir-Am, Phina G., & Outram, Dorinda. (1987). *Uneasy careers and intimate lives: Women in science, 1789–1979.* New Brunswick, NJ: Rutgers University Press.

Abram, Ruth J. (1985). *Send us a lady physician: Women doctors in America, 1835–1920.* New York: W. W. Norton.

Aldrich, Michele L (1978). Women in science. *Signs, 4,* 126–135.

Alic, Margaret (1982). The history of women in science: A women's studies course. *Women's Studies International Forum, 5*(1), 75–82.

Alic, Margaret. (1986). *Hypatia's heritage: A history of women in science from antiquity through the nineteenth century.* Boston, MA: Beacon Press.

Arnold, Lois B. (1984). *Four lives in science: Women's education in the 19th century.* New York: Schocken Books.

Baldwin, Richard S. (1981). *The fungus fighters: Two women scientists and their discovery.* Ithaca, NY: Cornell University Press.

Balka, Ellen. (1986, November). Calculus and coffee cups—Learning science on your own. *Resources for Feminist Research, 15,* 11–12.

Blashfield, Jean F. (1981). *Hellraisers, heroines, and holy women.* New York: St. Martin's Press.

Briggs, Shirley. (1981). Rachel Carson: A corrective memoir. *Heresies, 13* (Feminism and Ecology) *4*(1), 2.

Brody, Judit. (1985, February). The pen is mightier than the test tube. *New Scientist, 105,* 56–60.

Brush, Stephen G. (1978, June). Nettie M. Stevens and the discovery of sex determination by chromosomes. *Isis, 59,* 163–172.

Burlew, Ann Kathleen. (1982, Spring). Experiences of black females in the traditional and nontraditional professions. *Psychology of Women Quarterly, 6,* 312–326.

Crossley, Louise & Richards, Evelleen (1978, May). A women's place in science: Rosalind Franklin and DNA. *Refractory Girl, 16,* 19–28.

Davis, Audrey. (1974). *Bibliography on women: With special emphasis on their roles in science and society.* New York: Science History Publications.

Davis, Marianna W. (Ed.). (1981). *Contributions of black women to America* (Vol. 2). Columbia, SC: Kenday Press.

Dawson-Medina, Leslie. (1988, January). Patricia Donahoe: Healer and groundbreaking research scientist. *Ms., 16,* 58–98.

Donegan, Jane B. (1978). *Women and men midwives: Medicine, morality, and misogyny in early America.* Westport, CT: Greenwood Press.

Downs, Robert B. (1982). *Landmarks in science—Hippocrates to Carson.* Littleton, CO: Libraries, Unlimited.

Fins, Alice. (1979). *Women in science.* Skokie, IL: VGM Career Horizons.

Flexner, James Thomas. (1984). *An American saga: The story of Helen Thomas and Simon Flexner.* Boston, MA: Little, Brown.

Gornick, Vivian. (1983). *Women in science: Portraits from a world in transition.* New York: Simon & Schuster.

Gornick, Vivian. (1983, October). Women in science: The passion of discovery. *Ms., 12,* 50–52.

Harding, Sandra, & O'Barr, Jean F. (Eds.). (1987). *Sex and scientific inquiry.* Chicago: University of Chicago Press.

Harrison, Michelle. (1982). *A woman in residence.* New York: Random House.

Herzenberg, Caroline L. (1986). *Women scientists from Antiquity to the present: An international reference listing and biographical directory of some notable women scientists from ancient to modern times.* West Cornwall, CT: Locust Hill Press.

Herzenberg, Caroline L. (1987, November). Women in science during Antiquity and the Middle Ages. *Journal of College Science Teaching, 17,* 124–127.

Hubbard, Ruth. (1979). Reflections on the story of the double helix. *Women's Studies International Quarterly, 2*(3), 261–274.

Kahle, Jane Butler. (1985). *Women in science: A report from the field.* Philadelphia and London: Falmer Press.

Keller, Evelyn Fox. (1983). *A feeling for the organism: The life and work of Barbara McClintock.* San Francisco: W. H. Freeman.

Kien, Jenny, & Cassidy, David (Eds.). (1984). The history of women in science—A seminar at the University of Regensburg, FRG. *Women's Studies International Forum, 7*(4), 313–317.

Knudsin, Ruth B. (1974). *Women and success: The anatomy of achievement.* New York: Morrow.

Kohlstedt, Sally Gregory. (1978, Autumn). In from the periphery: American women in science, 1830–1880. *Signs, 4,* 81–96.

Leavitt, Judith Walzer. (1984). *Women and health in America: Historical readings.* Madison, WI: University of Wisconsin Press.

Lichty, Wemara. (1984, Summer). On being a woman in science. *National Women's Studies Association Newsletter, 2,* 18–19.

Love, R. (1979). Alice in eugenics land—Feminism and eugenics in the scientific careers of Alice Lee and Ethel Elderton. *Annals of Science, 36*(2), 145–158.

Love, R., & Grasset, N. (1984). Women scientists and the Great Barrier Reef—A historical perspective. *Search, 15*(9–10), 285–287.

Malcolm, Shirley M., Hall, Paula Quick, & Brown, Janet Welsh. (1976). *The double-bind: The price of being a minority woman in science.* Washington, DC: American Association for the Advancement of Science.

Mandelbaum, Dorothy Rosenthal. (1978, Autumn). Women in medicine. *Signs, 4,* 136–145.

McBeath, Lida W. (1978). Eloise Gerry, a woman of forest science. *Journal of Forest Science, 22*(3), 128–135.

Moldow, Gloria. (1987). *Women doctors in gilded-age Washington: Race, gender, and professionalization.* Urbana, IL: University of Illinois Press.

Morantz, Regina Markell. (1982, Winter). Feminism, professionalism, and germs: The thought of Mary Putnam Jacobi and Elizabeth Blackwell. *American Quarterly, 34,* 459–478.

Morgan, Elizabeth. (1980). *The making of a woman surgeon.* New York: Putnam.

Mozans, H. J. (also John Augustine Zahm). (1974 reprint). *Women in science: With an introductory chapter on women's long struggle for things of the mind.* Cambridge, MA: MIT Press.

Newman, Louise Michele. (1985). *Men's ideas/women's realities: Popular Science, 1870–1915*. Elmsford, NY: Pergamon Press.

Noble, Iris. (1979). *Contemporary women scientists of America*. New York: Julian Meissner.

Noyce, Ruth M. (1980, November-December). Women in science: Biographies for young readers. *Science and Children, 18*(3), 24–26.

Ogilvie, Marilyn Bailey. (1986). *Women in science: Antiquity through the nineteenth century*. Cambridge, MA: MIT Press.

Ogilvie, Marilyn Bailey, & Choquette, Clifford J. (1981). Nettie Maria Stevens (1861–1912): Her life and contributions to cytogenetics. *Proceedings of the American Philosophical Society, 125*(4), 292–311.

Ogilvie, Marilyn Bailey, & Choquette, Clifford J. (n.d.). *Alice Middleton Boring (1883–1955): An American scientist in China*. Unpublished manuscript.

O'Hern, Elizabeth Moot. (1985). *Profiles of pioneer women scientists*. Washington, DC: Acropolis Books.

O'Hern, Elizabeth Moot. (1973, September). Women scientists in microbiology. *Bioscience, 23*(9), 539–543.

Opfell, Olga S. (1986). *The lady laureates: Women who won the Nobel Prize* (2nd ed.). Metuchen, NJ: Scarecrow Press.

Rawson, Donald M. (1983). Caroline Dormon: A Renaissance spirit of twentieth century Louisiana. *Louisiana History, 24*(2), 121–139.

Richards, Evelleen. (1978, May). Bibliography: Women and science. *Refractory Girl, 16*, 46.

Richter, Derek. (1982). *Women scientists: The road to liberation*. London: Macmillan.

Rossiter, Margaret W. (1982). *Women scientists in America: Struggles and strategies to 1940*. Baltimore, MD: The Johns Hopkins University Press.

Rossiter, Margaret W. (1980, September). "Women's work" in science, 1880–1910. *Isis, 71*(258), 381–398.

Roth, Mark. (1978). The photographs and travels of Modern Schaffer Warren. *Beaver, 309*(3), 28–33.

Sarasohn, Lisa T. (1984, Autumn). A science turned upside down: Feminism and the natural philosophy of Margaret Cavendish. *Huntington Library Quarterly, 47*, 289–307.

Sayre, Anne. (1975). *Rosalind Franklin and DNA*. New York: W. W. Norton.

Schacher, Susan, (1976). *Hypatia's sisters: Biographies of women scientists—Past and present*. Seattle, WA: Feminists Northwest.

Siegel, Patricia Joan, & Findley, Kay Thomas. (1985). *Women in the scientific search: An American bio-bibliography, 1724–1979*. Metuchen, NJ: Scarecrow.

Sloan, Jan Butin. (1978). The founding of the Naples Table Association for Promoting Women. *Signs, 4*(1), 208–216.

Spender, Dale. (1982). *Women of ideas—And what men have done to them*. London: Routledge & Kegan Paul.

Stearner, S. Phyllis. (1984). *Able scientists—Disabled persons*. Oakbrook, IL: John Racila Association.

String-Boag, Veronica (Ed.). (1980). *A woman with a purpose*. Toronto, Ontario: University of Toronto Press.

Tuana, Nancy, &, Imber, Barbara. Bibliography—Women in science. (1988, Spring). *Hypatia, 3*, 145–155.

Vetter, Betty M. (1975). Women in the natural sciences. *Signs, 1*, 713–720.

Warner, Deborah Jean. (1978). Science education for women in antebellum America. *Isis, 69*(246), 58–67.

Wystrach, V. P. (1977). Anna Blackburne (1726–1793): A neglected patroness of Natural History. *Journal of the Society for the Bibliography of Natural History, 8*(2), 148–168.

Part Two: Recruiting Women Scientists

Aldrich, Michele L., & Hall, Paula Quick (compilers) with assistance of Karen L. Ehrlich, Roger Long & Rachel Warner. (1980). *Programs in science, mathematics and engineering for women in the United States: 1966–1978.* Washington, DC: American Association for the Advancement of Science. (Eric Document Reproduction Service No. ED 199 049)

Briscoe, Anne M., & Pfafflin, Sheila M. (Eds.). (1979). Expanding the role of women in the sciences. *Annals of the New York Academy of Sciences. 323.*

Carter, Carol J. (1987). Strategies for recruiting and retaining minorities and women in non-traditional programs. *New Directions for Higher Education, 57,* 75–82.

Chew, Martha. (1982, Summer). A survival course for women entering a male-dominated profession: Women's studies at the Massachusetts College of Pharmacy and Allied Health Sciences. *Women's Studies Quarterly, 10,* 19–21.

Checkich, Elaine, & Abramowitsch (Producers). *Count me in: Educating women for science and math.* (1978). Newton, MA: Education Development Center. Videotape documentary and brochure.

Chinn, Phyllis Zweig (compiler). (1979). *Women in science and math.* Washington, DC: Office of Opportunities in Science, American Association for the Advancement of Science.

Clark, Julia V. (1988, March/April). Black women in science: Implications for improved participation. *Journal of College Science Teaching, 17,* 348–352.

Conaway, Larry E. & Weiss, Iris R. (1979). *Manual on program operations for the Visiting Women Scientists Program.* Durham, NC: Center for Educational Research and Evaluation, Research Triangle Institute.

Connolly, Terry & Porter, Alan L. (1978). *Recruitment and retention of women as undergraduate engineers.* Georgia Institute of Technology, Atlanta, Georgia: School of Industrial and Systems Engineering.

Connolly, Terry & Porter, Alan L. (1978). *Recruitment and retention of women in engineering: Development of policy guidelines, final report.* Georgia Institute of Technology, Atlanta, Georgia: School of Industrial and Systems Engineering.

Connolly, Terry & Porter, Allan L. (1980, May). Women in engineering: Recruitment and retention. *Engineering Education, 70*(8), 822–827.

Cromwell, Robert A. (1986, May). The effective recruitment of women students in engineering technology. *Engineering Education, 76*(8), 755–757.

Davis, Barbara Gross & Humphreys, Sheila M. (1985). *Evaluating intervention programs: Applications from women's studies programs in math and science.* New York: Teachers College, Columbia University.

Dewitt, Diane, & Colasurdo, Elizabeth. (1980). *Careers for women in science and technology: A model treatment program, final report.* Midway, WA: Highline Community College. (ERIC Document Reproduction Service No. ED 186 652)

Hall, Paula Quick. (1981). *Problems and solutions in the education, employment, and personal choices of minority women in science.* Washington, DC: American Association for the Advancement of Science.

Harding, Jan, Hildebrand, Gaell, & Klainin, Sunee. (1988). Recent international concerns in gender and science and technology. *Education Review, 40*(2), 185–193.

Harding, Jan. (1983, September). How the world attracts girls to science. *New Scientist, 99,* 754–755.

Harlen, Wynne. (1985). Girls and primary-school science education: Sexism, stereotypes, and remedies. *Prospectus, 15*(4), 541–551.

Humphreys, Sheila M. (Ed.). (1982). *Women and minorities in science: Strategies for increasing participation.* Boulder, CO: Westview Press.

Ivey, Elizabeth. (1988, May). Recruiting more women into engineering and science. *Engineering Education, 78,* 762–765.

Jump, Teresa, Heid, Camilla, & Harris, John J. (1985). Science and math careers for women. *Feminist Teacher, 1*(3), 18–20.

Kahle, Jane Butler. (1988, March/April). Recruitment and retention of women in college science majors. *Journal of College Science Teaching, 17*, 382–384.

Koltnow, Joanne. (1980). *Expanding your horizons in science and mathematics. Conference for young women interested in new career options. A handbook for planners.* Oakland, CA: Mills College.

Kreinberg, Nancy. (1981). *Ideas for developing and conducting a women in science career workshop.* Berkeley, CA: Lawrence Hall of Science.

Lantz, Alma. (1979, Autumn). Strategies to increase the number of women in science. *Signs, 5*(1), 186–189.

Leach, Juliette D., & Roberts, Shirley L. (1988, October/November). A soft technology: Recruiting and retaining women and minorities in high tech programs. *Community, Technical, and Junior College Journal, 59*, 34–37.

Levine, Dana. (1985, October). Encouraging young women to pursue science and engineering careers through chemistry. *Journal of Chemical Education, 62*, 837–839.

McDonald, J.B. (1983, June). Recruiting high school girls for careers in chemistry and other sciences. *Abstracts of Papers of the American Chemical Society, 186*, 107.

Moche, Dinah L. (1976). Development of educational materials to recruit women into scientific careers. *American Journal of Physics, 44*(4), 390–391.

Place, Carol, Conaway, Larry E., Weiss, Iris R., & Taylor, Mary Ellen. (1979). *The Visiting Women Scientists Program, 1978–1979, highlights reports.* Durham, NC: Center for Educational Research and Evaluation, Research Triangle Institute. (ERIC Document Reproduction Service No. ED 179 399)

Place, Carol, et al. (1979). *The Visiting Women Scientists Program, 1978–1979, final report.* Durham, NC: Center for Educational Research and Evaluation, Research Triangle Institute. (ERIC Document Reproduction Service No. ED 179 400)

Rutherford, F. James. (1978, March 8). *The role of the National Science Foundation.* Paper presented at the annual meeting of the New York Academy of Sciences.

Shuchman, Hedvah. (1984, September). A science policy for women. *New Scientist, 103*(1422), 33–36.

Skolnick, Joan, Langbort, Carol, & Day, Lucille. (1982). *How to encourage girls in math and science: Strategies for parents and educators.* Englewood Cliffs, NJ: Prentice Hall.

Smith, Walter S., & Stroup, Kala M. (1978). *Science career exploration for women.* Washington, DC: National Science Teachers Association.

Strauss, Mary Jo Boehm. (1978). Wanted: More women in science. *American Biology Teacher, 40*(3), 181–185, 8.

Thomas, Gail B. (1986, January). Cultivating the interest of women and minorities in high school math and science. *Science Education, 70*, 31–43.

Torge, Herman. (1978, March 27–31). *A fast-track late-entry program for women in engineering.* Paper presented at the annual meeting of the American Educational Research Association, Toronto, Canada. (ERIC Document Reproduction Service No. ED 157 691)

Weiss, Iris R., et. al.. (1978). *The Visiting Women Scientists Pilot Program 1978, highlights report.* Durham, NC: Center for Educational Research and Evaluation, Research Triangle Institute. (ERIC Document Reproduction Service No. ED 164 290)

Weiss, Iris R., Place, Carol, & Conaway, Larry E. (1978). *The Visiting Women Scientists Pilot Program 1978, final report.* Durham, NC: Center for Educational Research and Evaluation, Research Triangle Institute. (ERIC Document Reproduction Service No. ED 164 291)

Whyte, Judith (1986). *Girls into science and technology: The story of a project.* Boston: Routledge and Kegan Paul.

Author Index

Alexander, Richard D., 24
Arditti, Rita, 58
Arnold, Karen, 70
Association of American Colleges, 1, 12, 15, 20, 76
Astin, Alexander, 11
Avoiding Stereotypes: Principles and Applications, 74

Baker, Dale, 52, 70
Barash, David, 24
Barr, Rebecca, 73, 74
Bartlett, Katherine T., 5
Baxter, James Phinney, 41, 42
Becker, Joanne R., 75
Belenky, Mary Field, 35–36, 54
Bennett, William J., 16
Bentley, Diana, 70–71
Bernstein, I. S., 27
Birke, Lynda, 28, 34–35, 37, 48, 54, 58, 60–61
Bleier, Ruth, 24, 25, 26–27, 28, 34–35, 41, 42, 48, 49, 50–51, 55, 58, 65, 67
Bloom, Allan, 1–4, 6–9, 10, 18–20

Blumenfeld, Phyllis C., 75
Blum, Lenore, 57, 64, 69
Boyer, Ernest L., 1
Breiter, Joan, 74
Brophy, Jere E., 56, 73
Bryhni, Eva, 71–72

Campbell, Patricia, 56
Carson, Rachel, 44
Chodorow, Nancy, 37, 44, 65, 68
Clinchy, Blythe McVicker, 35–36, 54
Cole, Michael, 73, 74
College Placement Council, 55
Corea, Gena, 16
Cronkite, Ruth, 57

Daniels, Jane, 57, 59, 69, 70, 71, 72
Darrow, Charlotte M., 16
Dawkins, Richard, 24
Day, Lucille, 74, 75
Dearman, N. B., 56
Dede, C. J., 56
Dill, Bonnie T., 20, 49
Dowie, Mark, 40–41
Dresselhaus, Margaret, 69

Eccles, Jacqueline, 75
Ehrenreich, Barbara, 43, 61
Ehrhardt, Anke A., 48
English, Deirdre, 43, 61
Erikson, Erik H., 16

Fausto-Sterling, Anne, 42, 58
Fee, Elizabeth, 23, 28, 34, 43, 46–47, 48, 50, 57, 68
Feminist Women's Health Centre (Frankfurt), 53–54
Fennema, Elizabeth, 25
Fix, Dorothy, 16
Floden, Robert E., 56
Fossey, Dian, 38, 39, 59
Frazier, Nancy, 74
Freeman, Donald J., 56, 73

Gallup, George H., 37
Gazzam-Johnson, Virginia, 66–67
George, Yolanda S., 68
Gilligan, Carol, 37, 39, 44, 50, 51, 63, 68
Givant, Steven, 57, 64, 69
Goldberger, Nancy Rule, 35–36, 54
Goldsmid, Charles A., 73
Goodall, Jane, 38, 39, 59, 62
Goodfield, June, 65
Gornick, Vivian, 23, 27, 52
Gould, Stephen Jay, 5, 28
Grant, M., 71
Greed, Clara H., 109, 110
Griffin, Peg, 73, 74
Griffin, Susan, 65–66
Guide to Non-Sexist Language, A (AAC), 76
Gunnings, Barbara B., 88

Haber, Louis, 42
Haley-Oliphant, Ann, 89
Hall, Roberta M., 14, 20, 66, 71, 92
Halpin, Zuleyma Tang, 66
Hamilton, Jean, 43, 45–46, 48, 50, 64
Haraway, Donna, 28, 34–35, 48, 55, 65
Harding, Jan, 56, 65, 74

Harding, Sandra, 29–30, 35, 43, 58
Hardin, J., 56
Harmer, Jalna, 16
Harris, A., 70
Head, John, 75
Hein, Hilde, 28, 34, 50, 55, 58
Henley, Nancy, 47
Hirsch, E. D. Jr., 1, 16
Hoffman, Joan C., 25
Hoffman, Lois Wladis, 51
Hoffman, Nancy, 2, 15, 46
Holaday, J. W., 27
Holliday, Laurel, 60
Holmes, Helen B., 16
Holy Bible, 95–96
Horner, Matina S., 51, 69
Hoskins, Betty, 16
Hrdy, Sarah B., 27, 38–39, 59, 62
Hubbard, Ruth, 24, 25, 26, 28–29, 34, 41, 48, 49, 58, 67
Humphreys, Sheila, 35, 57
Hunnerberg, Catherine, 75
Hynes, H. Patricia, 43, 44, 61

Jaggar, Alison M., 5, 27
Jenkins, Mercilee M., 12
Johnston-Gazzam, Virginia, 13
Johnston, Tracy, 41

Kahle, Jane B., 21, 35, 52, 56, 57, 59, 66, 74, 75–76, 87, 88
Kamin, Leon J., 26
Keller, Evelyn Fox, 18, 23, 27, 35, 37, 43, 46, 48, 50, 55, 57–58, 63, 65, 109
Kelly, Alison, 56
Kirschstein, Ruth L., 41
Kishwar, Madhu, 16
Klein, Edward B., 16
Klein, Ethel, 41, 60
Klein, Renate D., 16
Kohn, Alexander, 52
Kramarae, Cheris, 13, 47, 74
Kramer, Sylvia, 75
Kreinberg, Nancy, 57, 69, 75
Kuhn, Thomas S., 27–28
Kuhs, Therese M., 56, 73

Lakes, Marsha K., 56, 59, 75
Lakoff, Robin, 47
Lancaster, Jane, 24, 38, 47–48, 62
Langbort, Carol, 74, 75
Leavitt, Ruth R., 24
LeBold, William, 57, 59, 69, 70, 71, 72
Leibowitz, Lila, 24
Levinson, Daniel J., 16
Levinson, Maria H., 16
Lewontin, Richard C., 26
Lie, Svein, 71–72
Lipsey, Mark W., 36
Lowe, Marian, 24, 25, 48, 58

McIntosh, Peggy, 15, 100
McKeachie, Wilbert J., 73
McKee, Braxton, 16
MacKinnon, Catharine A., 5
McLeod, S., 29
McMillen, Liz, 14, 15
McNamee, Harriet, 16
Maehr, Martin, 74
Malcolm, Shirley M., 60
Mallow, Jeffry V., 74, 75
Manning, Kenneth R., 13, 68
Marchman, Virginia A., 75
Martyna, Wendy, 11, 66, 95
Marwick, C., 40
Matyas, Marsha L., 35, 60–62
Max, Claire E., 35, 69
Means, Russell, 29
Meece, Judith L., 75
Melnick, Susan L., 87
Menand, Louis, 7
Menne, Jack, 74
Merchant, Carolyn, 37, 61, 65–66
Mergendoller, John R., 75
Messing, Karen, 42, 43
Miller, Kathy, 56
Mitman, Alexis L., 75
Money, John, 48
Mozans, H. J., 40

National Assessment of Educational Progress, 59
National Institute for Education, 1

National Institutes of Health, 16, 64
National Research Council, 3
National Science Foundation, 3–4, 12, 53, 55, 56, 68, 76
National Women's Studies Association, 15
Needham, Joseph, 29
Noonan, John F., 14
Nulty, Peter, 11
Nussbaum, Martha, 8

Odum, H. T., 44
Office of Technology Assessment, 3–4, 36–37, 55
Ogilvie, Marilyn B., 38, 40, 50

Packer, Martin J., 75
Perl, Teri, 57
Pion, Georgine M., 36
Plisko, V. W., 56
Porter, Andrew C., 56, 73

Raymond, Janice, 16
Remick, Helen, 56
Rich, Frank, 22
Robinson, James, 69
Rose, Hilary, 28
Rose, R. M., 27
Rose, Steven, 26, 28
Rosser, Sue V., 48, 57, 64, 75, 101
Rossiter, Margaret W., 48, 57
Rowell, Thelma, 24
Rowland, Roberta, 16
Rubin, Vera, 40

Sadker, David, 14
Sadker, Myra, 14, 74
Sandler, Bernice R., 14, 20, 66, 71, 92
Sayers, Janet, 5, 49, 67
Schmidt, William H., 56, 73
Schuster, Marilyn, 15, 80–82, 100
Schwille, John R., 56, 73
Sells, Lucy, 56–57, 61, 71
Shapiro, June, 75
Shaver, Phillip, 69
Sherman, Julie, 25
Skolnick, Joan, 74, 75

Smail, Barbara, 56, 74
Stage, Elizabeth K., 75
Stallings, Jane, 56
Star, Susan Leigh, 25, 67
Steinbacher, R., 16
Steinkamp, Marjorie, 74, 87, 89
Stodolsky, Susan S., 89

Tarule, Jill Mattuck, 35–36, 54
Tetreault, Mary K., 15, 87, 100
Thorne, Barrie, 14, 47, 66
Towson State University, 62
Treichler, Paula, 47
Trivers, Robert L., 24

U.S. Department of Health, Education,
and Welfare, 12

Van Dyne, Susan, 15, 80–82, 100

Watson, James, 110
West, Candace, 13
Whatley, Mariamne, 74, 87, 88
Wheeler, Christopher W., 87
Wheeler, P., 71
Widnall, Sheila E., 3–4, 110
Wilson, Edward O., 24
Wilson, Everett K., 73
Winick, M., 27
Wright, Herbert, 84

Yerkes, R. M., 24

Zimmerman, Bill, 29
Zimmerman, Don H., 13

Subject Index

Achievement, scientific, girls' versus boys', 56
Activities, textbooks, sexism in, 83–87
African-American critiques, scientific research/theories, 29–30, 31
American Chemical Society, 57
"Anatomy is destiny" approach, to women, 6–7
Animal behavior:
    anthropomorphism, 24
    circularity of logic in interpreting, 48
    feminist critiques of, 24–25
Astronomy, women's observations and, 40
Attrition rate, natural sciences, 4

Behavior:
    classroom, 13–14, 20
    faculty, 13–14
    nonverbal, 14
    sex-appropriate, in language, 48
    verbal, 11–14
Betta spendens exercise, 62
Bias:
    in experiments, 58–59
    language and, 11–13, 20

in nonverbal classroom language, 14
science as reflection of society's, 28–29
of scientists, 28–29
See also Textbook sexism
Biological determinism, 6–7, 48–49
Biological Politics (Sayers), 49
Biology, 62–63, 64, 66, 75–76
Biology/environment dichotomy, 26–27
Black Apollo of Science: The Life of Ernest Everett Just (Manning), 68
Bloom, Allan:
    attack on feminism, 7–9
    biological determinism, 6–7
    Closing of the American Mind, The, 2–3
    critique of, 6–9
    gender neutral language and, 6
    Great Books curriculum, 18
    male/female relationships, views of, 7
    on natural sciences, 4
    women/women's studies, attitudes toward, 2, 6–9

Brain lateralization, sexist bias in, 25, 49–50

Cannon, Annie Jump, 40
Career opportunities in science, 70–71
  women's avoidance of, 61
  women's unawareness of, 57
Carson, Rachel, 44
"Chilly Climate" series, 93–99
  Defining Sexism and Its Relationship to Chilly Climate Issues, 93–94
  Gender Differences in Experiences with Chilly Climate Issues and Sexism, 96–100
  Incorporating Scholarship on Women into a Traditional Disciplinary Course, 99–101
  Pronouns as Power, 94–96
  Stereotypes Affect Discussion of Sexual Harassment Policy, 102–104
Chromosome karyotyping, 45
Classroom behavior, 13–14
  sexism and, 20
"Classroom Climate, The: A Chilly One for Women?" (Hall/Sandler), 20
Closing of the American Mind, The (Bloom), 1–3
Combined qualitative/quantitative methods, in data gathering, 44–45, 63–64
Commitment, to science, 52
Committee on Women in Physics of the American Physical Society, 57
Communication:
  of scientific information, 70–71
  students–faculty, 12
Competitive models, in practicing science, 51–52
Constructed knowers, women as, 36
Cooperative methods, in class/laboratory, 69
Critiques:
  of scientific research/theories, 23–30, 35
  differences among, 30–32

from standpoints other than feminist, 29–30
  nature/nurture dichotomy, 26–29
Cultural Literacy: What Every American Needs to Know (Hirsch Jr.), 1
Curricular content, 8–9
  sexism in, 80–82
Curriculum, 14–21
  curriculum integration projects, 15
  effect of women's studies on, 14–15
  funding women's interests, 16
  McIntosh model, 15–21
    redefined/reconstructed to include all, 18–21
    womanless curriculum, 15–16
    women as addition to curriculum, 16–17
    women as focus for studies, 17–18
    women as problem/anomaly/absence from curriculum, 17
  reforms needed for, 2
  womanless, 15–16
  women as addition to, 16–17
  women as focus of, 17–18

Dalkon shield, observation findings, 40–41
Data-gathering methods:
  combined qualitative/quantitative methods, 44–45
  experimental subjects, using women as, 45–46
  interdisciplinary approaches to problem-solving, 45
  women scientists and, 44–47
Degreeholders, science, 3–4
Depersonalization of knowledge, 2, 19
Direct qualitative methods, of data gathering, 44–45
Discrimination, See Bias; Textbook sexism; Sexism in nonverbal language
Disease:
  importance of gender to, 43
  stereotyping of, 43–44

Disengagement/disconnection, students/faculty, 1–3

Dualistic scientific research/theories, 68–69

Dysmenorrhea, women's personal experience and, 41

Education, See Higher education

Elitism/racism, 20

Endocrinology, 46
feminism critiques of, 25–26, 27

Engineering:
degreeholders, 3–4
salaries of engineering majors, 55–56

Environmentalists, women as, 44

Equal Rights Amendment, 5

EQUALS program, 69–70

Equipment, scientific, disparity in use of, 59

Experimental designs, screening of, 66

Experimental observations, acceptance of women's personal experience and, 40–41

Experimental subjects, using women as, 45–46, 64–65

Experiments, bias found in, 49–50, 58–59

Faculty:
behavior, 13–14
eye contact, 14
handling students' discomfort with experiments, 61, 63
review of verbal/nonverbal communication, 14
teaching mathematics, 71
women's studies, 12

Federally funded programs, to attract women to science, 56

Feeling for the Organism, A (Keller), 65

Female-friendly characteristics, in textbooks, 91

Feminist critiques, See Critiques

Feminist scholars, bias criticisms, 49

Feminist scientists, 34–35, 58

Feminist Women's Health Centre (Frankfurt), 53–54

Fetal development, shortcomings of nature/nurture dualism in, 51

For Her Own Good (Ehrenreich/English), 43

Fragmentation of knowledge, 2, 18

Fraud, in science, 52

Funding, for women's curricular interests, 16

Gender-gap polls, women's preferences in, 41

Gender neutral language, 6
in data gathering, 47–48
disease and, 43
scientific research/theories and, 23
in textbooks, 74
versus gendered language, 6–7

Gender referencing, 11, 66

Generic pronouns, 6–7, 76

Girls and Science and Technology (GASAT) conference, 34, 72

"Good Science: Can It Ever Be Gender Free?" seminar, 106

Great Books curriculum, 18

Guide to Nonsexist Language, A (AAC), 12

Hands-on experience, in laboratories, 59–60

Herschel, Caroline, 40

Herschel, Sir William, 40

Hierarchical scientific research/theories, 68–69

Higher education:
crisis in, 1–9
curricula reforms, need for, 2
emphasis on curricular content, 8–9
exclusion based on differences, 5

Hormone level studies, 25–26

Hormone secretion, in males/females, 46

Human values, scientific research/theories dichotomized from, 27–28

Hypothesis development:
  focusing on gender in, 62
  observations and, 39–40

Illustrations, textbook sexism and, 77–79
Imagined World, An (Goodfield), 65
Inclusionary methods, for attracting women to science, 55–72
Initials approach, to scientist identification, 13
Interaction:
  female–female, in primatology observations, 59
  nonverbal, 14
  verbal, by faculty, 13–14
Interactive methods, of observation, 46–47, 63
Interdisciplinary approaches, to problem-solving, 45
International GASAT Conference (1987), 34, 72
Interruptions in classroom, male versus female, 13
Investigation, scientific, 75
IUD (intrauterine device), observation findings, 41

Knowers:
  constructed, 36
  procedural, 35–38
  received, 35–36
  silent, 35–36
  subjective, 35–37
Knowledge:
  dualist approach to, 31
  fragmentation of, 18–19

Labeling, 11
Laboratory:
  equipment, use of, 59–60
  exercises, decreasing destruction of animals/reducing harsh treatment, 65–66
  hands-on experience in, 59–60
  partners, 59

Language:
  breaking biases through, 13
  nonparallel terminology in, 11
  as obstacle to learning, 11
  sex-appropriate behavior expressed in, 48
  sexism and, 11–13, 20
  textbook sexism and, 76
  See also Gender neutral language
Last-names-only approach, to scientist identification, 12–13
Leavitt, Henrietta Swan, 40
Life sciences, 75–76
  women and, 60
Logical reasoning, 75

McClintock, Barbara, 46, 50, 65
McIntosh curriculum model, 15–21
  curriculum redefined/reconstructed to include all, 18–21
  womanless curriculum, 15–16
  women as addition to curriculum, 16–17
  women as focus for studies, 17–18
  women as problem/anomaly/abscence from curriculum, 17
Male-female laboratory partners, 59
Male/female relationships, Bloom's view of, 7
"Manhattan Project," 42
Marxist critiques, scientific research/theories, 29, 31
Mary Baldwin College, 64
Masculine terminology, generic use of, 11
Mathematics, teaching styles, 71
Maximization/minimalization, discrimination and, 4
M. Butterfly dilemma, 22–33
Meitner, Lise, 42
Midwifery, as science, 43
Mills College, 64, 69
Minorities, natural sciences and, 4–5
Motivational problems, women's study of science and, 75

National Institutes of Health (NIH), 64
National Research Council (NRC), 3–4
National Science Foundation (NSF), 3–4, 12
National Women's Studies Association, 15
Natural sciences, 3–6
  attracting women/minorities to, 4–5
  attrition of women in, 4
  Bloom's view of, 4
  breaking stereotypes in, 12–13
  maximalization/minimalization, 5
  sexism and, 20
Nature/nurture dichotomy, 26–29, 50–51, 65–66
  shortcomings in fetal development theory, 51
Neurosciences, feminist critiques of, 25, 26–27
Nonparallel terminology, in language, 11
Nonscience careers, 61–62
Nonverbal behavior/interaction, sexism in, 14
Numerical problem solving/applications, 75

Observations:
  critique of, 48
  experimental subjects, women as, 45–46, 64–65
  interactive methods, 46–47, 63
  women scientists and, 38–44, 48–49
Office of Technology Assessment (OTA), 3–4, 36–37, 55

Paternalism, in language, 12
Pedagogy/theories, developed for women's studies, 10, 21
Personal experiences, incorporated into class discussion/laboratory exercise, 19, 59–60
Photographs/drawings/outlines, in sexist textbooks, 77–81

Physics:
  boys'/girls' attitudes toward, 71–72
  problem-solving workshops, 70
  women and, 60
Practice of science:
  barriers between science and lay community, 53
  competitive models, use of, 51–52
  perception of scientist's role, 52
  positive control over scientific discoveries, 53–54
Primatology, 24–25, 47–48, 59
  female–female interaction in observations, 59
  female primatologists, observations of, 38–40
  feminist critiques of, 24–25
Problem-solving, women's approach to, 50–51, 64
Procedural knowers, women as, 35–38
Psychological stressors, direct qualitative data gathering and, 44–45
Purdue University, 57, 71
  Program in Engineering, 70

Qualitative/quantitative methods, in data gathering, 44–45, 63–64

Received knowers, women as, 35–36
Reductionistic scientific research/theories, 68–69
Report of the Public Health Service Task Force on Women's Health Issues, 45
Research funding, for women's curricular interests, 16
Research/theories:
  African-American critiques, 29–30, 31
  dichotomized from other human values, 27–28
  differences among critiques of, 30–32
  feminist critiques of, 23–26
  animal behavior, 24–25

Research/theories: (*continued*)
  basis of, 26
  endocrinology, 25–26, 27
  mainstream scientists' reaction,
    35
  neurosciences, 25, 26–27
  gender neutrality and, 23
  hierarchical/reductionistic/dualistic,
    68–69
  Marxist critiques, 29, 31
  sex differences research, 28
  stereotyping in, 43
  women's way of knowing and, 34–
    38
Richard, Ellen Swallow, 43
Role models, of successful women scientists, 70

Sabin, Dr. Rena, 39–40
Salaries, science/engineering majors,
  55–56
Schuster–Van Dyne scheme, 80–82
Science:
  as a masculine province, 58
  barriers between lay community
    and, 53
  career opportunities in, 70–71
  commitment required, 52
  degreeholders, 3–4
  future of, 53–54
  girls'/women's reluctance to study,
    75
  proportion of women in, 55
  as reflection of society's bias, 28–29
  salaries of science majors, 55–56
  See also Career opportunities in sci-
    ence; Natural sciences; specific
    branches of science
Science anxiety, 60, 75
Science faculty, *See* Faculty
Science instruction, hands-on activities
  included in, 74
Science Question in Feminism, The,
  29–30
Scientific achievement, girls' versus
  boys', 56

Scientific discoveries, positive control
  over, 53–54
Scientific equipment, disparity in use
  of, 59
Scientific fraud, 52
Scientific information:
  communication of, 70–71
  and practice of science, 51–54
Scientific investigation, 75
Scientific research/theories, *See* Re-
  search/theories
Scientific terminology, 70–71
Scientists:
  bias of, 28–29
  perception of role, 52
  shortage of, 3–4, 55–56
  works:
    initials as identifiers, 12–13
    last-name-only references to, 12–
      13
Separation of academy from polity, 2,
  19
Sex-appropriate behavior, expressed in
  language, 48
Sex differences research, 28
Sexism:
  in curricular content, 80–82
  and language, 11–13, 20
  natural sciences and, 20
  in nonverbal classroom language,
    14
  in textbooks, *See* Textbook sexism
Sexual harassment policy discussions,
  effect of stereotyping on, 102–104
Siamese Fighting Fish exercise, 62
Silent knowers, women as, 35–36
Silent Spring (Carson), 44
Silhouettes, textbook sexism and, 77–
  79
Society of Women Engineers, 57
Sociobiology, feminist critiques of, 24
Spatial visualization, 74–75
Stereotyping:
  effect on sexual harassment policy
    discussions, 102–104
  in language, 11–12

Stereotyping: (*continued*)
  paternalism, 12
  of research, 43
Stressors, psychological, direct qualitative data gathering and, 44–45
Student–faculty communication, guidelines for, 12
Subjective knowers, women as, 35–37

Teaching styles, mathematics, 71
Terminology:
  masculine, generic use of, 11
  nonparallel, 11
  scientific, 70–71
Textbook sexism, 73–92
  discussion, 87–91
  methods/results, 76–87
    activities, 83–87
    curricular content, 80–82
    language, 76
    pictures, 77–79
  subtle sexism, 87–88
Theories, *See* Research/theories
"To Reclaim a Legacy: A Report on the Humanities in Higher Education" (Bennett), 1
Toxic shock syndrome (TSS), women's personal experience and, 40
Traditional disciplinary course offerings, incorporating scholarship on women into, 99–102
TSS, *See* Toxic shock syndrome
Tutoring by peers, 71

Unparallel treatment, of scientists' names, 13

VDTs, *See* Video display terminals
Verbal behavior:
  differences in classroom, 13–14
  differences in language, 11–13

Verbal interaction, by faculty, 13–14
Video display terminals (VDTs), birth defects and, 43
Visualization, spatial, 74–75

Watson, James, 110
Womanless curriculum, 15–16
Women in Science: Portraits from a World in Transition (Gornick), 52
"Women in Science and Engineering: Changing Vision to Reality" conference (GASAT), 34
Women scientists:
  commitment to pursuit of careers in science, 52
  data-gathering methods, 44–47
  observations, 38–44, 48–49
  as procedural knowers, 37–38
  as role models, 70
Women's Educational Equity Act,

Women's studies:
  curriculum, effect on, 14–15
  depersonalization of knowledge and, 19
  elitism/racism and, 20
  fragmentation of knowledge and, 18–19
  overcoming disconnections through, 18–20
  pedagogical methods, 10–11
  revitalization of curricula and, 14–15
  scientific disciplines and, 10
  separation of academy from polity and, 19
  teachers of, 12
Women's Ways of Knowing (Belenkey/Clinchy/Goldberger/Tarule), 35–54ff

About the Author

Sue Rosser is Director of Women's Studies at the University of South Carolina at Columbia, and is Associate Professor of Family and Preventive Medicine in the Medical School. She has edited and authored books on the theoretical and applied problems of women and science, including *Teaching Science and Health from a Feminist Perspective: A Practical Guide* (1986), *Feminism Within the Science and Health Care Professions: Overcoming Resistance* (1988), and *Female-Friendly Science: Applying Women's Studies Methods and Theories to Attract Students* (1990), all from Pergamon Press. She is also the Latin and North American Co-Editor of *Women's Studies International Forum*.

THE ATHENE SERIES
An International Collection of Feminist Books
General Editors: Gloria Bowles, Renate Klein, and Janice Raymond
Consulting Editor: Dale Spender

MEN'S STUDIES MODIFIED The Impact of Feminism on the Academic Disciplines
Dale Spender, editor

WOMAN'S NATURE Rationalizations of Inequality
Marian Lowe and *Ruth Hubbard*, editors

MACHINA EX DEA Feminist Perspectives on Technology
Joan Rothschild, editor

SCIENCE AND GENDER A Critique of Biology and Its Theories on Women
Ruth Bleier

WOMAN IN THE MUSLIM UNCONSCIOUS
Fatna A. Sabbah

MEN'S IDEAS/WOMEN'S REALITIES Popular Science, 1870-1915
Louise Michele Newman, editor

BLACK FEMINIST CRITICISM Perspectives on Black Women Writers
Barbara Christian

THE SISTER BOND A Feminist View of a Timeless Connection
Toni A.H. McNaron, editor

EDUCATING FOR PEACE A Feminist Perspective
Birgit Brock-Utne

STOPPING RAPE Successful Survival Strategies
Pauline B. Bart and *Patricia H. O'Brien*

TEACHING SCIENCE AND HEALTH FROM A FEMINIST PERSPECTIVE
A Practical Guide
Sue V. Rosser

FEMINIST APPROACHES TO SCIENCE
Ruth Bleier, editor

INSPIRING WOMEN Reimagining the Muse
Mary K. DeShazer

MADE TO ORDER The Myth of Reproductive and Genetic Progress
Patricia Spallone and *Deborah Lynn Steinberg*, editors

TEACHING TECHNOLOGY FROM A FEMINIST PERSPECTIVE
A Practical Guide
Joan Rothschild

FEMINISM WITHIN THE SCIENCE AND HEALTH CARE PROFESSIONS
Overcoming Resistance
Sue V. Rosser

RUSSIAN WOMEN'S STUDIES Essays on Sexism in Soviet Culture
Tatyana Mamonova

TAKING OUR TIME Feminist Perspectives on Temporality
Frieda Johles Forman, editor, with *Caoran Sowton*

RADICAL VOICES A Decade of Feminist Resistance from *Women's Studies
International Forum*
Renate Klein and *Deborah Lynn Steinberg*, editors

THE RECURRING SILENT SPRING
H. Patricia Hynes

EXPOSING NUCLEAR PHALLACIES
Diana E.H. Russell, editor

THE WRITING OR THE SEX? or why you don't have to read women's writing to know
it's no good
Dale Spender

FEMINIST PERSPECTIVES ON PEACE AND PEACE EDUCATION
Birgit Brock-Utne

THE SEXUAL LIBERALS AND THE ATTACK ON FEMINISM
Dorchen Leidholdt and *Janice G. Raymond*, editors

WHENCE THE GODDESSES A Source Book
Miriam Robbins Dexter

NARODNIKI WOMEN Russian Women Who Sacrificed Themselves for the
Dream of Freedom
Margaret Maxwell

FEMALE-FRIENDLY SCIENCE Applying Women's Studies Methods and Theories to
Attract Students
Sue V. Rosser